HALF-TIME

Steve Devereaux

To Jason
From the author,

Steve
Devereaux

gringo latino
books

Published by Gringo Latino Books
57 Darracott Road, Bournemouth
BH5 2AY, Great Britain

ISBN   0-9550515-0-9

Printed and bound in Great Britain by
Antony Rowe Ltd, Chippenham, Wiltshire

ACKNOWLEDGEMENTS

First and foremost, thanks to my father for all his love and support during what was probably the toughest chapter in the story that is my life; without him I would never have put pen to paper. Thanks to my mother Lyn and my sister Nikki for all their help and guidance, and most of all, for their patience with me as I struggled to recover from the physical and psychological injuries of a major trauma. Many thanks to the staff of Arrecife General Hospital for helping me cheat my extinction, to Doctor Ruiz for rebuilding my left leg, and to Mr Ilankovan and Doctor Cronin at Poole General Hospital for rebuilding my face. And finally, I can't finish without expressing my gratitude to all of my 'editors', an international group of family and friends who allowed me to bully them into giving vast amounts of invaluable constructive criticism of my manuscript. Lastly, thanks also to P. J. O'Rourke, the man who opened my eyes to travel writing and someone whom I've been quoting for so long now that I'm sure some of his ideas appear in this book because I can't seem to remember which are his and which are mine ... but I hope he takes this as a compliment.

In memory of Clifford Devereaux, the man
who gave me my 'gypsy' blood.

Contents

Prologue

'So we're rapidly approaching the conclusion of an action-packed first half. Just one minute of injury time to be added on. The home team in possession again. Ronaldson turns well, picks out Martin, back to Ronaldson. Looking for Forder but goes the other way, getting more joy down the right hand side. A long ball to Rawlings and Bournemouth start to put the pressure on. Forder makes room for himself. Rawlings finds him. Good control from Forder. Now they're getting into the flow of things. Forder to Martin then a cross towards Ronaldson. The ref glances at his watch. Ronaldson chases the ball down towards the corner, playing well in an attempt to recapture some of the form he displayed last season. Controls it, turns, choosing his moment. Makes a deep cross and a struggle in the box as they all jump in unison. A deflection and a man is down. He's clutching his left leg and the ref blows the whistle for half-time.'

1 *Offside*

I went to a football match once. It was a pleasant evening at the tail end of summer, that time of year when the sunscreen has been safely stored away in the bathroom cabinet while the woolly hat and gloves still lie hidden beneath folded T-shirts in the bottom drawer. The kind of day that could pass by almost unnoticed, yet one that remains in my mind as a day when I did something a bit different. You see, I'm not really a football fan.

However, when I say I went to a football match, it wasn't just a start-of-season provincial game. It was a friendly international at Wembley Stadium – England versus Colombia. To be honest, I simply couldn't imagine attending anything as mundane as an everyday football match. It had to be at least a little out of the ordinary. I mean, I never do things by halves.

My reason for going was also far from usual. Although it was that back-to-school time of year, I'd spent all summer at a school teaching English to foreigners, a job I had been doing for several years and a profession that put me among people of many different nationalities. But in addition to my cosmopolitan environment at work, I often mixed socially with my students because after spending a large part of my adult life abroad, I now felt most at home when in the company of foreigners. I soon began to look upon some of these students as friends, and due to my weekend job as a salsa DJ the majority of my new companions were South American.

Consequently, through a summer of socializing with a great many Colombians I'd learned all about their lifestyle, customs and Latin American passion for football. So when they told me about the forthcoming fixture, I thought it might be fun to accompany them. As the only Englishman in our group, I also offered to arrange tickets and transport to my nation's capital, and on the big day we set off in two rental cars, tickets in hand, having planned exactly where we would park before boarding the London Underground to complete our journey to the famed stadium.

Even so, in spite of my thorough planning of transportation and ticketing, I had given very little thought to the game itself. In fact, I only show a limited interest in this sport for two weeks every four years – the World Cup holds the same inescapable appeal for me as I imagine it does for many people – though back in 1986 I became noticeably more attentive during the Mexico World Cup. But it wasn't the football that had caught my attention; it was the fans. This was inspired by my interest in Latin American percussion, an obsession my father instilled in me at a very early age, and ever since then the thought of football has always filled my mind with many fond memories of those rhythmic Mexican spectators. As a result, when we packed the cars for our trip, I had believed it appropriate to take my *surdo*, an enormous hand-held bass drum used by Brazilian samba bands.

Upon arrival in London, we met a few more Colombian friends at a pub and took the tube to Wembley Stadium. It was a journey I found somewhat troublesome, since it wasn't that easy to travel on an overcrowded train hugging an oversized drum, but I considered this burden to be more than worthwhile. I fully expected to be surrounded by Latinos with similar rhythm-making apparatus once we'd arrived. Yet when we eventually reached the turnstiles of the stadium, my path became blocked by a heavy-set security guard.

'I'm sorry, sir, I cannot allow you to enter with that, er, *thing*,' he politely announced. 'It's too dangerous.'

'What? It's only a drum! And don't worry, I promise not to hit anyone with it,' I joked in the hope of easing the situation with a bit of humour.

'I know you won't, sir,' he replied indifferently, 'because you will leave it in our office.' Then he proceeded to request backup on his radio while I waited with my Colombian entourage, feeling rather bewildered by this unforeseen outcome.

Just at that moment a female security officer arrived and asked our disobliging 'doorman' what he was doing. He explained the problem but her immediate response caught everyone by surprise: 'What do you mean? Of course he can come in with a drum. He's Colombian!'

Well, it appeared there was someone else who still remembered the Mexico World Cup. She truly believed me to be a passionate South American football fan, here to support my nation in the only way I knew how. And I wasn't about to correct her misconception. To tell the truth, the love I had of Latin America played such an important part in my life that I almost felt privileged to be perceived as a citizen of the country whose team I had come here to watch.

We were subsequently permitted entry – with the drum – and made our way to the Colombian end. After taking our seats and getting comfortable, I looked across the immense stadium before me and found myself momentarily enthralled by this enchanting vista. Illuminated in blazing floodlights, row upon row of bright red chairs surrounded a pitch as green as a billiard-table creating a view very remote from my own associations with the game of football. It was really quite beautiful.

Finally, the players came on to the pitch, the referee blew the whistle and the game began. His whistle was also the cue to start beating my drum, and even though the official attendance for this match was the lowest ever recorded at Wembley Stadium, that night the Colombian end was crowded with several thousand South Americans, all clapping in time to my rhythms. On the evening of September 6th 1995, I started to think that I might have actually found a good reason for going to a football match.

The high point of the game came in the first half. It was when the charismatic Colombian goalkeeper Higuita did an extraordinary trick that had earned him the nickname 'The Scorpion'. The English forwards managed to slip past the offside trap, making a creative attack that climaxed with a powerful, 25-yard shot on goal. Higuita took a half-step backwards, then launched himself into the air, diving forwards with outstretched arms, an arched back and legs curled up behind him, and made an unbelievable save by striking the ball with the soles of his boots. It was so gracefully and masterfully executed that there was a brief moment of silence before the spectators could react to his unexpected display of dexterity. Then the stadium filled with deafening applause and this remarkable incident was repeatedly shown on television as the highlight of the nil-nil draw.

I never actually saw it happen. At that time I was too preoccupied with percussion. Nevertheless, several months later my memories of that day returned whilst I was walking down a street in the Colombian city of Medellín and I happened to bump into the acclaimed goalkeeper.

'Wow! You're Higuita!' I exclaimed in broken Spanish. 'I was at Wembley Stadium last year when you did the Scorpion!'

He seemed at a loss for words, perhaps through the surprise of being recognized by someone who clearly *wasn't* from his part of the world. Even so, he still went ahead and shook my hand, gave me a bemused smile and then continued on his way.

Higuita's magnificent save was the high point of an otherwise uneventful first half, and when the 45 minutes were up . . .

. . . the referee blew the whistle for half-time. Then Miguel turned to me and asked, 'Do you mind if I change the channel?'

'No, you go ahead. I wasn't watching it anyway,' I replied in effortless Spanish.

No, I wasn't watching the game. I didn't even know who was playing. What is more, my own whereabouts were also a complete mystery to me. I appeared to be in a small, two-bedded, hospital ward with a Spanish lad in the adjacent bed and a man seated at my side, but I felt so confused that nothing made any sense. Was it half-time?

2 *Cayo Hueso, Yes or No?*

'So, Stevie, are you enjoying the football?' my father tentatively asked.

'What? . . . The football? . . . Er, no, I'm not all that interested in football,' I replied.

'Yes, I know, but do you– do you understand where you are?'

As I looked around the room, I saw nothing that generated any feelings of recognition. In fact, I was finding it quite difficult to even understand his simple question. My mind seemed to be clouded with a fuzzy confusion that obscured any sense of comprehension.

'I . . . I don't know, don't remember, but I'm . . . I'm not at home, am I?'

'No, that's right,' he said with a little smile, 'we're definitely not at home. But can you tell me, are we still in Key West?' he asked in the voice of a schoolteacher addressing a class of five-year-olds.

'What? . . . Key West? No, I . . . I don't think so.'

'Good, yes, that's good,' came his enthusiastic response, 'because you've sort of spent the past few days there really.'

'Have I . . . have I been to Key West?'

'Well, yes, you have, we both have, except you're not there any-more; that was a long time ago. You're here now Stevie, in Lanzarote, the Canary Islands,' he patiently explained.

'Lanzarote? . . . Oh, right . . . yeah, 'course, I'm in Lanzarote,' I agreed.

'You know what? A couple of hours ago you were chatting to Miguel's grandad and then you turned to me and whispered, "He's from the Canary Islands too! I can't believe there are so many people in Key West from the Canaries." I don't know why, but you really thought you were in Key West!'

13

I really thought I was in Key West, a small island in a group called the Florida Keys that stretch down into the Caribbean from the base of the Florida peninsula. While the name relates to geography in so far as this island is the westernmost of the group, it's actually a corruption of the Spanish name: Cayo Hueso – 'Island of Bones' – chosen by the Spanish explorers who had encountered a landscape littered with the human bones of Calusa Indians.

I liked Key West. I had a lot of good memories there. Many years earlier I had spent seven months there; seven marvellous, formative months.

It was 1986, and just as I was finishing a course at art college I started to consider the possibility of travelling for a while before going to university. I don't know where this idea had come from. At that time nobody I knew had done anything similar and the phrase: 'A gap year' hadn't yet entered the national lexicon. Anyhow, it was a thought that wouldn't go away and eventually I decided to make a six-month trip across the United States, west coast to east.

I first spent the summer working very long hours to save enough money to get me there. Then I bought a ticket, packed a bag and took a flight to California. That part was easy but in truth I had almost no idea of what I was intending to do. I had never travelled in this way before and was completely oblivious to the world of 'backpacking', a term that would come to describe my way of life over the next few years. The only thing I did know was that I had very limited funds for the proposed journey and would definitely need to find work en route in whatever positions were available to someone who didn't possess a work permit. It was the start of a big adventure, a wonderful trek into the unknown, a voyage that would take my life along a learning curve much steeper than I'd experienced during my 19 years to date.

Shortly after arriving, I managed to start earning a bit of cash cleaning cars in Los Angeles. But it wasn't a proper job; no one had actually hired me. Despite many hours spent pounding up and down the streets of this city, making enquiries and filling out application forms, I soon discovered that finding employment without papers in America was not an easy task.

The United States has a southern border some 2,000 miles long that separates a fully developed nation from the chaos of the Third World. It's like a sweet shop window with thousands of poor kids, noses pressed hard against the glass, enviously gaping at everything they've ever dreamed of having. Of course, not all of them remain 'in the street'. Each year about three to four million of these wetbacks illegally cross this border in search of a better life, and who can blame them.

Unfortunately, the resultant immigration problem had made it quite difficult for a travelling foreigner to pick up a few weeks casual work, though I wasn't prepared to give up that easily. Moreoever, I was spurred on by the determination displayed by all these disadvantaged souls around me. They were struggling to survive in Los Angeles, 'The City of Angels', a conurbation where cars outnumber people, and I soon began to realize that there might be a way to use this automobile attribute to my advantage. I went out and bought a bucket, a sponge and a chamois-leather and started knocking on doors.

It took a few weeks to find the right neighbourhood for my new business venture. Then I rapidly built up a healthy client list including a couple of Hollywood directors and producers who were more than happy to have their quality European cars cleaned by a lad with a limey accent. I imagine it could have developed into quite a profitable little enterprise, had I chosen to stay longer, but I hadn't come to the States 'in search of a better life'. My dream was to travel, so less than two months later I decided it was time to move on.

It was during the course of my journey across the southern states of Arizona, Texas and Louisiana that I first began hearing about Key West. I invariably stayed at backpackers' youth hostels, where I heard more and more people talking about this island as a great place to get work due to its highly transient population. It was a thriving tourist resort and finding work there without papers was easy because there weren't enough permanent residents to fill all the positions. There was also something far more significant than the simple prospect of easy employment that made this destination appear so desirable.

Although born in London, I had lived in Bournemouth, the UK's premier south-coast beach resort, since the spring of 1976. This was the year of that long and lethally hot summer that had caused a chronic water shortage with temperatures high enough to crack the pavements. But for a city boy now living no more than a stone's throw from the beach, it was fantastic.

I learned something very important about myself that summer. Some people are drawn to the excitement of vibrant cities while others dream of majestic mountain ranges, but in 1976 I found that *my* ultimate passion is the simple combination of sun, sea and sand. Without a doubt, I'm a 'beach boy'. It's something that has influenced the course of my adult life in many ways, though Key West was the first place that would take me from a stick-of-rock seaside experience to a truly exotic, under-a-palm-tree-sipping-a-piña-colada tropical paradise. Consequently, following a bus ride from New Orleans to Miami, the last major city before the Florida Keys, I arrived in ecstatic contemplation of this 'treasured island'.

I spent the first couple of nights at The Clay Hotel, a backpackers' hostel on South Miami Beach. Then I had the good fortune to meet a local girl who offered me a place to stay in North Miami. This new friend was kind enough to show me the sights of the city, as well as telling one or two stories of holidays she'd taken in the Keys that reinforced my romantic image of the little island that lay about 160 miles to the south. Then once my brief stay in Florida's most famous city had come to an end, I set off with a backpacker's excited energy in anticipation of discovering new experiences.

I had decided to try and hitchhike to Key West, seeing as cost had now become my primary consideration when planning any journey. My friend dropped me off at the side of the freeway where I planned to hitch a ride, bypassing the city centre, to the highway that led to my ultimate destination. However, I quickly realized I was on the wrong side of this freeway and had to cautiously cross a flyover with no pavement before reaching a place where I could start hitching. Then I waited for ages, without success, so I decided to hike further down and try by the junction. It was the first time I'd tried this particular form of travel but I soon began to understand why people called it hitchhiking: obviously it entailed hitching *and* hiking.

About an hour or so later I managed to get a ride and, ironically, it was an English guy who'd stopped to pick me up. He couldn't take me far because he was turning off a couple of miles down the road, and just as he was dropping me off he also happened to mention that it was illegal to hitchhike in the state of Florida. Nevertheless, after waiting no more than a few minutes, I was picked up again and taken a little further. Then my third short ride left me in Miami city centre.

I hadn't planned a route including a visit to downtown Miami. This had come about when I'd simply felt it impolite to refuse a lift from someone who'd been kind enough to stop and offer me one. Even so, I soon discovered that hitchhiking out of a city centre is virtually impossible, so I started a long walk across town carrying a heavy backpack in the stifling heat of a humid Florida afternoon. It was extremely demanding, not quite the exciting experience I had been anticipating, and after a very short time I began to feel rather fatigued and decidedly dehydrated.

As I was trudging along a waterfront highway trying to sneak a look at millionaires' pleasure boats through the incessant passing traffic, I suddenly noticed that this lavish subtropical dual carriageway was lined with coconut palms. Even though it was my first time in the tropics, I remembered a conversation with a well-travelled backpacker who had gone to great lengths to explain the difference between coconut *milk* and coconut *water*. The former is the contents of a fairground coconut, one that has fallen from a tree and lain in the sun, thus causing the husk to dry out, the flesh to solidify and the fluid to ferment into a liquid resembling milk. The latter is contained by a coconut whilst still on a tree, and this experienced tropical traveller claimed it was a more refreshing beverage, always cool no matter the climate, and much easier to extract because the husk had yet to harden into the characteristic smash-with-a-hammer shell.

The chance of a cold drink (and one that didn't involve payment) was too great to pass up. I put my backpack down and stood in the shade of swaying palm fronds, surveying my quarry while a sea breeze dried my sweat-stained T-shirt. Despite feeling conspicuous amongst passing businessmen in elegant Armani suits and shimmering glass skyscrapers – a setting very different from the jungles of my fellow backpacker's story – I scrambled up the rough but readily

17

scalable trunk and plucked my prize.

It transpired that all the information I'd been given was correct. Using a pocket knife, I started cutting a small hole in the top of the husk around the stem that had attached it to the tree, and I found it to be easily penetrable. Within a matter of minutes, I had sculpted this perforation into an adequate mouthpiece and began gulping down a drink that was more remarkable for its temperature than taste. Then, feeling adequately refreshed, I threw the drained husk in a litter bin (an inappropriate end to such a 'primitive' experience) and gathered up my belongings to recommence the gruelling hike.

I continued walking for over two hours, soaked in sweat, and my feet soon became sore and blistered, ultimately forcing me to consider other options. Taxis were expensive and bus routes complicated, but the heart of Miami's public transport system was the Metrorail, an elevated train network. It only cost a dollar and there was a line that stretched to the south of the city, where I felt certain I would be able to find a good place to start hitching again.

After a brief rest in a comfortable seat, I got off the train and began hiking down the highway. I'd just reached a bus stop and was contemplating a bus ride to Homested, the last town before the Florida Keys, when someone stopped and offered me a lift. Eager not to miss the opportunity, I first double-checked he was going my way, then I threw my backpack onto the back seat and jumped in. It was another of those frustratingly short rides, lasting a matter of minutes, but following several more of a similar duration I eventually found myself at the end of the Florida peninsula.

My next ride took me onto Key Largo, the first and also the longest island in the Keys. In return for his help, the driver asked me for a dollar so he could buy himself a cold beer and then generously offered an invitation for some early supper back at his place. Fortunately, this allowed me to have a much-needed rest in addition to the first decent conversation in what was becoming a very long and lonely day.

My obliging host was an amiable fellow and for a reason I couldn't quite comprehend, he appeared to be terribly excited about picking up a 'hitchhiker from London'. (Why do Americans always assume that every Englishman lives in London?) We had a snack and a pleasant chat, then he took me back to the main highway and left me to continue with my journey, not before offering a place to sleep for the night if I became stranded.

By then it was early evening and even though I had almost a hundred miles left to travel, I still found time to enjoy the unfamiliar surroundings. These islands were very flat, having formed through sand collecting around the roots of mangroves until they eventually grew into islets. In fact, a piece of Florida Keys trivia I would hear repeated on numerous occasions is that the highest point in the entire group is only 18 feet above sea level. Nevertheless, their lack of elevation hadn't left them barren and there was a vast amount of vegetation including countless coconut palms and tropical fruit trees. There were even small forests of tropical hardwoods inhabited by Key deer (a subspecies of white tail deer) and although I hadn't yet seen one, the warning signs at regular intervals along the highway made it obvious their presence constituted a road hazard.

And the contrast of colours was breathtaking: pale blue sky, deep blue sea, white sandy beaches and dark green vegetation studded with brightly coloured flowers. But the most appealing thing to me was the sound: that incessant tropical hum. I later learned that it's made by tree frogs.

I waited just a few minutes for another ride, again only a short one, but the sun had long since slipped below the horizon before I was taken a further 15 miles to Plantation Key, the place where the *real* nightmare began. Here I started to think that maybe hitchhiking wasn't such a thrilling adventure, a thought that went on to fill a lot more time than it deserved.

I waited, and waited, and waited. I was extremely tired, my back was aching and my feet were throbbing. I had no idea where I would sleep that night and my feelings of desperation were so great that I was almost on the verge of tears. Finally, I realized I had no other choice. I would have to start hiking again, so after struggling to shoulder my backpack I began an agonizing walk. There was no other alternative, short of sleeping at the roadside, an option I had already discarded after careful consideration of many impractical factors such as the thick swarm of mosquitoes that were currently feeding off every inch of my exposed flesh.

As I walked, in an effort to take my mind off the pain, distress and panic that was mounting within me, I tried to think of an acceptable solution to this unexpected dilemma. Even though I was nearly half way through *my* journey, the mid-point of the Greyhound bus route to Key West was on Islamorada, about a 50-minute hike down the highway. I knew that the last bus of the day had a rest stop at the Burger King on this island at 10pm, so I decided to sacrifice my backpacker's pride and get there in time to take the bus the rest of the way. I marched on bravely, ignoring the blisters, until about 20 minutes later when the bus roared past me. I wasn't going to make it. I would be sleeping at the roadside with mosquitoes as room-mates.

I wandered on aimlessly, feeling completely drained of all the confidence and enthusiasm that had filled me at start of that day. While crossing another of the many bridges that connects the chain of Keys to the mainland, I paused and looked down into the crystal-clear water below. Even in the moonlight it was possible to make out the coral bed some 20 feet below the surface. This beautiful seascape was home to an enormous variety of colourful tropical fish, a few of which ventured up to investigate some unusual ripples at the surface but encountered nothing more than teardrops falling from the eyes of a boy on his first big adventure.

Just at that moment, consumed with despair, a bright red convertible screeched across the bridge and skidded to a dramatic halt on the gravel of the hard shoulder just a few yards to my left. I was immediately thrown into a state of shock and before I'd even had the chance to regain my bearings, I was greeted with a cry of, 'Hey dude! Are you gonna get in or what?'

My feelings of desperation suddenly became polluted with confusion. I hadn't had my thumb out, so why had they stopped? Was the simple presence of a backpack at my side enough to confirm that I was hitchhiking or had they thought I was about to throw myself off the bridge? It took a moment for my mind to catch up with my mouth until I finally managed to stutter, 'But– er– yeah. Yes, of course!'

'Well, come on then. Get it in gear, turkey!'

'What? Oh right, you mean hurry up,' I replied, hoping this was the correct *British* English translation of his request. 'Just let me get my things.'

'Wow! That's one hell of a bag you got there, man. Looks like you's *travelling*!'

'Yeah, you know, just trying to see a bit of the world.'

'All right! So what we got here is an explorer! Welcome to the New World, dude. I'm Brian the Lion and this is Pistol Pete,' he said, gesturing towards the man at his side. 'Nice to meet you.'

'Yeah, nice to make your acquaintance, Columbus,' echoed the passenger.

'Colum– oh right, yeah, I get it,' I chuckled. 'But my name's Steve, actually.'

'So, Steve, where are you from?' asked Brian.

'I'm English.'

'English! Cool, a hitchhiker from London. Let's get going then!'

These two characters were considerably livelier than my previous 'chauffeurs', and this served as the perfect tonic to drag me out of my melancholy mood. Brian the Lion, the man at the wheel, was the shorter and stockier of the two, and I also got the impression he was the 'lion' in their friendship. I wouldn't describe him as domineering, it was just that he was a lot more vocal than his passive passenger Pistol Pete, and he tended to dictate the course of conversation. His companion was more of a gentle giant, a role that befitted him well, though he did have the appealing capacity to demonstrate a pistol-quick sense of humour with perfect timing.

Both of them worked as ground crew at Fort Lauderdale airport, about 20 miles north of Miami, and they had set off late that afternoon with the grandiose plan of spending a thousand dollars in one night. This excessive undertaking made my situation feel even more extreme, since that amount of cash was roughly equivalent to my budget for almost two months of backpack travels. They'd rented the sporty open-top roadster for the occasion and had equipped it with an enormous cooler resembling the trunk of a genuine 'New World explorer', full of ice-cold beers. As soon as I was seated, they politely asked me to replenish their brews, which were warming in the heat of a tropical evening, and invited me to help myself. They also told me they were destined for Key West, which came as a great relief after the endless hours of intermittent short rides that had brought me this far.

A few hours later we reached this pretty little tourist haven, dubbed 'The Last Resort' on account of being the southernmost point of the continental USA. As we drove down the island towards the town centre, a question from my companions caught me by surprise. I was an Englishman in Key West for the first time, with two guys from southern Florida, yet *they* asked *me* if I knew of anywhere to stay. Many of the travellers I'd met who had talked about Key West had also mentioned the Casa Marina Hotel as a great place to get work in the kitchens. It was a good hotel and they always needed people.

'I've heard the Casa Marina isn't too bad,' I suggested with the air of a seasoned traveller.

'That sounds perfect,' said Brian. 'Let's go for it!'

It wasn't difficult to find but when we arrived, much to my embarrassment, we discovered it to be a five-star hotel, reputedly the most expensive and luxurious on the island. However, this didn't deter them in the slightest. Brian the Lion marched straight up to the reception desk and asked for the best suite presently available.

I couldn't remember ever having been in a five-star hotel before, much less having a suite for the night. The previous few months had been spent in a number of backpackers' hostels that provided a variety of austere accommodations. Yet now, through a strange quirk of fate, I was at the other end of the spectrum. Now I was in five-star luxury.

This elegant, top-floor suite consisted of a plush lounge complete with TV, video, stereo and mini-bar; a couple of bedrooms with en suite bathrooms; a fully equipped kitchen and a balcony overlooking the swimming pool. I was suitably impressed with all the modern comforts of my new surroundings but was given very little time to enjoy them before my companions invited me to take a tour of the local taverns.

The small town centre of Key West is traversed by Duval Street, described by the locals as 'the longest street in the world' because it runs from the Atlantic Ocean at one end to the Gulf of Mexico at the other. In reality, it took us no more than about 20 minutes to walk its

22

entire length . . . but what an enchanting walk! A local by-law decreed that all buildings be painted in colours selected from a list at the Town Hall, a law that had turned Key West into a medley of pastel hues that blend so pleasingly with the dark green, tropical vegetation.

On reaching Mallory Docks at the Gulf end of the street, we went into Key West's oldest and best known bar. It's called Sloppy Joe's and in past times was frequented by the island's most famous resident, Ernest Hemingway, a man who lived on the island from 1931 to 1940. The moment we entered, Brian the Lion bought each of us a souvenir T-shirt printed with a portrait of this literary giant, and his generosity continued when we ordered our first round of drinks. From there we went to Rick's Bar, a more modern hostelry across the street, and once again I didn't need to put my hand in my pocket. The night progressed along the same theme until we eventually returned to our hotel suite and ran up a tab on the mini-bar that would have paid for a couple of weeks of my travels.

The following day, feeling rather delicate, we were awakened at noon by a chambermaid who wanted to clean the room, so we hastily packed our bags and checked out. I spent the afternoon with Brian and Pete (our friendship having transcended the need for macho monikers) and we rented bicycles to see the sights at a leisurely pace. Finally, early that evening they bade farewell to their 'hitchhiker from London' and left me outside the Seashell Motel, Key West's youth hostel.

My original plan had only been to spend three or four weeks there, but things went so well that I didn't move on until some seven months later. I found employment in construction as a painter with absolutely no trouble at all. I simply read an advertisement on the youth hostel notice-board that first night and went to the specified address the next morning. Despite my limited experience of this profession – my father was a painting contractor and I'd helped him out once or twice – I was an art student who always felt at home with a paintbrush in his hand and subsequently took to the job very quickly.

I started work along with two guys called Hans and Colin, a couple of Australian backpackers who were also staying at the hostel. Some people pass through your life like waiters in a restaurant, yet the memory of these two guys is still with me, even today. At that time I hadn't met many Aussies and I knew very little about their country, but over the following months, through a continual stream of amusing anecdotes, I learned a great deal about life down under and we soon established valuable friendships.

In addition to this, my new employer gave me some assistance in renting an apartment. It was a modest, one-bedroomed, ground-floor flat, which I shared with another backpacker recruited from the youth hostel and was situated in the Cuban part of town known as Bahama Village, where monthly rentals were very reasonably priced.

The time I spent there is extremely precious to me. A new part of my life started in Key West and in many respects I became an adult there. It was my first exposure to the joys of an independent lifestyle in my own flat, and I was also earning considerably more money than I'd ever had the good fortune to earn in the past. Consequently, this new-found freedom and wealth afforded me a very active social life, and the cosmopolitan make-up of the island led to friendships with a multitude of people of differing nationalities and backgrounds, people who could also open my eyes to the wonders of many other parts of the world.

It was a time that infected me with life, but the best thing of all for a boy who'd grown up on the beaches of Bournemouth was that all of this was happening on a beautiful, small, subtropical island, 90 miles north of Cuba. Things could have been worse.

Things were worse. I wasn't in Key West. I was on Lanzarote, in hospital, and I had no idea why I was here or what had happened to me. I don't really know why, in my mind, I had returned to Key West. Maybe it was a combination of the memories of my hospitalization for an appendectomy whilst living on the island and of the month my father spent there with me when I got him a job as a carpenter. I'd been in hospital in Key West and I'd been with my father in Key West. Now I was in a foreign country, in hospital once again, and my father was at my side.

On the other hand, it could have simply been due to the need to be anywhere I'd felt better than I did right now; anywhere that could take me out of the nightmare of the present. I needed to be in a place that provoked happy memories, vivid enough to overpower reality, and in my mind I had chosen Key West.

Though I suppose things could have been even worse. At least I wasn't in this nightmare alone. My father was here with me too.

3 *Cuba Libre*

So I understood I wasn't in Key West. I was in the Canary Islands, on Lanzarote, and I was in hospital. But that was the limit of my comprehension. I could see that my left leg was in traction, several IV tubes were coming out of my arms and chest, and I had severe double vision in my left visual field. Yet I had absolutely no recollection of anything preceding that moment. It was as if I'd been in a dark place devoid of any concept of time or consequence, and just as I was returning to the 'real world' the first thing I'd seen that had made any sense was the face of my father.

'So, Stevie, are you starting to feel a bit better?' he softly asked.

'Yeah . . . er . . . I'm OK.'

'Good, yes, well at least you know where you are now,' he said in a voice that conveyed relief. 'I mean, it's nice to have you back. We kinda lost you for a while there and– oh yeah, look who arrived last night!' he added, pointing to the lady seated next to him.

'What? . . . Oh, it's mum . . . Hello.' Although happy to see her, I was still far too bewildered to give a warmer greeting and was more preoccupied with the unfamiliar surroundings.

This room was smaller than a typical British hospital ward and only accommodated two patients. My room-mate Miguel lay in the bed to my left, watching the football on a television fixed high on the wall opposite us. He was younger than I was, maybe 17 or 18, and there was an elderly gentleman in a chair on the far side of his bed, presumably his grandad. Beyond them was a window that appeared to look out over a central quadrangle, though it was difficult to get a good sense of geography from such a restrictive position.

My parents were seated to my right. Behind them I could just make out the far edge of the door to our room but I was unable to see through the doorway into the corridor beyond because my path of vision was obscured by the wall of an internal cubicle. As my focus of attention moved further to the right, I started to realize that this cubicle was an en suite bathroom, the door of which was open.

'I'm just going to the loo,' I said and made ready to get up.

'No! Wait! You can't get up!' my father exclaimed. 'You've got a broken leg.'

'But I want to go to the toilet.'

'Look, you have to stay here and use this bottle,' he explained.

'I can't get up?'

'No, Steve, not at the moment.'

Whilst struggling to digest this piece of information, suddenly I was confronted with another familiar face. Even though I was in a very confused state of mind, I immediately recognized the boyish, beaming grin of the man in front of me, who, like so many of Latin descent, had the appearance of someone much younger than his years.

'Hey, Leonardo! What are you doing here?' I drawled in a morphine-induced haze.

This man was something akin to a flying doctor, since the geographical nature of the islands occasionally engendered the need to fly a patient from one island to a hospital on another that housed the required specialist department. While unable to comprehend anything so complicated, I was about to be sent to Gran Canaria, where it had been deemed necessary I underwent assessment in the neurology department, and Leonardo was going to take me there.

From the moment he entered my room, I was sure I already knew him. I felt certain I'd met him at the carnival in Tenerife, and he reciprocated with a friendly greeting, though this may have been through politeness rather than the product of a genuine acquaintance. Nevertheless, as we set off on our journey to the airport, my mind began racing through memories of the carnival in Tenerife four years earlier.

It was February 1995 and I was spending a month on this Spanish island, the largest and perhaps most well known of the Canaries, a group of seven islands lying off the north-west coast of Africa. It was longer than a typical holiday, but I was between jobs with time on my hands and it was still considerably shorter than other trips I had made. The previous year I had returned from Venezuela, where I'd been working as an English teacher for about six months after travelling around a few islands in the south of the Caribbean. In fact, my Venezuelan adventure had been one of the two reasons why I'd decided to visit Tenerife.

On my travels through this South American country I had met numerous Canarian immigrants, the majority of whom were from Tenerife. Many of them had emigrated in the early seventies to escape poorly-paid employment in the Canaries at a time when Venezuela's petroleum-based economy was rapidly expanding due to escalated oil prices. This had produced strong social and cultural ties between the Canaries and Venezuela, so through visiting Tenerife I'd felt it would be, at least to a limited extent, like returning to the environment of my first South American experience.

The other reason was the carnival. I'd heard many stories about this very Latin-flavoured festival from some of the friends I regularly met at the salsa club where I worked as a DJ. Consequently, following a week of relaxation at a campsite in the south of the island, I was waiting at the airport in excited anticipation of a wild week of non-stop partying with two British guys, Dave and Neil, also coming over for the carnival.

Although they were both friends of mine, they lived in different parts of England and had never actually met each other before. My friendship with Dave began not long after I'd moved to Brighton to start university. We initially became acquainted at a local pub, where he was performing as a guitarist with a flamenco band. Then a few years later he invited me to join another band he was with.

However, during the four years I spent in Brighton I only ever saw him at pub gigs and band practice, and our friendship didn't really begin to flourish until I had gone on my trip to Venezuela. Like me, Dave was a keen traveller with an interest in Latin America, so we occasionally corresponded while I was away and once I returned we started to visit each other from time to time. Whenever we got together, our shared passion for music and travel always led to long conversations into the early hours, though we also had one more important thing in common: both of us taught English as a foreign language.

Neil and I shared a slightly different musical connection. He was one of a group of people I referred to as my 'salsa friends' because we only ever met at the nightclub in Bournemouth. I didn't know him nearly as well as Dave, he was little more than an acquaintance, and apart from salsa there wasn't much else we talked about. Even so, it transpired that he'd booked a ticket on the same flight as Dave but had been unable to organize accommodation, so I'd offered to let him join us, despite my concern that I knew too little about him to be sure if he and Dave would get along.

I needn't have worried. They finally met at the airport, and during the four-hour flight they discovered that a love of Latin music and a shared party spirit were enough to produce easy-flowing exchanges, which proved to be sufficient to guarantee a great holiday for all three of us.

Once they'd arrived and collected their luggage, we picked up the rental car and started driving north. Unlike most visitors to this island, who prefer the reliably sunny tourist centres of Los Cristianos and Playa de las Américas in the south, I'd booked an apartment in a town named Puerto de la Cruz. This picturesque resort lies at the mouth of the Orotava Valley, on the much greener, northern coast of Tenerife, in a landscape of luxuriant vegetation. It's a pretty little town, criss-crossed with narrow streets of beautiful, old, Canarian-style houses, and was the first holiday centre to develop in the Canary Islands, originally discovered by well-to-do British people at the end of the nineteenth century.

During the drive north, we discussed our plans for the week and exchanged many stories we'd heard about the carnival in Tenerife. None of us had had any firsthand contact with this Canarian *fiesta*, though I'd seen one or two similar celebrations in other parts of the world. I'd been fortunate enough to enjoy a truly Caribbean carnival in Trinidad, a very commercial Mardi Gras in New Orleans, and our own English version in Notting Hill. But nothing had prepared me for the South-American-style festival I was about to sample.

On reaching Puerto de la Cruz, we checked in to the apartment, did some shopping and then decided it was time to eat, so we began making a few sandwiches. However, another recent purchase quickly caught my attention. On our brief shopping trip we had also bought a bottle of my favourite Venezuelan rum, and the temptation proved too great to resist. I took three tall glasses, filled each with an ample helping of ice, over which I poured a good measure of rum, added a slice of lemon and then topped them up with Coca-Cola to produce that classic Caribbean cocktail: Cuba Libre.

Feeling refreshed and inspired, Dave then suggested indulging in some live music. He never travelled without his acoustic guitar and I had a pair of maracas and a cowbell in my backpack, so we adjourned to the terrace, tuned up and began playing one of Dave's favourites, the Gypsy Kings song *Bamboleo*.

It wasn't an unsociable hour and our rendition was fairly re-strained, but after a short time a man appeared on the terrace of the adjacent apartment. He was a mature gentleman, perhaps in his mid-fifties, with greying hair and a small moustache. Indeed, it was obvious from his untidy hair that our performance had interrupted his afternoon *siesta*, and this concerned me a little. I'd read that Puerto de la Cruz was popular amongst the more senior, middle-class tourist, not the type of person who took kindly to musicians on their doorstep, so I felt sure we were about to receive a severe reprimand.

I couldn't have been more wrong.

'Cor blimey! Fer a minute there I fought the Gypsy Kings 'ad moved in next door!' he exclaimed in a broad cockney accent.

'Er, sorry, we didn't mean to disturb you,' I apologized, at the same time finding myself impressed by the accuracy of his musical knowledge.

'No, that's awright lads, don't worry 'bout that. So, 'ave yer fellas just arrived then?'

'Yeah, we've come over here to check out the carnival,' explained Dave.

'Oh, right. Well, yer 'ave come ter the right place. Me 'n me 'ole lady come 'ere evry year fer carnival.'

'Really?' came my involuntary response in a voice that expressed disbelief rather than interest. He didn't exactly epitomize my precon-ceived concept of a regular carnival carouser.

'Yeah, yer know, it's a right good laugh. Lot's a music an' plenty a dancin', plus the chance fer a bit uv a booze up o'course. An' I see yer fellas 'ave made an early start,' he added with a nod towards the open bottle of rum on the table. 'Mind if I join yer for one?' he asked as he lifted a patio chair over the knee-high wall that separated his terrace from ours.

His name was John and he worked as a pilot on the River Thames taking ships inland from the estuary to the centre of London. He said that he was here with his wife Fay, told us that they were musicians as well, and subsequently invited us to join the two of them for an evening of live music at an Irish bar in town.

Later that day, they took us to Molly Malone's, a bar owned by a musician called Des who commenced the evening's entertainment with some Celtic tunes. However, this bar also operated an open-floor policy, and no sooner had he vacated the stage than John and Fay got up to repay us the favour we had done them that afternoon. To be honest, they gave a well-rehearsed performance and once the Cuba Libre had begun to take effect, Dave and I even went and played another Gypsy Kings number, much to the amusement of the Spanish-speaking bar staff, who graciously assisted with backing vocals.

It was an enjoyable start to the evening, but we hadn't come to the Canaries to pursue careers as musicians. Eventually, we left this bar and went down to the town square in search of the real carnival action. It was only a short walk down a winding, cobbled street and the moment we arrived I realized all my hopes, dreams and expectations of this carnival were certainly going to be fulfilled.

At one end of the palm-lined plaza, a large stage had been erected that was currently filled with a group of about a dozen musicians. They comprised a brass section, a percussion section, a pianist, a bassist and three vocalists, all dressed in shiny, cabaret suits, and they were blasting out a driving rhythm of Latin sounds. The area in front of this stage was jammed with a frenzied mob, swinging their hips to the constant thump of percussion and a hypnotic bass line punctuated with the wail of trumpets, saxophones and trombones. The majority of these revellers appeared to be locals, most of them dressed in carnival costumes, but through this crowd of gyrating bodies I could also make out one or two other tourists, like myself, all wearing the same dizzy euphoric expression and their eyes glittering with excitement.

Down the middle of the streets on either side of this plaza ran elongated bars, each of them a series of booths full of rum, whisky, vodka and beer, and manned with teams of bartenders feverishly working to supply the surrounding hordes of happy people with drink. It was a street party unmatched by any I'd previously experienced.

The next day was Saturday and traditionally an important night in the carnival calendar. Having enjoyed an evening in the tourist town of Puerto de la Cruz, we decided to visit Santa Cruz, the island's capital, seeing as coming to Tenerife during the carnival and not going to the capital was like paying for an English course and not attending the classes. According to the *Guinness Book of Records*, Santa Cruz is the 'Capital of Carnival' and holds the record for the most people dancing in the same place at the same time. That place was the Plaza de España and that time was Carnival.

We left Puerto de la Cruz at around ten in the evening and drove across the island, through the university town of La Laguna, to the capital on the other side. After parking on the edge of town, we joined the throngs of people heading down towards the Plaza and one thing I noticed almost immediately was that everyone was in fancy dress. The previous night in Puerto de la Cruz a significant number had been dressed up, yet here absolutely everyone was, everyone except the three of us: three tourists.

Despite feeling a little conspicuous through our lack of appropriate costume, we still enjoyed ourselves immensely and danced until dawn in streets filled with the same happy excitement we'd experienced on our first night of Carnival. However, we also realized that more effort would be required if we were to return to Santa Cruz.

The following night we partied more conservatively in Puerto de la Cruz in preparation for Monday, the biggest night in carnivals all over the world. We'd decided to return to the capital but had additionally agreed that fancy dress was an absolute necessity. Unfortunately, this presented me with a problem. As was usually the case, I was travelling on a limited budget and couldn't stretch to the expense of a shop-bought costume. But I wasn't prepared to let this minor complication spoil our fun. Consequently, I told Dave and Neil that I was sure we could put something suitable together, completely free of charge, with whatever we could find in our apartment.

Since the theme of Carnival that year was 'A Thousand Arabian Nights', we decided on a bed sheet with a leather belt as an Arabian robe, and a tea-towel tied on with a bandanna as a head-dress. Even though the end result was a costume with a rather thrown-together nature, one element made it very appropriate for Carnival in the Canaries. A recurrent image we'd seen the previous three nights was that of cross-gender dressing – men dressed as women. Virtually every Canarian man would spend at least one night of Carnival in drag, so we were certain that our costumes wouldn't look out of place because the sheets we had used were bright pink, thus giving a very effeminate feel to our portrayal of 'Three Arabian Knights'.

It was a truly memorable night, although my memories of the latter part were drowned in Cuba Libre. Even so, we managed to return safely to our apartment the next morning, with time to hide the soiled sheets before the arrival of the chambermaid, and spent the rest of the day sleeping off the excess of alcohol.

But at about six that evening, at breakfast, we did receive a small visual reminder of our activities the previous night. During Carnival in the Canaries the local TV stations always broadcast the highlights of festivities from the night before, and as we munched on toast and sipped hot coffee, there, on the TV screen in front of us, were three wild-eyed effeminate Arabs, all doing their best to dance merengue!

'It sounds like you had a good time,' said Leonardo.

'Yes, I did,' I confessed. 'I even went back again the following year.'

'Really? Well, it's time to get you out of this ambulance now. So, are you ready to move?'

'Yeah, but, er, I'm in quite a bit of pain at the moment, actually.'

'Let me give you something for it first, then,' he said, taking a syringe out of his bag of medical supplies to give me another dose of morphine.

Once I had been lifted out of the ambulance and onto the tarmac of the runway, my head began floating to a drug-induced state of euphoria. As I lay there, contemplating the clouds, I could feel a strong breeze blowing across my face and hear a strangely familiar *thwacka thwacka thwacka* of propellers. Then, slowly, I turned to my left and became transfixed by the image on view before my eyes – the coolest aircraft of any schoolboy war game – a helicopter!

The combination of being so close to such a powerful machine with a potent narcotic flowing through my veins produced a bizarre reaction in my confused mind. For a brief moment, I had been transported to the setting of a war film I've never been able to forget. It was as if I were really there; surrounded by body-strewn bomb craters, post-combat chaos and Charlie Sheen on the stretcher next to me. I had been wounded in action and was about to be airlifted out, my ears resounding with that haunting, Oscar-winning soundtrack.

'Yeah, man!' I screamed in a carnival of excitement. 'Ours is not to do or die. Ours is to smoke and stay high!'

'What did you say?' asked Leonardo, unable to understand my English.

'This is just like Vietnam!' I shouted in Spanish.

'What?'

'Vietnam, the Vietnam War!' I replied, still struggling to contain myself.

'Oh, the Vietnam War. Yes, I understand, but you're not in Vietnam, Steve. The war is over; *your* war is over now,' he said, and then he loaded me into the helicopter and we flew to Gran Canaria.

4 *Last Dance*

My first few days on Gran Canaria are a series of disjointed recoll-
ections. I knew that my surroundings had changed, that I was in a
different hospital on another island, but I still didn't understand what
had happened to me. I remember feeling a mixture of frustration,
panic and fear, and just as I was emerging from a confused period of
delirium I'd been taken from those who were close to me and left to
confront this fear alone.

The previous day these emotions had been temporarily abated
when I'd received a visit from my mother. She had flown over from
Lanzarote and although unable to stay long, it had been very com-
forting to have her at my bedside, albeit for only a few hours. She's a
woman of great compassion and, as a nurse, was familiar with caring
for someone in my condition, so I'd enjoyed her visit immensely.

I had also felt quite touched that she'd taken the trouble to come,
travelling 2,000 miles from England to Lanzarote and then catching an
internal flight to Gran Canaria, particularly considering she wasn't my
real mother. In truth, I didn't expect or even want a visit from the
woman who had actually borne me because Lyn, my stepmother, had
long since become the woman I always thought and spoke of as 'my
mum'.

My biological mother, a troublesome woman called Mary, lost the
right to this title many years ago. She has always been partial to pre-
meditated acts of malice and eventually the place where my love for
her had once been soon grew very cold and hard and dry. In the end, I
decided that the blood we shared would no longer tie us in affection
and I chose the 'mother' who deserves this name rather than a woman
whose only claim to it is through childbirth.

I know this may seem quite a harsh decision, but I'm not the sole member of our family who has found this woman to be an eternal source of heartache. We've all endured countless years of her lies and deceit, and in recent times her lack of respect for moral values even escalated to breaking the law. Not long ago, her youngest sister fell victim to a very nasty piece of hate mail that she'd sent to her place of work, an incident that led to police involvement, though she proved to be capable of much worse crimes. Her last boyfriend had to contact Interpol after she'd stolen thousands of pounds from him in the Greek islands and then fled back to England to buy a flat with her ill-gotten gains! Even my maternal grandmother no longer enjoys her company, preferring to spend the Christmas holidays with her ex-son-in-law (my father) and his wife than with her own daughter.

The list of people she's hurt and the problems she has created is endless, and my own personal grievances are far too numerous to recount here. Nevertheless, there is one particular wound she inflicted that I find impossible to forgive. It all started with a divorce, although I had no idea what had happened until many years later. It's also something that involves my sister and to understand the damage our mother did, you first need to know what it was like between the two of us before the problems began.

When our parents divorced we stayed with our mother. Nikki was eleven and I was nine and, as is usually the case, a mother's care was considered more important at that stage of our lives. Until then we'd enjoyed a healthy brother-sister relationship and in many ways, during the first few years following the separation, this bond became much stronger. Even though we attended different schools, we spent most of our free time together with our little group of friends – she didn't have her friends and me mine, they were *our* friends – and, of course, the weekends were spent with Dad.

Despite having disparate personalities (we were made from the same raw materials but put together differently) we both shared the same adolescent preoccupation with popular culture. And this was at a time, a unique period, when England was the world centre of youth fashion and music. I imagine most people look back on their formative years with affection, yet we were members of a special generation, the first children to experience so many things that are now considered quite ordinary. Since then, what was new for us and much of what had come before has endlessly been recycled and repackaged because, it seems, no one is able to come up with anything better.

In the world of music, I had watched my sister paper her bedroom walls with posters of Jimmy Osmond, then Donny Osmond, David Cassidy, then David Soul, but when *Saturday Night Fever* brought 'disco' to the UK, we finally had a musical interest we could share. It came across the water from America – the Vietnam War had drawn to a close and the Yanks wanted rhythm without the blues – though in Britain the musical reaction to politics was punk rock.

During the year of our parents' divorce, we found ourselves at the start of a radical period of revolution in popular culture. Suddenly, our wardrobes weren't restricted by financial constraints, by fashions dictated by designers. We would spend every Saturday afternoon rummaging through clothes in second-hand shops and then hours sat at a sewing machine producing our own personal fashions. We had the complete freedom to choose exactly what we wore. Labels weren't important, creativity was what counted.

Then the synthesizer gave birth to the New Romantics and New Wave (very avant-garde concepts of fashion and music) and Bob Marley's concert at the Lyceum had recently brought reggae to the UK, which had combined with punk rock to produce the ska revival Two-Tone. There were so many different musical styles around that it was the only time the Pop Charts have actually offered a *variety* of music. It was also a period when music and fashion were so closely intertwined that the clothes a person wore told you exactly what their record collection comprised.

And the choices were manifold. Every Saturday night my sister and I would go to an under-eighteen's disco, where there were always several distinct groups of youngsters. There would be tight-knit clusters of mods, punks, new romantics, skinheads, alternatives, rude boys, trendies and ratsas, and it was all progressing so rapidly that you virtually had to change your entire wardrobe every six months or so.

Together with music and fashion, we were the first children to have experience of many new technological advances. We played the first video games (Space Invaders, Asteroids and Pacman are the ones anybody my age will remember). We owned the earliest domestic video-game console, the ludicrously named Pong, that now looks positively archaic alongside contemporary technology but no child since has experienced the pure, unbelievable, virgin fascination of actually being able to control something on your own television set. We were the first to have pocket calculators, digital watches, televisions in our bedrooms and video recorders in the lounge; the first to cruise the streets on skateboards whilst listening to music on personal stereos. We were the first children to have access to computers.

Then there was foreign travel. The package holiday had been born during our childhood days, and I remember in the mid-seventies a group of our primary school classmates sitting around us in silent awe while we recounted the details of our two-week summer break in Benidorm. Nowadays, no one bats an eyelid when you tell them you went to Sydney for your summer holiday. Back then, a trip to Spain was like visiting another planet.

Everything today's kids take for granted – the things that they assume have always been there – we experienced as they were brought into existence. And all of this I shared with my sister. Those memories are beyond value, something I will always treasure at a time before mother started making our relationship so much more complicated than it ever should have been.

The problems began after I started grammar school. Nikki had made that nerve-racking transfer to secondary education the previous year, except she hadn't passed the eleven-plus exam and had consequently been placed at one of the comprehensive schools in town. There was a certain amount of resentment felt by many kids at the local comprehensives towards 'the select few' at grammar school, but unbeknown to me, this feeling had been magnified ten-fold in our family home due to mother's obsession with academic success. Every end-of-term report card, every end-of-year exam result was used by our mother to make my sister feel like a chronic under-achiever, and I was continually held up as an example of a model student.

This was grossly unfair, not behaviour one would consider as good parenting, but what made it even more unjust was that Nikki *wasn't* a bad student. Admittedly, of the two of us, I'd always been the more 'scholastic' thinker – I mean, we all learn in different ways and Nikki had to struggle hard to get the results she needed – but the differences between our schools were enormous. Bournemouth Grammar School was an intensive learning centre designed to groom students towards the ultimate goal of passing a string of O and A level exams, and possibly even acceptance at one of the prestigious universities of Oxford and Cambridge. Consequently, our mother had absolutely no right to expect Nikki to compete with me academically, yet in her mind this was the only thing that held any value.

At that time, I had absolutely no idea any of this was happening. Most of what I've just written is an assumption on my part based on things that occurred later, as we were entering adulthood. I think it was a more private, subconscious resentment that my sister carried round inside her throughout our secondary education. In fact, I only remember one occasion when it actually came to the surface: she stole all my chemistry books the day before my O level chemistry exam.

It was such a gradual process that it enveloped our relationship without even provoking an inkling of our awareness. Nikki was, and still is, a loving sister and I always accepted her reactions to various situations as the normal response of a caring sibling. I never thought it strange that she didn't congratulate me on passing my O level exams, or two years later my A levels, or even when I graduated at university. I remember telephoning her with news of passing my driving test and all she could say was, 'I really wanted to see you fail this time.' I simply laughed and took it as a joke, even though I couldn't hear the slightest hint of humour in her voice. I saw all of this as acceptable behaviour, something to which I'd become accustomed, and it's only now, when look back on our childhood, that I begin to understand the damage done by our mother.

Ironically, Nikki studied beauty therapy at college and went on to open her own salon, becoming a very successful businesswoman in the process – I'm incredibly proud of her – whereas I, the 'intellectual giant' of the family, probably ended up as a failure in the eyes of our mother. Foregoing the fruits of academic success, I spent many years bumming around the world, got a university education that never led to any kind of prosperous career and finished up scratching a living as a lowly English teacher on Lanzarote.

But I don't regret the choices I made. I don't feel that my education was wasted because I've never considered my little collection of certificates and diplomas as a thing of any great value. I believe education is like travel. It's the opportunity to enjoy a learning experience that shouldn't be missed and not just something we use as a means of getting somewhere. I studied hard for the same simple reason I travelled: I don't want to discover when I come to die that I haven't lived.

Yet the thing I find most frustrating is that Nikki doesn't understand I've never prized academic success in the way that our mother did; in the way that she forced my sister to value and ultimately resent it. What really hurts, though, is that our mother created a daughter who can't seem to praise her little brother for anything he's ever achieved in life. The one person whose approval I would cherish the most has never been able to congratulate me.

I don't blame Nikki for any of this. I don't even know if she is conscious of what happened as I have never spoken or written of it until now. But deep in my heart, all I want is for my sister to be able to see me as a normal human being; someone with feelings just like her; a man who needs an occasional pat on the back. Unfortunately, our biological mother has made it impossible for my sister to even combine the three short words 'Well done, Steve.' She's removed any possibility of Nikki ever again being able to perceive me as the little brother who would always turn to his big sister for comfort, advice and support.

So my mother isn't 'mum'. My stepmother, the woman with whom I live as her son whenever I'm in the UK, who treats me as her own, who flew over from England to be with me in my moment of need, she's *my* mum.

However, when she walked into my room the previous day she hadn't received a greeting worthy of her status. In my mind, I was still floating back and forth between reality and fantasy, and the moment I saw her I demanded a pen and paper and proceeded to do a detailed diagram of the 'ice-cream-making machine' I'd just 'invented'.

'It would be really useful for a hospital in the Canary Islands,' I enthusiastically proclaimed on showing her the finished drawing.

'Yes, I suppose it would,' she agreed.

'No, you don't understand,' I continued. 'It's very hot in the Canary Islands and ice-cream is very cold, so it would be quite nice for the people in hospital to eat something cold, wouldn't it?'

'Yes, of course it would,' she replied, successfully appearing to take my puerile proposition seriously, and our conversations that day proceeded pretty much in the same muddled manner.

Nevertheless, she had managed to explain one important thing to me: I'd been in a car crash. I had been involved in a very serious car crash, although the details, circumstances and consequences of this accident were still way beyond my mental capacity at that time.

Anyhow, despite my struggle to maintain a lucid state of mind, my recent memory didn't seem to have been affected. I felt sure I'd been in this hospital for three days and during that time had experienced nothing more than the usual hospital routine. I had no idea why I'd been brought here and I hadn't even seen a doctor yet. This bothered me a little because I assumed a patient would see their doctor every day. That was how it worked in hospital, wasn't it?

While these and other, more crazy thoughts continued to run through my mind, a man in a white coat entered my room.

'Good morning, I'm Doctor Mendoza,' he announced. 'How are you today?'

'I'm OK.'

'Good, good. Well, we're going to do a CAT scan this afternoon,' he said, making no effort to explain what this actually invloved.

'Oh, er, all right,' I consented.

'OK, we'll come and get you later on,' he said and then turned to leave. But he paused for a moment at the door and asked, 'Are you a dance teacher?'

'Yes, I teach salsa,' I replied. I assumed he'd heard this from one of the nurses, who in turn must have heard it from Leonardo, who had found it fascinating that I was teaching Latin American dance to Spaniards.

'Well, I hope you realize that you won't be able to dance again once you've had the operation on your leg.'

'What? I don't understand. No, wait!' I cried but it was too late, he'd already gone.

As I lay there, alone and scared, I became engulfed in a multitude of emotions. I was angry with this doctor for revealing information with such far-reaching consequences in such an unfeeling way, and frustrated that he had left without offering the chance for further discussion. I was confused because the words I'd just heard had been spoken in a foreign tongue, though I knew I hadn't misunderstood him. It wasn't a difficult phrase for me to comprehend. But above all, I felt an overpowering sense of despair. If that really were the truth, if I would never dance again, I would rather have died in the car crash. Dancing had become the most important thing in my life, a thing I couldn't bear to lose. I had to dance again. I simply *had* to dance.

The only thing I truly missed here was the opportunity to dance. I'd been living on Lanzarote for more than a year and I still hadn't found anywhere to pursue my passion for salsa.

Latin music has always been an important part of my life. Through my father's guidance, I grew up listening to the music of many groups with South American influences and before reaching my teens I followed in his footsteps as a Latin percussionist. As time passed, I began to realize that my feel for rhythm was something worth cultivating, and by the age of 17 I was regularly performing with a couple of bands in pubs around town.

My interest in Latin American dance developed a few years later. Not long after starting university, I met a salsa disc jockey and began going to his club on a weekly basis. The initial attraction had only been the music, but after a short time I decided to take a few dance classes and discovered that I learned very quickly. I had always been a keen dancer, having grown up through the disco and break-dance eras, but I also had a significant advantage over the other novices who attended these classes. I'd spent so many years playing and listening to Latin music that I could understand these complex dance rhythms without the difficulty that many westerners experienced. As I started to dance more and more, my love of salsa continued to grow and I eventually became a Latin disc jockey. Then, in the fullness of time, I ultimately progressed on to teaching dance as well.

When I made the decision to move to Lanzarote, this again was inspired by a Latin American connection. I had spent the previous year in Colombia and the year before that in Venezuela, and on both occasions I had been forced to return to my homeland due to the political and economic instability of these countries. But the Canary Islands are like a 'cultural bridge' between Spain and South America. They offer the opportunity to adopt a Latino lifestyle – the customs, culinary preferences and musical influences are similar, and the dialect of Spanish is much closer to that of Latin America than mainland Spain – yet they are in Europe. In the Canaries one can feel a South American ambience whilst still having the peace of mind permitted by the stability of the West.

Consequently, following two failed attempts at building a life in Latin America, I concluded that Lanzarote should be an adequate compromise. It had the climate I preferred, a language I spoke and would almost certainly allow me to continue dancing to the music that had become a defining facet of my personality. Whenever family and friends thought of Steve, they inevitably thought of salsa.

Shortly after arriving, I learned that this was not to be the case. It appeared that merengue was popular here, though it was a simpler dance and I found the music rather less inspiring. Salsa, on the other hand, wasn't very fashionable and none of the discos ever included any on their play-lists. But what surprised me most was that, in spite of the recent worldwide success of Latin music, I couldn't even seem to find anyone here who knew how to *dance* salsa.

Finally, after a year on an island I had come to love, yet one that deprived me of my musical obsession, I tried to think of a way to surmount this dilemma. If I started giving dance classes, might it generate enough interest amongst the locals to solve my problem? I felt sufficiently confident that my teaching experience in England at least warranted an attempt, so I began translating the instructions I used and started looking for a suitable venue.

Some time later I was introduced to Chicho and Paqui, a friendly couple who owned a bar called the Rincon del Majo. It wasn't a bar I usually frequented and I'd only been there once before during my first month on the island. It was a beautiful, old, Canarian building with high ceilings, thick stone walls and tiled floors, and was situated in my favourite part of town on the edge of a tidal lake. It had a very warm and welcoming atmosphere, and I'd also remembered that there was a large room at the back of the building with a small stage and a dance-floor, thus making it perfect for dance classes.

When I began explaining my idea to the owners, they seemed to be listening with a polite attentiveness that I hadn't expected. They had a wonderful capacity to make everyone in their bar feel like they really belonged – in a place where everybody knew your name. In addition to this, they were local Canarians, not from mainland Spain, and as a result they were always keen to support any new ideas on their island.

Paqui seemed particularly interested, feeling it an unusual but alluring twist that an Englishman would teach Latin American dance. So great was her enthusiasm that when I started teaching in their bar, she even invited the local TV station to come and film one of my classes and an interview with me. This generated some very beneficial publicity and my once-a-week classes soon became twice weekly to accommodate the demand.

Due to my rapid success in teaching salsa to the locals, I began to consider a way of extending this new vocation. Why not teach the tourists? The popularity of Latin music and dance had grown consid-erably throughout Europe in recent years. In England we had even started to see salsa classes featured in soap operas along with hearing the music used in more than a few television advertisements. There was a big market out there, ready to be exploited.

I made some enquiries through one or two friends who worked in the hotel business and a meeting was arranged with the entertain-ment's manager of a hotel in Costa Teguise, one of the three tourist centres on the island. At that meeting I outlined my plans for a dance class, possibly followed by a Latin DJ night to give people a chance to practise what they'd learned. To gain credibility, I also mentioned the success of my classes in Arrecife, the capital of Lanzarote, and he seemed quite sure we could come to an arrangement.

I walked out of that hotel into the warmth of a Canarian evening feeling very contented. I'd negotiated a third night of classes and was a step closer to changing my job of teaching English to Spanish kids for the more exciting career of a Latin dance teacher and disc jockey. I was a step closer to becoming 'El Gringo Latino' on a full-time basis. I got into my car, put on my favourite Colombian salsa cassette and began the short drive back to Arrecife, where I planned to meet a friend and go to the cinema.

I never went to the cinema that night. I didn't even make it back to Arrecife. That evening a local lad had been drinking very heavily in a bar in the capital, then he and his friends had set off in their cars to hit a tourist bar. Unfortunately, as they were racing along the straight stretch of road that led into Costa Teguise, he hit me.

I have no memory whatsoever of the crash itself, the moment of impact, just a faint recollection of the glare of headlights shining directly into my face as I was approaching the brow of a small hill. Then nothing – game over – nothing for the following two weeks until Miguel asked me if he could change the television channel and I found myself in a hospital bed with my father at my side.

But I hadn't been in a coma. I wasn't even unconscious when the emergency services had arrived at the scene of the accident. This trauma had put me into a state of delirium, as well as putting an end to my dream career as a salsa dance teacher. In fact, it had almost put an end to me, full stop.

But as I lay in my hospital bed, the one thought that wouldn't leave my mind, the one revelation that continued to haunt me was that I would never again be able to dance. If that really were the truth, if this accident had taken away the one form of self-expression I considered intrinsic to my own personal fulfilment, I didn't know how I could go on living. It made the future appear so dark and intimidating that the only thing I could do was shut my eyes and return to all the places I had been in my past.

5 Bacchanal

At long last, my stay on Gran Canaria was coming to an end. I'd spent twelve days at this hospital while the neurology department made a comprehensive assessment of my condition, and now they'd decided I could be sent back to Lanzarote.

I was very anxious to leave. Over the past week I had become consumed with an intense feeling of loneliness. Apart from my mother, I'd only seen one other visitor and it wasn't even somebody I knew. This had come about when the secretary of my English school on Lanzarote, a lady from Gran Canaria whose extended family still lived on this island, had asked one of her nieces to come and visit me. A few days after I arrived, a young lady had come to see me and although my mental condition must have made it quite a difficult visit for her, she still returned again, bringing books, drinks and snacks in an effort to make my stay as comfortable as possible.

Nevertheless, despite talking to my family by phone every evening, I'd been in the company of strangers for a long time. I knew that my father was still on Lanzarote, awaiting my return, so now that I had regained complete lucidity I was desperate to be with him. There were so many questions I wanted to ask. I still knew very little about my accident and it scared me to feel so uninformed about such a formidable, life-changing event.

As a nice surprise, when my discharge forms had been prepared and signed I was collected by my carnival companion Leonardo.

'Are you taking me back to Lanzarote?' I asked with anticipation as he entered my room.

'I certainly am,' he replied, his boyish beaming grin very much in evidence.

'Oh, that's great! I can't wait to see my dad again.'

'Well, you won't have to wait long now,' he assured me as I was gently lifted off my hospital bed and onto a gurney. Once we were in the ambulance and on our way to the airport, the topic of conversation quickly slipped into the one thing we had in common.

'Last year I flew back to Tenerife for Carnival, but this year I was planning to stay in Lanzarote,' I said.

'Really?'

'Yeah, well, seeing as I'd started teaching salsa, I thought it would be better to spend the week doing some promotion for my classes.'

'Oh, right, good idea,' he agreed.

'I know Tenerife's a lot bigger, so it probably isn't as good in Lanzarote, but it's still Carnival, isn't it?'

'That's right,' he replied. 'It's still Carnival, no matter what island you're on.'

'Yeah . . . Carnival!' I screamed.

'Carnival! . . . *Bacchanal*!' roared Erik.

'What does bacchanal mean?' I asked. 'Is it a Trinidadian word?'

'Yeah, it's something everyone shouts here during carnival, you know, like *PARTY*! You hear it in a lot of carnival songs as well.'

'Oh right, I get it . . . *Bacchanal*!'

Erik had been born here but adopted by a family in Sweden. On reaching adulthood, he had returned to the Caribbean to find his biological family and we had met a few months earlier on the neighbouring island of Tobago. Now we were in Port of Spain, the capital of Trinidad, where we were preparing for the carnival and Erik was tutoring me and another carnival novice in the traditions of this very special West Indian celebration.

I'd never contemplated visiting Trinidad and Tobago. It had been a spontaneous decision brought about through a chance meeting with another adopted Swede in Venezuela. The decision to go to South America, however, was by no means a sudden flash of inspiration. This was a desire that had slowly and steadily developed and matured during my university years in England.

I started my degree about six months after returning from my first trip around the world. Initially I socialized with other students from my course but I found it quite difficult to establish any close friend-ships. I was only about three years older than most of my classmates, an insignificant difference at that age, but I'd spent those years doing very different things.

My problem arose whenever we were in a social environment, away from the pressure of university life where conversations usually revolved around college work. Sitting in a pub, a club or at a party, we would chat on a more personal level about our own lives. Someone would tell a funny story, maybe a crazy thing that happened one time when they were trying to get a taxi to wherever, and this might remind me of a similar experience. I would start to recount my tale, though reference to location would often be necessary for the story to make sense – it happened in Bangkok, Hawaii, Guatemala City or Jamaica and involved language, local customs, landscape or climate. But this was at a time when it was still uncommon to take a gap year, and my classmates soon began to tire of hearing me 'brag' about my travels as they perceived it. Consequently, they would usually lose interest the moment a distant destination was mentioned, which limited my input in conversations about our past lives and ultimately reduced my part-icipation in any exchanges during social situations.

Then I met two Brazilians, Pedro and Bebeto. One evening I had gone out alone to find a live music bar and on arriving it appeared to be another typical Brighton pub. Yet the atmosphere inside was far from English. It was as if I'd walked onto Copacabana Beach. Even though it was the middle of winter, as soon as I entered I could feel an incredible warmth that radiated both from the patrons packed in wall-to-wall and the music that united their rhythmic motion.

As I peered through this cosmopolitan crowd of gyrating bodies, I could just make out two musicians in the far corner. On the left, closer to the bar, was a calm, controlled guitarist with thin, greying hair tied back in a small ponytail, and to his right I could see a long-haired, round-faced, bouncing body, simultaneously playing a flute with one hand and a shaker with the other. It was my first introduction to a very different side of Brighton.

That night my life as a student started to change. During the week I studied graphic design but the weekends would be spent with Pedro and Bebeto, developing my understanding of Latin American music. Through these two Brazilians I also met many more South Americans. They introduced me to Venezuelans, Bolivians, Nicaraguans and, of course, numerous Brazilians, and they were people I could talk with about my past. They were doing exactly what I had done – living in a different part of the world, working without permission, struggling with a new language and unfamiliar customs – so my stories didn't seem at all out of place in our conversations. Finally, I had met some people I could socialize with in comfort. That night a seed was planted which, four years later, resulted in me boarding a flight bound for Venezuela.

I spent the first couple of days in Caracas with the family of a Venezuelan friend I had met in England. It was quite a daunting city situated 30 miles from the coast in a rift valley of the thickly forested central highlands, and very densely populated with over four million inhabitants who spoke a language I didn't understand. Since the war it had been the fastest growing Latin American capital, which had produced an incongruous mix of architecture and in many parts the old colonial buildings had given way to massive, modern, multi-storey edifices. It was also a dangerous city by European standards, and the neighbourhood I was in was one that my guidebook recommended to avoid after dark.

At the end of a few particularly anxious days, I decided to visit a coastal town called Puerto la Cruz about 170 miles east of Caracas. Then, on the advice of my Venezuelan friend in Brighton, I made the short ferry crossing to Margarita Island. This island had become the jewel of the Caribbean Coast in the eyes of many Venezuelans due to a massive tourism boom in the early eighties when the dramatic fall in value of local currency had forced most of them to start spending their holidays 'at home'.

It wasn't a destination recommended for budget travellers and on arriving in the main town, Porlamar, I found it to be very developed with many new shopping centres and Miami-style hotel complexes. Eventually, I managed to secure accommodation on the cheaper, less commercial side of town in a friendly neighbourhood with narrow, litter-strewn streets and a more local atmosphere. It was on my first night there that I met Mattias.

Matt had been born in India and adopted by a Swedish family. He'd grown up in Sweden, done his military service and then decided to see a bit of the world. He spoke absolutely no Spanish, and I understood very little, so it came as a welcome relief to both of us to meet someone with whom conversation was easy – like many Swedes of his generation, he spoke English quite competently.

We also quickly discovered that there was plenty to talk about, since we shared an interest in world travel. One thing I liked about him almost immediately was the way he spoke with such modest pride about his birthplace, a country I'd never actually visited. I got the impression that his trips to India hadn't been inspired by the usual backpacker's desire to learn more about the world in which we live. I felt he'd seen it as a way of learning more about himself. He'd gone there to discover his roots.

'Do you fancy going over the road for a beer?' I asked, once we'd completed the customary where-and-when conversation of two backpackers becoming acquainted.

'Oh, is there a good bar near here?'

'I only arrived this afternoon, so I haven't been there yet, but it looks quite friendly and they've got a couple of pool tables too.'

'Yeah, why not. That sounds like fun.'

'Great! So let's go and get 'polarised' then.'

'Polarised? What does that mean?'

'Well, the local brew is called Polar, you know: Polar *Beer* – polar *bear*, though I can't understand why Spanish speakers would choose a name that only makes a joke in English. I guess they must think it gives the impression of a beer that's always ice cold.'

'But why *polarised*?' he asked, still noticeably confused.

'Oh, that's just me. A bit of English humour.'

During the course of conversation over a few frames of pool, Matt told me his travel plans. He'd come to this island with the intention of travelling on to Trinidad, where he wanted to try and find an old friend. It was someone he had met during his military service when they had worked together as chefs. But they also had something else in common: both of them had been born elsewhere and then been adopted by Swedish families. His friend Erik had returned to his birthplace the previous year and now Matt was planning to try and find his old military kitchen mate.

We spent the next few days exploring the island but for me it was very disappointing. Margarita was nowhere near as beautiful as my Venezuelan friend had led me to believe. His travel-brochure descriptions had conjured up the image of a lush, tropical paradise, yet in reality the landscape was quite barren. Apart from a few small wooded areas, the majority of vegetation was made up of mangroves, scrub and marshes interspersed with undulating sand dunes. We came across one or two nice beaches, although the most popular ones were very crowded and patrolled by vendors who had all adopted an aggressive sales pitch that made it virtually impossible to actually relax and enjoy the sun, sea and sand.

In addition to this, we were visiting this popular holiday resort at a somewhat inopportune time. It was during the lead up to the general election that Sunday, which wouldn't have been a problem in Britain, and Matt had said the same about Sweden. However, during elections in Venezuela the bars and discos were not permitted to open. On the Friday evening before the big day, whilst on our way to a backstreet *bodega* to purchase a bottle of rum, I asked our taxi driver about this.

'Is because in Venezuela we are drinking more whisky than in all the world,' he replied.

'Oh, right, I understand. The government doesn't want people to be drunk when they vote.'

'No, no, is not for this reason. Is because the government is worry if the people are drinking much they . . . er . . . I not know the word. Boom, boom, boom!' he gesticulated.

'Ah! Violence!'

'*Sí, sí, violencia!*' he replied.

On hearing this, one thing started to make a lot more sense. I'd seen a lot of policemen cruising the streets on motorbikes, two to a bike with the pillion passenger carrying a machine gun. It was something I'd thought to be a little unusual in a tourist resort, and even though I now understood they were here to keep the peace until the election, I still couldn't help thinking that they looked more like a

51

gang of homicidal gay bikers.

On the eve of the election we sat in the hotel restaurant with some other guests for a quiet evening of conversation over a few drinks. This hotel was one of the cheapest in town, so quite a few of the residents weren't tourists, they were locals who hadn't yet found permanent accommodation. Consequently, the day before the citizens of Venezuela made a very important political decision, we spent the evening chatting with two waiters and a chambermaid about such issues as the cost of alcohol and tobacco here compared to prices in our countries. The more acute economic problems currently facing Venezuela weren't very high on their list of priorities.

Towards the end of an entertaining evening's conversation, I decided to change my travel plans. I had seen enough of Margarita Island and I thought it might be fun to accompany Matt on his trip to Trinidad. I'd visited Jamaica and the Bahamas a few years earlier but I now had the opportunity to see a Caribbean island much further to the south. Also, Christmas was almost upon us and I considered it appropriate to spend the festive season in an English-speaking part of the world. Once the decision had been made and the election brought to a close, we began the pursuit of a passage to Trinidad.

At the first travel agency we tried, they offered us a one-way flight via Caracas for about $200 and also claimed that there were no direct flights from the island and no ferry service. Finding this hard to believe, we went to look for some Trinidadians and a couple we met in a clothes shop told us they'd paid about $100 for their return flight to Margarita. They went on to explain that many Trinidadians, like themselves, frequently came to this island to buy vast amounts of the incredibly cheap clothing available here, which they then sold in their shops in Trinidad. As a result of this thriving export trade, there was an abundance of direct flights.

We went to another travel agency, where an elegantly dressed, older gentleman, who spoke very good English, was pleased to offer us a direct flight for $127 one-way or $170 return. This was still way beyond our budget, so to demonstrate our financial constraints we recounted a few tales of arduous but economical journeys we had made such as Matt's 56-hour train ride across India and my three-day bus trip through Mexico.

'But why do you do it?' he asked. 'You're from Europe, you have money. I certainly wouldn't do it. I like my comfort; I like my air-conditioning.'

While unable to comprehend the concept of a 'backpacker', he appreciated our needs and proceeded to tell us about a ferry service to Trinidad. Apparently, it left once a week and for more information he suggested that we go to Hotel Super Ocho, ask for Agustín Nuñez and say that Gustavo López had sent us.

We followed his instructions and on finding Mr Nuñez we were told that this ferry arrived in Pampatar, the principal port of Margarita, at seven the next morning. He said that tickets (which cost $70) could be bought on board and that it set sail at six in the evening. He also advised us to ask for Alfonso and say that Agustín Nuñez had sent us.

The following morning, we awoke early on what we thought would be our final day on the island and took a bus to Pampatar. It was only a few miles north-west of Porlamar, set around a large bay full of fishing boats and foreign yachts. When we reached the port we found the ferry quite easily, though unfortunately we discovered there were no more tickets available. It appeared that now was one of the busiest times of the year, seeing as many Trinidadians chose to do their Christmas shopping on Margarita.

We decided to return to Hotel Super Ocho and see if it was possible book tickets for the ferry the following week. In the reception, an English-speaking Venezuelan advised us to consult a man called Ali Asgar at Los Roques Hotel because he had the only Trinidadian travel agency on the island. Finally, on the third attempt, we managed to speak to Mr Asgar at about half past seven that evening after he'd returned from a trip to Caracas. He was a sharp-faced little man who gave the impression of being an influential businessman with more important things on his mind, but he told us he would see what he could do and that we should return at half past five the next day.

As we left his shop, wondering if we would ever leave this island, we were stopped in our tracks by the harmonious tones of a sweet-sounding West Indian voice. On the other side of the street we could see a rotund, middle-aged, Trinidadian lady dressed in floral patterns and a petite straw sun-hat who was beckoning us over to join her.

Once we had crossed the street, she confessed to overhearing our conversation with Mr Asgar and said that she might be able to help. Basically, she had two tickets for a flight to Trinidad to sell and told us she would be happy with $60 for each of them. She proceeded to explain that two of her friends had bought so much on Margarita that they'd returned by ferry because it would have been impossible to fly. Before departing, they'd given her the tickets for their return passage by plane and they were ours if we wanted them.

'But can we travel on a ticket that's in the name of another person?' I asked.

'Dat be no problem, mon,' she replied. 'At de airport we check in togeda, one big group. Me collect all passport an' ticket an' gi dem de mon. By den it be ram wid people, so dis mon only count dem, 'im nah worry if all name be de same.'

'But are you sure it will work?'

'Yeah, no problem, mon. Me dun it many time. All me axe be you permit me use any you luggage allowance dat you no need. I dun bought many ting 'ere too!'

'Sure, no problem,' I replied, finding her lyrical accent infectious. 'We've only got one backpack each.'

'Dat be good, tanks mon,' she said with a beaming, ivory-toothed smile. 'Lissen me nuh. Dis plane a-go leave timora af'noon, but me a beg you meet me inna mornin' at Hotel Torino. You make it dey eight o'clock?'

'Hotel Torino, eight o'clock. No problem, we'll be there. See you tomorrow then.'

The following morning we got up early again and went to meet our friendly Trinidadian. We paid her for the tickets, made the necessary plans and returned to Hotel Torino at three that afternoon to travel with Indra, her sister Molly and sixteen other Trinidadian ladies to the airport. When we arrived, Indra collected all 20 tickets and passports and checked everyone in for the flight. Then after waiting more than four hours, we were invited to board the plane in a typically disorganized, Latin American fashion.

As I surveyed the chaos before me, I noticed a security guard who was pointing at me and signalling that I join the front of this haphazard queue. Feeling a little confused, I looked round and saw a whole line of 'whites' coming from the back to board the plane first. Very quickly I understood his mistake and shouted, 'I'm not with them. I'm with the locals. I can wait!'

So we flew to Trinidad with our native travel companions, a short flight of only 30 minutes that somehow didn't feel a sufficient reward for all the problems we'd overcome to get the tickets. But upon arrival we were presented with a new complication. The exchange bureau at the airport had already closed, thus leaving us stranded in a foreign land with no local currency.

Luckily, a few of the ladies were still close by and on realizing our predicament we were offered a lift with Molly and her husband, who had come to the airport to collect her. They were a charitable couple and during the drive into Port of Spain they even bought us dinner at a fast food restaurant. Eventually, they dropped us off outside La Calypso Hotel, an establishment described in Matt's guidebook as 'a backpackers' hostel in disguise', where we managed to check in by leaving a passport at the reception as a deposit and retired to our room feeling relieved to have reached our destination.

The next day I awoke to a bright Caribbean morning, green and lazy and full of sun, and was amazed by the dramatic contrast in scenery after such a short distance travelled. A week earlier I'd taken a ferry to Margarita Island, hoping to find a succulent garden of delights and encountered a desolate, barren landscape. But dreams are never in the place you expect them to be, and here was an island – no further from the Venezuelan coast than Margarita – so rich and lush that it would have been difficult to find somewhere more similar to my imagined tropical paradise.

I also perceived the people to be considerably more benevolent than I had initially anticipated. My most recent Caribbean experience had been on Jamaica, where my interaction with the locals had led me to form the impression of an island inhabited by a very insular community with rather aggressive tendencies. In contrast, here the locals seemed more than willing to accept outsiders and it had come as an additional surprise to be helped on arrival instead of robbed, as had been the case in Kingston, the Jamaican capital.

Once we'd resolved the more immediate need for money and food, we embarked on the search for Erik. Matt had his family's address, which was in a neighbourhood on the edge of the city's suburban sprawl. It was half way up a small mountain called Dundonald Hill, so we took a bus to the outskirts of town and started hiking up a winding, mountain roadway. It was an enjoyable walk that offered panoramic views of Port of Spain in the coastal valley below, allowing me to build a better mental picture of the geography of a city until then only seen from the opposite perspective.

We were looking for house number 246, so on reaching the two-hundreds we began asking people for help. We were repeatedly told to continue climbing until we started meeting people who said we would find this house further back down the road. Then we met a man who realized he knew the family (once we'd told him about the Swedish connection) but he wasn't sure exactly where they lived. In the end, we happened across another man, who explained that he was certain we needed to go all the way back down the mountain and up again on another road. Finally, after following his directions and asking a few more people for help, we managed to find Erik's house.

It was a modest, detached, flat-roofed abode, as were the majority of dwellings we had passed on our walk, although no two houses in this neighbourhood appeared to be identical. Unfortunately, no one was home so we waited for about half an hour until his little sister arrived and immediately told us that Erik had moved to Tobago. She went on to explain that her mother had his telephone number there, but she wouldn't return home until early evening. Consequently, we asked for her number, explaining that we would call that night, and then began the long trek back to our hotel.

Later that evening, Matt got Erik's phone number from his mother and subsequently managed to speak to him. He was working at a Swedish restaurant on the island and suggested that we take the ferry to come over and visit him. The next day, we went down to the port to get information about departure times and made plans to leave the following day. In the afternoon, we relaxed by the swimming pool of a hotel on the edge of the beautifully exuberant, botanical gardens, and after nightfall we ventured out to a local bar but avoided buying popcorn from a street vendor who had a sign which read: 'Cholera free with fresh butter!'

Early the next morning, we packed up, checked out and returned to the port. Once inside the small ferry terminal, we quickly discovered they had a wonderfully confusing system for buying tickets, though this came as no surprise. Previous travel experiences had shown me it was just another example of a developing country trying to reduce unemployment levels.

It commenced with taking a ticket from a machine like those found at the delicatessen counter of a supermarket and waiting for our number to be called. However, it didn't take us long to realize that our number didn't correspond at all with what was on the display screen so we decided to join a queue. Shortly after joining one, a member of the port staff announced that the ticket machine didn't work and that all passengers should first join the queue furthest to the left.

After changing to the correct queue and waiting for about twenty minutes, the clerk at the counter told us if we wanted to buy tickets for the ferry to Tobago, we needed to join the next queue to the right. The only tickets on sale at this terminal were for the ferry to Tobago, yet it had still been deemed necessary to employ someone to tell you this.

Following another long wait, we were greeted by a clerk who wanted the names of the people requiring tickets, which he wrote on a piece of paper and passed it along to the clerk on his left. By this stage we were beginning to understand how their system operated and went straight to the back of the next queue of people to our right.

This time our patience was rewarded by making the acquaintance of the cashier, who took our money, wrote our names on two tickets and passed them on to the next clerk. Feeling we were close to a conclusion, we joined the final queue to the right and were ultimately presented with our tickets, complete with validating stamps.

There was still one more queue to join, though, and this one consisted of a menacing mass of bodies, aggressively mingling by a door marked 'Gate One'. (The port only possessed one gate but a sign had obviously been considered necessary.) At the end of an apparently pointless wait, a security guard opened this door just as a tropical downpour began and we started racing through the rain to board the boat and find a seat.

By the time we got there we were completely soaked through and we also found there wasn't a single seat available. But this wasn't due to the number of people on board. Each row of seats consisted of one passenger and a vast number of bags placed on the other three seats in order to save them for friends. As a result, we spent the entire six-hour crossing sat outside on a rusty metal deck, despite many of these bags remaining on the otherwise unoccupied seats. Maybe the Trinidadians weren't that accommodating after all.

At eight that evening we docked at the port of Scarborough, the capital of Tobago, and there, on the quay, awaiting our arrival was the elusive Erik. At long last, I was introduced to the man whom it had been so difficult to find and any preconceived impressions I'd formed of him through conversations with Matt were instantly forgotten. There was only one conclusion I could make: Erik was Eddie Murphy with a West Indian accent!

Even though my original plan had been to spend nothing more than the Christmas holidays on Tobago, I finished up staying for almost two months. I discovered it to be an incredibly beautiful island – the verdant haven of my dreams – and the three of us rented an apartment together on the beach at Crown Point, the western tip of the island.

My days were spent sunbathing and swimming, and I occasionally went surfing on the north coast as well as taking a couple of boat trips to snorkel on the reef. I even hitchhiked around the island to explore the jungles of the eastern end, where on one particular occasion I managed to trip over a snake about six feet long that was hidden in the dense vegetation. Luckily, a little earlier that very same day I'd been told there were no venomous snakes on Tobago, so my heart only stopped beating for a short time.

However, my best memories of the time I spent there are of the people I met. Throughout all my previous travels I had never encountered such an endearing community. Our landlord and his family lived in the apartment above ours and were always eager to help out with anything we needed. Our neighbours were, ironically, a Swedish family, so due to this Nordic connection we spent a lot of time with Magnus, his wife and their baby daughter. I also became friendly with a rasta called Ako who liked to smoke *sensi* but would always turn down the offer of a glass of rum with the same excuse: 'It leave me well overhung, mon.'

On one of my hitchhiking trips I was picked up by George, an ageing taxi driver who had worked the streets of New York City for 15 years. I declined his offer of a trip around the island for $100, and instead he accepted a packet of cigarettes as payment for a ride to the next town, where we called in on his brother-in-law for a chat and, in true Trinidadian style, several glasses of rum. The fact that it was only ten o'clock in the morning didn't seem to bother them.

Everywhere I went I was greeted with smiling faces, and after spending a few weeks surrounded by such happiness it was difficult not to be swept along in this tide of joy. No matter where I was on the island someone would always strike up a conversation with me, and along with all these brief encounters with numerous locals there were, of course, my two flatmates Matt and Erik. During those few special months we became great friends and eventually we all travelled back to Trinidad together when the time came for the biggest party of the year – Carnival . . . *Bacchanal*!

'So, was it good?' asked Leonardo.

'Yeah, it was great, but not as good as Tenerife. I mean, that's got to be the best carnival in the world, hasn't it?'

'Well, I haven't seen any other carnivals, though I think it would be difficult to find a better one,' he agreed as he lifted me out of the ambulance and onto another gurney.

Then, as he started wheeling me across the runway, I began to feel a sense of calm growing within me. It had been a long, tough and lonely trip but now I could see the end. There, on the tarmac before me, was the gleaming white plane that would take me back to Lanzarote . . . back to my father.

6 *No Name*

Following a 30-minute flight, I was back in Lanzarote and initially I felt extremely relieved to be in more familiar surroundings. But this feeling was very short-lived. The reception I received upon arrival soon revived all the feelings of frustration and confusion I had only recently managed to suppress. There was still so much I didn't understand about my accident, but on the journey from the airport to the hospital something came to light that made me begin to comprehend the gravity of my misfortune.

It happened after I'd been loaded into an ambulance to make this short journey. I was desperate to call my father to let him know I was back, and since I had seen a mobile phone clipped onto the ambulance driver's belt when he lifted me aboard, I asked if I could borrow it. Unfortunately, he explained that he wasn't permitted to lend this phone because it could only be used for work-related calls but, showing a little compassion, he asked about my current situation.

'So, you were in a car crash,' he repeated on hearing the limited information I had at my disposal. 'What were you driving at the time?'

'A Seat Ibiza.'

'Was it black?'

'Er, yes, it was,' I replied, feeling rather surprised by this question.

'Ah, I remember you. I attended to you at the accident.'

'Really?' I asked in amazement.

'Yes, and do you know what you did once they'd got you out of the car and onto the road?'

'No, what do you mean?'

'Well, while I was at your side trying to keep you alive, you kept trying to hit me!'

'What?' I exclaimed in disbelief.

'You kept trying to punch me in the face.'

I imagine to most people this would sound strange, but to me it seemed absolutely preposterous. I'm by no means a violent man and could probably count on one hand the number of times I've actually hit another person, yet this was exactly what I'd tried to do to the very person who'd been trying to help me. With little time to absorb this startling news, we arrived at the hospital and as I was wheeled through a maze of corridors I was continually greeted with, 'Hi Steve, how are you? How was Gran Canaria?'

It appeared that almost every nurse in the hospital knew who I was.

Some time later we reached my allocated room, where I was lifted onto a bed and left feeling completely bewildered by the apparent 'fame' I had acquired amongst the hospital staff. The desire to see my father became intensified by my confusion, as I felt sure he could give an explanation, and this dire need for paternal enlightenment began to provoke an odd sense of déjà vu. Except this time the roles had been reversed. With this homecoming it was my father, not me, who would reveal all once we had been reunited.

It was 1989, and I was finally returning home to begin my university education after two and a half years of travels. I'd always maintained contact with my family while away and on two occasions my father had even come out to join me. However, when my return home had become imminent I decided to withhold the date of my arrival. I'm not too sure why I did this. Maybe I wanted to demonstrate the independence I had attained through my travels by getting home without parental assistance . . . or maybe I just wanted to be dramatic.

I was flying home from Australia and had bought a ticket that included a four-week stopover in Thailand, my last opportunity to sample a different culture before returning to the familiarity of the life I had temporarily escaped. It was at a time when this country was becoming established on the backpackers' circuit while still offering the chance for an authentic, south-east Asian experience. It would be a few more years before it built its current reputation of an inexpensive sex-drugs-and-rock-and-roll tourist destination.

I arrived early evening and spent the first night in Bangkok at a backpackers' hostel on the now legendary Khao San Road – a street of cafés, bars, budget accommodation and countless stalls offering bootleg cassettes, watches, jewellery and clothing. The next morning, I travelled a few hours west to Kanchanaburi and realized a childhood dream to see the bridge on the River Kwae. The following day, I went to a national park nearby and spent the afternoon in a tropical forest laced with streams cascading into deep, crystal-clear pools. I had also considered a trip north to Chiang Mai to make a trek by elephant, but my world trip was coming to an end and it was time to find the one geographical feature I had pursued with the most vigour throughout my travels: The Beach.

I'd read about an island in the south-west of the Gulf of Thailand off the coast of the narrow strip of land that leads down to Malaysia. It's called Koh Samui and had been highly recommended by many of the travellers I'd met in Australia who had arrived via Asia. I first consulted my guidebook for travel information, then bussed back to the capital and took an overnight bus south. The next morning, feeling a little drained due to an uncomfortable journey spent trying to digest some rather spicy noodles, I made the four-hour ferry crossing to my final destination.

Unfortunately, when I arrived I was very disappointed at what I found. Although it must have once resembled the picture-postcard photos I'd seen, this island was brimful of backpackers and far too many reminders that I still hadn't escaped from that part of the world that was 'real'. I was looking for a beach resort for people who don't like beach resorts. Koh Samui certainly couldn't offer this but I'd read about another island close by that had only recently been discovered by backpackers. I concluded it might well be a suitable alternative, so I took a bus to a small village on the northern tip of Koh Samui where there were boats that made the short crossing to the island of Koh Pha-Ngan.

While sitting in a homely rural restaurant, waiting for the next boat, I spotted a familiar face. It was an English girl I'd met about a month earlier at the Thai Embassy in Melbourne when I'd been applying for my visa. This was something that had happened quite frequently during my travels, yet chance meetings with familiar faces still never ceased to amaze me. I knew just one person in Thailand and *here* she was, in the same restaurant as me!

I went over for a chat and had to ask her name, even though I was sure she'd told me when we first met at the Embassy. She was called Sue and after a brief exchange of travel stories – a custom that soon becomes protocol for any long-term traveller – we took the boat to Koh Pha-Ngan.

As we landed on Hat Rin beach, the sight of naked hippies playing Frisbee on acid made me think that, perhaps, this wasn't the type of place I was looking for. While set in a beneficial location on a lowland peninsula at the eastern end of the island and noticeably less developed than Koh Samui, I didn't feel that the obvious presence of a 'drug culture' would be conducive to the experience I was pursuing. I only stayed there for one night and the following morning I headed up the coast in search of somewhere a little less contaminated by the shortcomings of the West.

Eventually, I came across an appealing hamlet of about a dozen bamboo huts – 'bungalows', as they were called by the locals – and a rustic restaurant. They were situated on a stunning stretch of beach with a barrier reef breaking the surf about a hundred yards out, and the whole complex blended beautifully with a backdrop of coconut fields rising up to mountains enshrouded in a canopy of jungle. It was about midway between the 'hippie-zoo' of Hat Rin and the island's main town, Tong Sala, so was also relatively tranquil. Believing it would be impossible to find anywhere more comparable to my desired utopia, I rented an A-frame hut at a very reasonable rate and began three glorious weeks in a setting so idyllic that my mind almost refused to accept it.

The days quickly slipped into a relaxed routine of a short swim before a fruit salad for breakfast, and then a long snorkel over the reef followed by endless hours of sunbathing, sketching and swimming. On my second day there, my watch even stopped, thus enhancing the easy-going atmosphere of a place where time wasn't important.

Around late afternoon, I usually wandered down to Hat Rin to enjoy the sunset from the top of a wooden lookout tower. It was always a very social event and invariably led to a meal with whom-ever I'd met, at one of the inexpensive but enchanting restaurants that catered for Hat Rin's community of backpackers. These restaurants all served a variety of tasty Thai cuisine, and very soon I discovered a delightful dish that I found almost addictive. It was a vegetable deep fried in batter, served with a sweet and sour sauce, and was simply called 'no name'.

On one of my sunset excursions I met Chris and Aden, a couple of guys from England. They were about the same age as me but had begun travelling *after* university and had chosen a route opposite to my global circuit, thus making Thailand one of their first destinations. Nevertheless, they were certainly far more familiar with this country than I was, having toured extensively before arriving on the island a few weeks earlier.

Chris seemed to possess a natural reticence, but I felt an excitement flicker somewhere inside me when Aden talked of all the experiences he'd encountered during his first few months of travel. Listening to him recount some of his stories, it was as if I were looking into a mirror at a young man just starting out on the big adventure I was now on the point of completing.

Towards the end of an enjoyable evening of Thai food, travel chat and rice whisky, they invited me to join them on a hike into the jungle the following day. This sounded like an unmissable opportunity and as I wandered back to my hut along a moonlit beach, my mind became pervaded with exotic images of the proposed tropical trek.

The next morning, I gathered together some food, a bottle of water, my sketch-book and a camera, and set off down the coast to meet the others. When I reached Hat Rin there was still a freshness in the morning air, but I had to patiently wait for Chris and Aden to get ready until we eventually embarked on our expedition in the heat of the midday sun.

The first part of the trek was very easy, a gentle stroll through the coconut groves encircling this backpackers' resort, but it progressively became harder as we started to penetrate the interior of the island. It took a lot of stamina to hike up a mountain through dense jungle, and for Aden this was particularly arduous. He was quite small in stature, whereas Chris and I shared the same tall, slim build. Consequently, after struggling to keep up for an hour or so he chose to return to Hat Rin, leaving us to continue with our battle through the incredibly beautiful landscape.

We had to ask for directions from locals a couple of times because the overgrown trail wasn't that easy to follow, and at one point it led us right up to the front door of a small hut. This door was open, so we announced our presence and entered in the hope of receiving some guidance.

As we peered into the semi-darkness of this modest dwelling, we discovered it to be inhabited by a blond-haired English guy who was currently sitting cross-legged on the floor 'wearing' nothing more than the guitar he was strumming. He introduced himself as Gavin and told us he'd been living there for several months, so he was able to give us clear directions to the coast on the other side of the island. We thanked him for his help and continued on our way until we finally broke through the jungle onto a completely isolated, exquisitely beautiful beach with not a naked hippie or Frisbee in sight.

By then we were both completely exhausted but we still managed to find enough energy to pick a few coconuts for a refreshing drink much cooler than what remained in our water bottles. Then we sat ourselves down on the warm, inviting sand and gave our weary limbs a very welcome rest.

Some time later we were joined by Gavin, now clothed in the unusual combination of brightly coloured Bermuda shorts and a black trilby. He'd thought that a trek through the jungle had sounded quite inviting and had decided to catch up with us. Having spent several years travelling throughout Asia, he'd amassed a wonderful repertoire of travel tales, a few of which he recounted with the finesse of an experienced storyteller. Then we all set off to hike further along the undeveloped coast of Koh Pha-Ngan.

After a few hours, we came across a secluded cove with a virgin beach hidden by a curtain of coconut palms. In the centre of this beach there was a shimmering, freshwater pool fed by a fast-flowing stream that had eroded a deep gorge into the enclosing mountain ridge. It was like we'd come to the far side of paradise, and I loved it.

Even though our expedition had begun as a day-trip, we all agreed it was the perfect place to set up camp for the night, as it was now far too late to return to 'civilization'. We left our bags on the sand, picked a few coconuts and then set about collecting some driftwood to make a camp-fire for the evening meal. Gavin had some rice and local condiments with him and I had some tinned fish in my daypack, so he started cooking while Chris and I bodysurfed in pounding breakers not found on the other side of the island. After an invigorating swim, we bathed in the freshwater pool and then dined under the stars, chatting until the early hours whilst sipping sweet coconut water.

Despite a full stomach and a tired body, I was afforded little sleep that night. We were completely exposed to the open air, which was thick with mosquitoes, and I felt quite cold as I was clothed in nothing more than a T-shirt and light cotton trousers. However, my discomfort was offset by the nocturnal chorus of the jungle combined with a full moon rising over a rippling ocean, and at the end of a long and almost sleepless night I saw the cool pink glow of sunrise too.

Following a quick breakfast, we collected our things together and resumed our hike. Here the coastline consisted of cliffs, forcing us to cut inland through the mountainous jungle for some more punishment. As we had discovered the previous day, trekking through this type of terrain was extremely demanding but the pleasurable views more than justified the pain.

Around mid-morning, we reached a charming little coastal settlement comprising only three or four huts and a small bamboo pavilion. Gavin could speak Thai quite competently, so he asked one of the residents if they could prepare some food for us and it wasn't long before we were each served an omelette with rice and a chilled bottle of Coca-Cola. Once we'd eaten our fill, enjoyed a moment's respite and reimbursed the locals for their hospitality, we recommenced our trek, this time over rocks at the edge of the sea.

Along the way we came across a Swiss guy living in a shack on the beach. By this time we were ready for another rest, so I had a nap in his hammock while Gavin chatted with him and Chris sat under a palm tree, engrossed in a book. When we eventually set off again, our group had grown to four, seeing as the Swiss guy had also decided to join us.

We continued on to Than Sedet, a small fishing village that could only be reached by first negotiating a steep, forested headland. The final descent was through very dense jungle, in some places virtually in darkness, but after a period of strenuous physical exertion we emerged from the thick vegetation into the brightness of a coastal valley.

This picturesque village was situated at the point where several small rivers converged before meeting the sea, making it a place of immense natural beauty due to the numerous waterfalls concealed in its environs. We crossed a rickety bamboo bridge that spanned these combined rivers and wandered through the huts until we came across the village restaurant. Then we slumped down onto a bench, soaked up the laid-back ambience and bathed in a blissful feeling of complete exhaustion mixed with a wonderful sense of achievement: we had survived two days in the wild!

At that moment of sheer satisfaction, I remember thinking about a book I'd read as a child. It was one of my own personal favourites, a book that had influenced my adult life significantly and in one sense had instigated the journey I'd just completed. It was called *Lord of the Flies* and told the story of a group of young boys, dropped into the wilderness of a desert island with no adults to supervise them, and their struggle to build a civilisation that ultimately ended in barbarism. It was the definitive 'beach-life legend' and would also form the basis of a novel to be written by another English backpacker, several years later, set in this very same group of islands.

We relaxed for a while in the shade of the restaurant veranda, and then set about organizing accommodation for the night. Gavin planned to sleep on the beach but both Chris and I decided we would rather stretch to the expense (and luxury) of a hut. That evening we sat on the beach with many other backpackers around the glowing embers of a camp-fire, all talking travel, telling jokes and singing songs until the early hours. Finally, the combination of a long day's hike followed by a late night produced a very good night's sleep, in spite of a mosquito net that was full of holes, not to mention the profusion of gaping cracks in the walls and floor of our hut.

The next morning, Chris and I chose the slightly easier option of taking a boat back to Hat Rin. I would have liked to continue with our expedition a little longer – I was enjoying my brief taste of life as 'Indiana Jones' – but my extended world trip was on the point of concluding and I had a flight to catch in a few days. When we reached the beach at Hat Rin, I said farewell to my fellow jungle explorer and began hiking back to my hut to prepare for the journey to Bangkok.

As I wandered along this now familiar stretch of beach for the final time, I felt a small pang of regret. The past few days had been the high point of my stay here, an experience I would never forget, and I'd shared it from beginning to end with Chris. Yet I knew so little about him. I wasn't even sure what part of England he came from.

I left Koh Pha-Ngan the following day on the night boat from Tong Sala to Surat Thani. This ferry was affectionately known as the 'Coconut Boat' by backpackers because the hull was always loaded to the water-line with coconuts before any passengers could climb aboard. During one stormy crossing the previous year, this boat's predecessor had sunk. It was a dreadful disaster that had resulted in the death of all passengers apart from three German girls who swam for five hours towards distant, glittering lights until they eventually reached the shores of Koh Samui. A German backpacker told me this story as we chugged across to the mainland lying on thin mattresses in the cramped, three-foot headroom passenger deck with the unnerving sound of coconuts rolling back and forth on the deck below us.

Upon arrival, I bussed back to the capital, found accommodation and spent my penultimate day abroad buying gifts in Bangkok's marvellously cheap markets. On my final night, I sat in a bar on the Khao San Road, a farewell glass of rice whisky in hand, thinking about all of my adventures around the globe. I realized I'd learned so much about the world that I could never have learned in any other way. But I also understood I'd discovered a great deal about myself and even though my travels were about to come to an end, I knew they were something that would always be with me.

As I sat there, contemplating the past few years of my life, I started to have a strange feeling that I was about to meet someone I knew. Just as I was becoming aware of this sensation, I turned around and there, at the bar, was a guy I felt sure I'd met before. It had happened again: another chance meeting with someone from my past.

Although I never forget a face, names have always been a problem for me. As I studied his familiar features, trying to at least remember where we had met, absolutely nothing came to mind. With no other option available, I got up, walked over to the bar, tapped him on the shoulder and simply said, 'I know you from somewhere.'

'Steve!' he replied without the slightest hesitation. 'What are you doing here?'

'Waiting for a flight, but w– where do I know you from?'

'The International Network Hostel, Los Angeles, about a year and a half ago.'

'Oh yeah, of course. You're Swedish, aren't you?'

'Yeah, I was the one who got stuck in LA when the Greyhound Bus Company lost my backpack and I got a job at the hostel as night security.'

'That's it! I remember,' I said as everything started coming back. 'I had to wake you up very late one night to let me in after I'd been to a party.'

'Yes, that's right,' he said with a friendly smile.

'But, er, I still can't remember your name,' I added with embarrassment.

'Petter.'

'Of course, Petter! How's it going, man?'

Unfortunately, we didn't have much time to reminisce about our time together in Los Angeles or catch up on our respective travels since then because I had a plane to catch. It was due to leave at midnight, so at around nine o'clock I said my goodbyes and went to get a taxi. At the airport, I found the Scandinavian Airlines desk quite quickly but just before checking in I realized there was one more thing I needed to do. I ceremoniously removed my well-used sandals, threw them in the bin and then laced up my hiking boots in preparation for my journey back to the rolling fields of England's green and pleasant land.

The comfortable flight home was via Copenhagen and the quality of in-flight service was what one would expect from a Scandinavian airline. I enjoyed a tasty meal with a nice glass of wine, watched a great movie and then slipped into a deep sleep. I didn't wake up until we were about 20 minutes from England and the first thing I heard was the pilot's voice informing us that, in London, the temperature was 2° C and it was snowing.

I couldn't believe it! On the very day I'd decided to return home after travelling for so long through so many hot countries, the south of England was being hit with a freak April snowstorm. I couldn't help but take it personally. Then suddenly I realized this posed a very serious problem. Despite changing my footwear for something more suitable at the airport in Bangkok, I was still wearing nothing more than a vest and a pair of light, cotton, beach trousers.

As we began descending through thick cloud, I sat with my face glued to the small circular window waiting for my first glimpse of Great Britain. The pilot repeatedly turned one way and then another, descended and then ascended a little, until eventually we broke through the cloud and into a raging blizzard. The pilot's weather report had been reliable and I felt obliged to explain to the confused couple seated next to me why I had burst out laughing on seeing the snow.

Once we'd landed I rapidly disembarked, rushed through immigration and raced to the baggage carousel. The moment my backpack arrived, I quickly pulled out my clothes except I found I didn't have anything remotely suitable for these unexpected climatic conditions. Consequently, I had to improvise with what was available and strode through customs into the arrivals lounge wearing three soiled T-shirts; a thin, ragged sweatshirt; a long, brown, Australian riding-coat; and a black, suede, Australian bush-hat. This unusual attire, combined with my deeply sun-tanned skin, must have presented a confusing image for those there to meet passengers who had boarded the plane in Denmark.

I changed the meagre amount of Thai currency I still had in my wallet and then went to find a bus home. It was freezing outside, as the snow continued to fall, and just as I thought I was about to cross the final hurdle I discovered I couldn't afford a ticket to Bournemouth. I only had enough money to get me as far as Southampton, a city some 25 miles short of my destination, and that left me with exactly 21 pence in my pocket.

The drive from Heathrow Airport down to the south coast was an amazing experience for me. I remember peering through a misted-up window at the snow-covered, rural, English countryside, and having a fantastic feeling I had felt on several occasions during my trip around the world. It was as if I were finally enjoying a view only previously experienced through photos or television. I had been away for so long that it truly felt like this was the first time I'd ever seen England. My homeland had never looked so beautiful.

On reaching Southampton bus station, I instantly abandoned any plans of trying to hitchhike the rest of the way due to the 'Arctic' conditions. I realized I would have to swallow my pride and telephone my parents. I tried but no one was home, so I called my sister and luckily she hadn't left for work yet. She was very surprised to hear that I was back in the UK and told me she would send her boyfriend to collect me right away.

I had never met Russell before, though I don't imagine it was difficult for him to identify me when he arrived at the station. I was also pleased to have a chance to get to know him during the drive back home, and once we'd reached Bournemouth he took me to the flat he shared with my sister and began preparing some lunch.

While we were chatting in the kitchen, I suddenly heard the sound of a key in the front door. Immediately, I rushed through to the hall and got there just as the door flew open and my sister's little body came bouncing in with a smile on her face as if all her Christmases and birthdays had come at once.

'Steve!' she cried as she ran towards me. Then she hugged me with a warmth and affection that had been absent since before I could remember.

'Hiya, sis, how are you doing?'

'Yeah– great– fine– I'm fine, thanks,' she stuttered. 'I just can't believe you're back! Why didn't you let us know you were coming?'

'I don't know. I guess I just wanted to be dramatic.'

'Dramatic? Yeah, that's typical of *you*!' she teased. 'But do you know what? I always felt I would be the first of the family to see you when you finally came home.'

'Wow! So did I!'

'Really?'

'Yeah, well, you were always the one who looked out for me when I was a kid, so it kinda made sense that you'd be here waiting for me when I came back.'

'God, Steve, sometimes you say the daftest things.'

A little later my mum just happened to pop by, so she became the second family member to witness my homecoming, but I asked her not to let Dad know I was back. Seeing *him* again would be a moment I wanted to savour.

Early that evening, we drove to my parents' house and I rang the doorbell while my sister and Russell kept out of sight. My father opened the door rather formally, fully expecting to meet a potential buyer of his house. Instead, he was confronted with a deeply-tanned, long-haired, 'Australian' bloke who was wearing a very strange hat and coat.

'Hello, Dad,' I said and moved forward to embrace him but he stepped back in a state of confused shock.

'What– who– who are you?' he mumbled.

'Come on, Dad. It's me, Steve. I'm back!' I exclaimed. 'Give us a hug then!'

Thankfully he did, then we went inside and I started to explain exactly what had happened.

'So I guess you still don't understand exactly what happened,' my father said shortly after arriving at the hospital.

When he had entered my room just a few minutes earlier, I almost hadn't recognized him. Although he'd been with me before I was sent to Gran Canaria, at that time I was still emerging from post-traumatic delirium and I hadn't completely registered his presence. Now that I'd returned both mentally and physically, I couldn't believe that the man before me was the same man I had spent the Christmas holidays with less than two months earlier.

He was dressed in his usual attire: a loose T-shirt under an open denim shirt, baggy tracksuit trousers, comfortable trainers and, as always, a San Diego baseball cap to protect his balding head from the cold in the winter and the sun's searing rays in the summer. The clothes were familiar; it was the face that had changed. He was like a hollow replica of the man I had known my whole life. He seemed to have lost that mischievous sparkle in his eyes and a naughty moustached smile that gave the impression of a man who was still very young at heart.

'You don't know how happy I am to see you,' I replied, struggling to contain my emotions. 'I know I've been in a car crash but I've, er, I mean I've got so many questions. Like, why do all the nurses seem to know who I am?'

'The thing is, Stevie, for the first two weeks after your accident you were pretty crazy. You said and did a lot of crazy stuff.'

'What do you mean? What kind of *stuff*?'

'Well, you constantly called all the nurses 'prostitutes', you also tried to hit quite a lot of them and you kept trying to get out of bed, even though your leg was in traction.'

'I don't believe it!' I exclaimed. 'Why did I do that?'

'In your accident you received a pretty hefty bash to the head and I guess it kinda knocked things out of place for a while,' he explained. 'One of the doctors here told me it wasn't uncommon behaviour for someone in your condition, so don't worry, you're OK now and I'm sure the hospital staff all understand.'

Then suddenly a shimmy of fear ran through me as I remembered those words of torment delivered by the doctor on Gran Canaria. My palms began to sweat, I felt an uncomfortable ache in my stomach and a persistent need to swallow but I knew I had to ask the question.

'W– what about my leg?'

'Well, it's broken, isn't it?'

'Yes, but, w– what are they going to do?' I stammered. 'What's going to happen?'

'They're going to screw it back together again,' he said in his DIY voice that conveyed the assurance of a true professional.

'But will it be all right? Will I be able to walk OK and stuff like that?'

'Of course you will, son!' he replied. 'Knowing you, you won't be walking; you'll be dancing again in no time at all. You and your dancing. It would take more than a broken leg to stop you doing that, wouldn't it? Don't worry, everything's going to be fine.'

Later that night, after my father had left, I started to think more about my situation. I'd been involved in a very serious road accident because a drunk driver had crashed into me head-on. I'd spent two weeks in intensive care, where my spleen had been removed due to internal bleeding and I'd received over four litres of blood. I had a broken foot, a shattered femur with a leg in traction, and a number of fractures around my left eye causing double vision and a degree of facial deformity. It had been a very demanding experience, particularly at the beginning when all the doctors were sure I was going to die. But I didn't . . . I was still here.

I had been fortunate enough to live a very full life, then one man's reckless disregard for safety had almost brought that life to an untimely end. He'd put me in intensive care, where I had surprised those men of medical science. I hadn't died, I was still in the game, but the whistle had been blown for half-time. Now I'd returned to the dressing room to recuperate from the first half and reflect upon the game so far.

Yes . . . it *was* half-time.

7 *Turtle Town*

Morning arrived with the traditional promptitude of hospital staff scheduling and I was woken at daybreak by a nurse dispensing medication before finishing her night shift. However, once she had discharged her duties I couldn't go back to sleep again because finally I had a reason to stay awake. Almost four weeks had passed since my accident but today was the first I would spend both lucid and not alone. I would spend the day with my father.

Throughout my entire life, I'd never longed for his company with the intensity I had felt over the past few days. Even though there had been long periods of separation when I'd been travelling or living in other countries, I couldn't remember ever having missed him in the way I did now. Maybe this was because it had been different in the past. Back then, we'd been apart due to things that were under my control and I had always known I could return home whenever I so desired.

In my childhood there had also been a brief period without paternal support, though it hadn't been so unbearable because I hadn't been alone, my sister had been with me. Yet as I thought back to that spell of turmoil in the relationship with my father, I felt an uncomfortable sense of guilt. At that time, I hadn't supported him with the loyal devotion he was currently exhibiting through a willingness to put his life on hold while I rebuilt mine.

During the first few years after the divorce he had gone through some immense difficulties. It was a distressing time for all of us but I think, for him, possibly even more so. He'd had to overcome all the problems in his personal life without the support of others, whereas we still lived in a family unit. And in addition to all this emotional stress, he'd been striving to keep his business afloat while a recession engulfed the nation.

It was a time when many people were struggling financially and at one point my father's situation became so acute that he couldn't afford the child-maintenance payments. It was a fact our mother zealously advertised at every possible opportunity, and eventually she convinced me that his lack of financial assistance indicated a lack of love for his own children. As a result, I refused to see him and although this situation only existed temporarily, I still felt culpable for believing that money was the only way he could show us what he thought.

'A penny for your thoughts.'

'Dad! I didn't see you come in,' I exclaimed. 'Hi, how are you?'

'I'm OK. Happier for seeing you, of course. So, did you sleep all right?'

'Yeah, fine thanks. Much better than in Gran Canaria. It's a lot quieter in this hospital and the nurses seem friendlier here as well. I feel like they really care about me.'

'Yeah, well, most of them saw you go through your . . . er–'

'Crazy period?'

'Your crazy period, yes, so I guess they're just relieved to see that you're back to normal again.'

'Yeah, that makes sense, and I suppose you know most of them pretty well by now.'

'The faces are familiar, Steve, but I don't speak the language so I haven't had the chance to chat any of them up yet, if that's what you mean.'

'No, of course not!' I sniggered. 'It's just that you've been here for quite a while.'

'Yep, I sure have,' he sighed. 'It's been nearly a month now and to tell the truth, this past week hasn't been all that easy, really.'

'Why not?'

'Well, since Lyn flew back to England I've been feeling a bit lonely, sat there in your flat waiting to see you again,' he confessed. 'But all that's changed, now that you're back.'

This was the moment when I realized we'd both been sharing the same severe sense of isolation. I began to understand that my accident hadn't involved me alone, I wasn't the only 'casualty', and this sudden realization inspired the desire to converse. That morning we chatted about everything and anything until our throats were dry and our voices hoarse. At long last, we could release all the emotional pressure that had been bottled up inside of us for days.

Soon after lunch, in the quiet lull before formal visiting hours began, a friendly bearded face appeared at the door to my room. It was Manel, one of the doctors at the hospital, only we hadn't met as a result of my accident. A mutual friend had introduced us during my first year on the island, and this had come about through a shared interest: Manel was a musician. He was a guitarist and on a couple of occasions he'd invited me to play percussion with his jazz band.

'Hi, Steve, how are you?' he asked and then immediately glanced over his shoulder as if he were being followed.

'I'm all right, thanks. What about you?'

'Er, OK . . . yes, I'm OK,' he replied, appearing distracted.

'So, have you met my dad, Paul?'

'No, we haven't been introduced,' he replied, extending his right hand across the bed towards my father. 'Nice to meet you. My name's Manel. I'm a friend of your son's.'

'Nice to meet you too. And it's also a pleasure to meet someone who speaks English so well!'

'Thank you, I've . . . er . . . I've spent some time in England. But anyway, I can come back later if now is a bad time,' he said with an unfamiliar reluctance to socialize. I was confused by his behaviour because it was very out of character for a man who usually enjoyed a friendly chat.

'No, really, it's fine,' I said. 'Please don't go.'

'Alright, but there's something, er, th– there's something I think you should know.'

'What is it?'

'Well, it seems there's a rumour about you being circulated here amongst the doctors. Basically, they're all saying that you were very drunk on the night of your accident.'

'What?' I exclaimed. 'That's complete rubbish!'

'Yes, I'm sure it is,' he replied with conviction, yet the discomfort evident in his facial expression didn't convey genuine belief.

'Really, it's impossible, and I can tell you why. I don't drink and drive. The police in England are a lot stricter about things like that,' I declared, at the same time looking to my father for collaborative support. However, Manel's immediate reply rendered it unnecessary.

'Yes, I know that, but there's something else.'

'What?'

'Well, it's quite simple really. The uncle of the man who crashed into you works here. He's a doctor at this hospital, so I think it's obvious who started the rumour.'

'What did you say?' exclaimed my father. 'Are you telling me that one of your colleagues is trying to make my son look bad in front of the very same people who saved his life?'

'I'm sorry, Paul, that's *exactly* what I'm saying,' replied Manel, his eyes firmly focused on the floor. 'And there's one more thing I think you need to know.'

'What?' demanded my father but Manel didn't answer right away. He slowly raised his head and looked at me with the face of a guilty child who knows he has to confess. Then he briefly glanced across at my father, turned back to me again and did something that increased both my confusion and my father's frustration. Despite speaking English fluently, he switched to Spanish.

'Everyone knows it was this doctor's nephew, not you, who was drunk that night,' he said. 'He's famous for it! You see, you're not the first person he's put in hospital and I was also told that the police confiscated his driving-licence after his last crash a couple of months ago. But, well, it seems he's got away with it again.'

'He's what? I mean, we already knew he was drunk,' I explained. 'I still don't understand.'

'Look, Steve, although I'm from mainland Spain, I've been living on this little island long enough to know how the system works here.'

'What's he saying?' interrupted my father, desperate to be included in the conversation.

'Wait a minute, I don't know. What *are* you saying Manel?'

'Well, after the accident they brought both of you here, to the hospital. Then, the other guy, he walked away scot-free. He didn't have a scratch on him.'

'So they took him to the police station for questioning?'

'No, Steve, they let him go home. It appears his uncle *bribed* the police.'

'No! I don't believe it!' I screamed, my whole body becoming charged with anger.

'But it's true, his uncle bribed them. I've spoken to a few other people and it seems that it's not the first time he's done it either. His nephew has been in the same situation on several occasions in the past, so I guess he just did what he'd done before: he bribed them.'

'Please tell me what he said,' begged my father, frustrated beyond control.

'He said his uncle bribed them!'

'He bribed them! Who? The other doctors?'

'No, Dad, he bribed the police. The guy who nearly killed me won't be prosecuted because his uncle bribed the police.'

'The police!'

'What?'

'The police!' he repeated, and as I looked up from my Spanish phrase book I suddenly became aware that we had been surrounded. Behind Scott was an unusually large Latin American holding a base-ball bat, behind me another of much the same build armed with a similar weapon, and between us a bearded police officer with a pair of handcuffs in one hand and an automatic pistol in the other.

We were in Costa Rica, Central America, and I'd travelled up from Panama in an effort to arrive in San José in time for the 21st birthday of my best friend Scott. My stay in Panama had been very brief. I'd flown from Jamaica to this lazy S-shaped country connecting South America to its northern neighbours and was eager to leave soon after arriving. This was due, in part, to my nervousness at being alone in a non-English-speaking country for the first time on my trip around the world. Until then I'd only travelled through the USA and to a few parts of the British West Indies. But it was also due to recent events that had been receiving international press coverage about a place only previously famous for a canal and a hat (although the hats are actually made in Ecuador!)

Panama had been going through a period of political instability – a popular trend in Latin America – and was now being portrayed as a military dictatorship loosely disguised as a democracy. I'd heard about numerous demonstrations by both the pro-General Noriega loyalists and the opposing *Cruzada Civilista Nacional* businessmen, and I didn't want to get caught in the middle of such political protests with absolutely no understanding of their beliefs, doctrines or even their language.

I arrived in Panama City late at night, found a secluded corner in the airport lounge and went straight to sleep. Early the next morning, I ventured out into the city, though I only stayed long enough for a quick breakfast and then took a bus 300 miles north to a small town on the border. The following day, I set off at dawn and after some communication difficulties at immigration and customs, I crossed into Costa Rica, a country reassuringly described as, 'An oasis of calm amidst turbulent neighbours'. Indeed, that very same year, President Oscar Arias had received the Nobel Prize in recognition of his efforts to spread Costa Rica's example of peace throughout Central America. Finally, I bussed up to the capital, San José, where Scott was staying at the house of a man who'd stayed at his own family home on a study trip in England several years earlier.

I first met Scott when we started secondary school, and back then we were very different in many respects. In fact, it was one of those differences that instigated our friendship. Of the hundred or so eleven-year-old boys who joined Bournemouth Grammar School that year, I was the third shortest and it would be a couple more years before I began the rapid physical development that came with pubescence. Scott, on the other hand, was among the tallest, and seeing as boys of that age will pick on others for any number of reasons, I'd considered it advantageous to cultivate a friendship with someone of such stature.

Nevertheless, there were one or two other differences that led to the strengthening of this friendship. While both of us were responsible students and quite adept in many subjects, my biggest weakness was one of Scott's greatest strengths: foreign languages. Fortunately, he was always more than willing to help me with any homework assignments I found difficult, and in return I assisted him in certain areas of 'education' that were not on the school curriculum.

Unlike him, I had an elder sister whose boyfriends were usually older than her, and from these young men I had received some invaluable guidance in such things as music, fashion and girls. Scott was quite a shy adolescent, yet keen to develop his understanding of such fundamentally important fields of enquiry, so we were able to grow up through those formative, teenage years with each of us somehow providing the other with what he was lacking.

Our close friendship continued through to adulthood and when I was six months into my world trip, he flew out and joined me in Key West. Once again, we could share many new experiences – living away from home, having our own flat, assimilating a different culture, mixing with people of diverse nationalities – but when we decided to move on, we made differing travel plans whilst still vowing to keep in touch if at all possible. Consequently, on arriving in the Costa Rican capital at about five in the afternoon of September 11th 1987, I called the contact number he'd given me and wished him a happy 21st. It was the best 'present' he got that year and he said he would come down to the bus station and collect me right away.

As I waited on a park bench opposite the bus terminal, I was very excited to be on the point of seeing him again. Even though only six weeks had passed since we'd parted company in Florida, an enormous amount had happened in that short space of time and I was desperate to share it with him. In addition to this, two whole days had gone by without actually being able to have a conversation in English, so I was quite keen just to talk to anyone about anything!

'Hi *compadre*, how's it going?' came a familiar voice from behind me.

'That sounds like Scott,' I said and turned round to find myself looking up at the tallest and palest skinned person I had seen in the last 48 hours. It was as if I were facing a gigantic blood donor who just couldn't say no. 'Happy 21st, mate! And what's with all this 'compy dray' stuff?'

'No, stupid, it's *compadre*. It means the same as *amigo*, except you only use it with your best friends.'

'You Central American gigolo, you. Speaking the lingo now, are

81

we?' I mocked.

'Come on, give me a break. I've been here for more than a month, so I'm bound to have picked up a bit, aren't I?' he replied in self-defence.

'Picked up a bit! You're probably fluent by now, knowing you.'

'Well, not exactly, it isn't that easy. But don't worry, you'll get the hang of it after a while.'

'Reckon it'll take *me* more than a while, Scott. So, how are you doing?'

We collected my things together and he took me back to the home of his Costa Rican host family, who were extremely welcoming and had already made up another bed for me in the guest room. That evening they prepared a birthday meal for Scott, complete with cake and candles, and then a little later the two of us went out to celebrate his coming of age. He took me to a nightclub close by that he had frequented on occasion since arriving, and we stayed there until the earlier hours, catching up on all the news of one another's recent adventures.

Scott had decided to stay on in San José for another month and possibly even enrol on a Spanish course, but in the end I managed to persuade him to accompany me on a trip I was planning. Before leaving the USA, I had bought a guidebook to Central America and during the intervening weeks I'd become captivated by what I had read about the Caribbean Coast. This littoral is poetically known as the 'Mosquito Coast', a name derived from that of the Mosquito Indians, one of the few remaining tribes of Amerindians who still inhabit the area. But it was more than just a romantic-sounding name that had made this region appear so attractive.

San José is racially homogenous with the vast majority of its inhabitants having Spanish blood. In contrast, the Mosquito Coast is far more culturally diverse and in addition to the Amerindian tribes, is home to a large number of Creoles, many of Jamaican decent, making it a bilingual province. Also, about 50 percent of this coastal area is protected by national parks, leaving it noticeably undeveloped compared to other parts of the country, and from all this information I had concluded it would definitely be a place worth visiting.

We first had to spend a few days in the capital before embarking on our expedition, as there were one or two visa, ticket and money problems that needed resolving. I felt this city had a very North American ambience, brought about by many of the department stores, fast food chains and shopping malls found all over the USA, but its climate was decidedly English. It seemed to rain every day, which helped me understand how Scott had managed to lose his Florida tan so quickly.

Once we were ready to leave, we were dropped off at the station to take a train to Puerto Limón, the principal town on the Atlantic Coast. At midday we boarded a battered blue train painted with the red and white stripes of the national flag, and commenced an eight-hour trip to the coast. I had seen some photos of the planned journey in my guide-book but this was one of those rare occasions when the reality was even better than the dream.

It started very slowly, as the locomotive struggled to haul its chain of clanking carriages up mountains planted with coffee bushes. Then it gathered speed on the decent through lush jungle, past banana plantations and tall fields of sugar cane, following the meandering course of a surging river. On reaching the coastal plain, the railway line diverged from the river, transforming our verdant window-seat view into an endless show-reel of small, decaying, wood-panelled shacks, all with rusty tin roofs and built on short stilts no more than 15 feet from the train rails.

And it appeared that this train was a daily attraction. The narrow verandas of these rustic provincial residences were crowded with silent staring natives, all intently watching the faces of 'city folk' pass by. However, the beaming visage of a foreigner must have triggered emotions other than mere interest because a young lad hurled a small rock through an open window that would have seriously injured me, hadn't it been for Scott's perceptive warning.

We arrived in Puerto Limón early that evening and the final part of our journey had been spent in complete darkness, since this train wasn't equipped with such luxuries as lights. We got a room at a cheap hotel close to the station, showered and changed, and then went out for some dinner.

While being the capital of the Caribbean Coast, Puerto Limón was still nothing more than a sleepy little town. There were a dozen or so wide, dusty streets arranged in the grid fashion of the USA, one or two grassy parks with limited landscaping, and the architecture resembled a larger, more solid version of what we'd seen by the railway lines.

Yet contrary to its small-town feel, it was absolutely teeming with people. They congregated on every street corner, bunched around park benches and grouped together in the doorways of those households that possessed a ghetto blaster. But they didn't seem to be doing anything. They were all just standing around, waiting. It was as if someone had changed the route of the carnival parade at the last minute but had forgotten to let them know it wouldn't be coming their way. We later discovered this was because there wasn't really very much to do after dark in Puerto Limón.

The next day we began discussing our plans, now that we had reached the Mosquito Coast. There were two possible options. We could take a bus south to the beach town of Cahuita and snorkel on the country's largest coastal reef, or we could take a boat trip north up an inland waterway to a coastal village very close to the Nicaraguan border. I'd read that this was the primary breeding ground for the green sea turtles of the Atlantic, which spawned on the beaches there in the month of September, an annual event that lent the village its name: Tortuguero – 'Turtle Town'. This sounded rather more 'educational', so although Cahuita was the number one coastal destination on the backpackers' circuit, we chose the turtles.

After bussing down to the small wharf, we found that there was a problem with the boat that day and the one o'clock departure had been postponed until five in the evening. This was quite frustrating because we had hoped to enjoy the journey in daylight, but a brief chat with a Swiss backpacker standing nearby revealed that another one would be leaving at nine the following morning. Consequently, we decided this would be a preferable alternative.

The next morning, we woke up early, packed our things and went to take our seats for a memorable passage on the Tortuguero ferry. It was a truly unforgettable tropical travel experience. We saw pelicans, monkeys, iguanas and even a few turtles as the boat carved its path along the turgid canal through rich, dense, jungle vegetation. The only minor disappointment was that, counter to the poetic description in my guidebook, we couldn't hear the crash of Atlantic waves on the hidden beach just 30 yards away. Obviously, the writer of this book hadn't actually bothered to make the journey himself because if he had, he would have discovered that even conversation with the person seated next to you was virtually impossible due to the incessant roar of the boat's engine.

Nevertheless, about half way through our trip we were granted the pleasure of hearing whitecaps tumble from the tops of waves for a few hours when this engine spluttered to a halt. As a result, an eight-hour journey that we'd prepared for poorly, not taking any kind of refreshments with us, soon turned into an eleven-hour marathon and when we eventually arrived in Tortuguero we were both extremely hungry.

It was a small village situated on the narrow strip of land between the canal and the Caribbean. There weren't any proper streets as such, just well-trodden paths amongst the haphazard jumble of houses, huts and assorted edifices that provided this isolated community with their basic requirements.

Even though it was early evening and we desperately needed some food, our first priority was accommodation. We quickly found what appeared to be a cheap hotel but the receptionist turned us away with surprising terseness for someone who worked in the hospitality industry.

As we wandered outside again, we happened to bump into the same Swiss backpacker we had met at the wharf in Puerto Limón the previous morning. After exchanging stories of our respective terrible ferry journeys – his ferry had also had engine problems, resulting in a four-hour delay in complete darkness on a river inhabited by a variety of wildlife, including crocodiles – we told him about our recent brief exchange with the unfriendly hotel receptionist.

'No, you guys won't get rooms there. They don't rent rooms to gringos,' he explained.

'Gringos? What the hell is a *gringo*?' I asked.

'Well, most Latin Americans call any foreigner a gringo, though it really means North American. You see, in the past there used to be a lot of American soldiers in Mexico but the locals didn't want them there. US soldiers wear green uniforms, so whenever a Mexican saw one they would always shout, "Green go!" Of course, with a Spanish accent it came out as, "Gringo!" So that's what every Latin American calls them now, and all of us Europeans as well.'

'Oh, right, I understand. Where I come from, that's the same as calling someone a grockle.'

'Really? Well that's a word I've never heard that word before. But anyway, if you want to get a room try the place next to that bar,' he suggested, pointing to his right. 'They seem a bit more tolerant over there.'

Following his advice, we succeeded in renting a small, economical room for the night. Then our next basic necessity of life was an evening meal. We made our way to the village restaurant, but on arriving we were stopped at the door by a waiter who explained that the kitchen was empty. They'd sold out of every dish on the menu and there would be nothing available until the boat arrived the following morning.

This left only one other option open to us. We set off to find the village shop and this time we were stopped at the door by the owner, who was closing up business at the end of his working day. Finding food was beginning to present a problem and it appeared that our desperate need for nourishment wasn't going to be satisfied, at least not that night, not in Tortuguero.

'This is absolutely ridiculous,' Scott sighed. 'What are we going to do now?'

'Well, I suppose we could always go down to the beach to find a couple of turtle eggs and make a big omelette,' I suggested.

'Look, Steve, I'm too tired and hungry to put up with your silly jokes right now,' he snapped. 'Besides, without a camp stove and a frying pan, how are we going to cook one?'

'Oh yeah, I hadn't thought of that,' I replied, relieved that he hadn't completely lost his ability to see the funny side of things. 'Well, there's only one thing for it, then.'

'And what's that?' he asked with a hint of sarcasm.

'I reckon it's time for a beer, although *you'd* better order them 'cause with my Spanish we'd probably end up with a couple of glasses of milk.'

'Hey, don't be so negative, it's getting better every day. Anyway, a glass of beer *or* milk sounds fine to me. So come on, let's go.'

We made our way back to the hostelry next to our hotel and ordered two beers and a couple of bags of crisps. We thought that the combination of alcohol and snacks would be enough to see us through until the arrival of the morning boat, but this was the point where a day that had been far from perfect took a turn for the worse. Scott opened his bag of crisps only to discover they were so stale that he could bend one double without it breaking. I suggested he went back to the bar to change it for a fresh packet, but as I sat there watching his attempts at negotiation I could see that the barman wasn't being very obliging.

For a reason I never fully understood, I suddenly found myself possessed with a strong desire to seek justice. Despite the fact that his limited command of the local language was far superior to my almost non-existent Spanish, I felt sure that my help was required. I got up, marched over to the bar and formally enquired, 'What appears to be the problem?'

'He doesn't speak English, so can you let *me* deal with it, please?' requested Scott.

'No, I want to know if he's going to give you a fresh bag,' I demanded.

'I'm not sure, but it looks like I might have to buy another one. Still, it doesn't matter, it's not important.'

'No! He's got to change it for a new bag!' I argued. 'You didn't pay good money for something that's virtually inedible, did you?'

But Scott wasn't disposed to confrontations. He was always more inclined to diplomacy, and simply shrugged his shoulders.

I, on the other hand, wasn't prepared to give up that easily. I turned to the barman and, addressing him with the intonation and enunciation used by many Englishmen when faced with a foreigner, said, 'Look *señor* . . you change . . bad crisps . . different bag . . *comprendo*?'

'Actually, Steve, *comprendo* means, "I understand" not, "Do you understand?"' translated Scott.

'I don't care if he understands. He's just taking the piss because he thinks we're Americans,' I yelled. Then as the frustration of this linguistic barrier began to cloud my sense of judgement, I grabbed the offending bag of crisps from Scott's hand and, straining to remember some of the Spanish he'd taught me, said very loudly, 'We *inglés*, not *Americano*, not gringo. We not *rico*, no have *mucho* money. *Tu* sell 'crispo' *mucho malo*. Now *tu sabes* we not *Americano, tu estás mucho* 'embarrassedo', no?'

Before I could finish my pathetic attempt at communication, the barman – actually the owner – burst out laughing, as did one or two others who were standing nearby.

'What happened?' I asked Scott, feeling completely bewildered by this unexpected response.

'You've just told him he's very *pregnant*,' he replied, struggling to stifle a giggle.

'Well, fuck him!' I shouted, simultaneously throwing the bag into the air in an attempt to vent my feelings of irritation, anger and humiliation. This somewhat theatrical gesture also resulted in the barman being showered with stale crisps and although not my original intention, I considered it an appropriate conclusion to our brief confrontation.

There is no other way to describe the outcome of my actions than to say it was like a scene from a low-budget spaghetti western. Ten minutes earlier we'd walked into a locals' bar and received nothing but unfriendly looks of disdain from the majority of its clientele. Now, as the landlord stood before me with his head and shoulders adorned with a patchwork of potato chips, the whole bar became filled with a tense silence. The regulars once again focused their attention on the two gringos, this time all glowering with a bug-eyed intensity.

All of a sudden I was overcome with a desire to be where other people weren't. I grabbed my beer, sucked it dry in a single swig, then slammed the empty frothing bottle back down on the bar and strutted out in a pathetic attempt to emulate Clint Eastwood. In hindsight my actions had been very foolish, particularly as we were in an extremely isolated part of a Latin American country, and even though by then I had spent nearly a year on the road, I realized I still had a lot to learn about world travel.

Scott came out very soon after my dramatic exit and we both agreed it was the perfect end to such a bad day. While discussing the absurdity of our little confrontation, we began making our way to the other bar. There was only one restaurant in the village and only one shop but Tortuguero boasted *two* bars. At least they had their priorities right.

This one was noticeably quieter than the first, which was rather reassuring under the circumstances, so we purchased some beers, avoided the bar snacks and then sat at an empty table, still laughing about our nightmarish day.

As a result of recent events, I decided it was time for another Spanish lesson and started thumbing through my phrase book to find out how being 'pregnant' could be 'embarrassing'. However, before I'd even had a chance to begin my studies, Scott said something that made me look up and I suddenly became aware that we had been surrounded. Behind Scott was an unusually large Latin American holding a baseball bat, behind me another of much the same build armed with a similar weapon, and between us a bearded police officer with a pair of handcuffs in one hand and an automatic pistol in the other.

There was a brief exchange of Spanish between Scott and our captors, then we were escorted from the bar through a field of long grass towards a hut that appeared to serve as the police station. Many alarming scenarios were running through my mind as I began to feel the web of sin and circumstance closing in, though one thing stood out above all other possible outcomes: I was sure they were going to take our money. At that particular moment, the amount of local currency I had on my person was only worth about $20, but to a backpacker in that part of the world, it was a lot of money to lose. Consequently, as I stumbled through the knee length grass in darkness, I casually took the notes out of my pocket and slipped them inside my underpants.

A few minutes later, two very nervous gringos were bundled into a shack in the back end of nowhere wondering if they would come out alive. Soon after the interrogation began, it became obvious that it was way above Scott's level of comprehension so the police chief sent for a Jamaican interpreter.

While we anxiously waited, there was a rapid dialogue between the chief and one of his 'sumo-baseball' officers and despite my problems with the local language, I managed to catch the word 'marijuana'. Almost immediately I realized I was wearing a T-shirt from Jamaica that depicted a rastaman smoking a very large cannabis cigarette. My original thoughts of money instantly returned, except this time in the form of extortion. I started to consider the possibility of being set up on a drug charge and having to change vast amounts of traveller's cheques in order to pay off enormous bribes.

Before I'd even had time to imagine the consequences of such a situation, the policeman at my side dropped his baseball bat, pulled my shorts down, shoved his hand inside my underpants and extracted a small wad of Costa Rican *colones*. Then he looked over to his boss for orders while I resigned myself to the loss of the money. It wasn't that bad, I could live without it. I also hoped that this small financial reward might ease the situation a little. Yet much to my surprise, once the chief had barked his demands the policeman shoved the money back where he'd found it and pulled my shorts up again. At that moment, I began to calm down. I realized everything was going to be all right. These coppers were good guys.

Following a short, almost embarrassing wait, the interpreter arrived. He was an elderly Jamaican man with thin grey hair, grey stubble and facial features that made him appear to be constantly smiling. He greeted both of us warmly and after mentioning how much he liked my T-shirt, he listened attentively to our account of recent events, scratching his wiry head from time to time. When he had all the pertinent details, he started to translate to the chief but he didn't have time to finish before our meeting was rudely interrupted by an uninvited guest.

At first I couldn't understand why this woman was shouting at us. Then eventually I realized she was the landlord's wife; he'd sent his old lady to fight his battle! I also sensed that the others present found this quite amusing – the macho disposition of Latin American men meant they didn't consider it appropriate to let a woman take control in a situation of conflict – but they all patiently waited, letting her have her say, and when she had run out of steam she was courteously escorted to the door.

The final outcome was that the police chief magnanimously conceded we had been treated unfairly by the proprietor. He should've changed the bag of crisps, so we were free to go, as long as we didn't return to that bar. We had been barred. Through the interpreter, we politely apologized for any inconvenience, said our goodbyes and then exited as rapidly as possible. We returned to the other bar, where we found our untouched beers gathering condensation on our empty table, and quickly finished them (and several more) before finally returning to our accommodation feeling lucky to have avoided incarceration.

We never saw the Atlantic turtles laying eggs on the beach. The next morning, we awoke at dawn and decided it would probably be better if we left Tortuguero as soon as possible. We gathered together our possessions, shouldered our backpacks and went straight down to the canal to catch the morning boat back to Puerto Limón.

When we arrived at the village wharf, a familiar figure stood out amongst the crowds of people waiting for the imminent departure. It was the police chief and his presence there was obviously a daily ritual demanded of a man in his position. However, on catching sight of us, his air of authority became replaced with a somewhat awkward discomfort. He immediately approached and greeted us with excessive warmth, giving friendly handshakes and pats on the back and making what I assumed were humorous comments about the previous night's misunderstanding. Then, with a sheepish bearded grin, he turned away and headed back to the village.

My father's undisguised anger fuelled Manel's somewhat awkward discomfort, and with a sheepish bearded grin, he turned away and headed out of the room. I watched him exit in silence, still needing time to digest the information I had just been given. I was desperately struggling to control feelings of anger and frustration. One side of me was consumed with the desire to seek justice, whereas my other, more experienced side understood that this wasn't always possible. On a small island such as this, I knew it would be impossible to prove the corruption of a police officer, so no matter how embittered I became I would have to surpress my desire to do so.

After gathering my thoughts, I turned to my left, expecting to find my father at my bedside but he wasn't there. He was standing by the window, silhouetted against the bright sunlight of a Canarian afternoon, and from his sunken stance I understood that now wasn't the time for discussion. I knew exactly what he was thinking, we didn't need to talk, and even though I was finding it difficult to accept what Manel had just told me, I felt a strong sense of reassurance through simply having shared it with him.

8 *Medicine Man*

It was nearly ten o'clock, so I knew my father would be arriving soon and in my mind I could clearly picture him on his daily 'pilgrimage' to Arrecife General Hospital. He would leave my flat and turn right towards La Granja, a convivial little bar at the end of the road, and then take a tiny side-street between the pub and a furniture shop, up to the local thoroughfare. This road was extremely cramped – a single lane of traffic constantly flowing past buildings jammed together three and four storeys high with overhanging balconies – but characteristic of Arrecife, a town that a visiting English friend had once described as 'a capital of backstreets'.

At the main road he would turn left, up the hill, along a lumpy pavement so narrow that he would be forced into the gutter whenever a pedestrian came the other way, since not only motorists in Spain always pass to the right. On this stretch of road there were occasional breaks in the overbearing architecture, where the 'grave' of a traditional Canarian house had yet to be replaced with a block of flats. Then finally he would feel a breeze on his face as he reached the top of the hill and the buildings opened out around an enormous roundabout planted with numerous cactuses, a profusion of flowers and a sizeable palm tree dominating its centre.

Here it would be important to follow the confusing permutations of a number of sets of traffic lights while he cautiously crossed the hub of several principal highways during the hectic morning rush hour. Once safely on the other side, he would pass the Red Cross ambulance station to his right before walking by a short row of whitewashed, stucco villas, all with tiny front gardens. At the end of this row, he would continue past the military base on his left, a place that was home to a couple of soldiers whose blood was now flowing through my veins. Apparently, just after I'd been admitted to intensive care, an ambulance was sent to this base in search of blood donors because there wasn't enough of my group in reserve at the hospital.

As he progressed up the highway towards a volcano peaked with radio antennas, he would cross under the town bypass that led to the place where my accident had happened. Beyond the dual carriageway there was a large, open area of cactus-filled flowerbeds, then he would pass through a commercial district of car mechanics and breakers' yards full of crashed vehicles. On reaching the next roundabout, he'd traverse the main road and take the exit up to the hospital. This slip-road would lead him past the taxi rank on the left and the car park on the right, shortly before he arrived at the main entrance.

As I lay in bed, awaiting his arrival, the highlight of my otherwise monotonous day, I couldn't help wondering what thoughts filled his mind. I'd suffered a very traumatic accident, but he had gone through the aftermath with me. So, what was it like for him? I tried to imagine what he was thinking and feeling, and the only way I could do this was to put myself in his situation. I had to try and see things through his eyes.

I got married in 1965, when I was still quite young, and we started a family almost immediately. My daughter Nikki was born first. Then a year and a half later my son Steve arrived and I worked hard trying to build a good life for them.

However, as the years passed I began to feel that maybe I had married the wrong woman and despite a change of scenery when we moved from London to a Devonshire village, things just wouldn't work out. Less than a year later, we moved again, this time to Bournemouth, but it was only a matter of time before I opened my eyes and saw the truth: the marriage wasn't going to work and my role as a father would never be the same again. We decided that Nikki and Steve should stay with their mother and I had to settle for becoming nothing more than a Saturday-afternoon-at-the-zoo dad.

It was a difficult time for me, trying to adapt to life alone again after more than a decade as a family man. I would see my children at the weekend and I always looked forward to spending time with them.

But it wasn't the same as before. I no longer felt like a real *father. Our trips to the cinema or the bowling alley, walks along the beach or picnics in the countryside were a poor substitute for having breakfast with them every morning before sending them off to school, and then talking about our day over the evening meal. I no longer played an integral part in their lives. I had become an 'accessory'.*

Alongside the struggle to deal with all these changes in my personal life, my hairdresser's salon was on the verge of going under. Mine wasn't the only business in that neighbourhood having financial difficulties – we were all just a little too far from the centre to get consistent trade – and the combination of wages, bank payments, other overheads and child maintenance often totalled more than the till contained at the end of each week.

This resulted in further heartache and I can still remember going to pick Steve up from his mother's house but he wouldn't let me in. 'You don't love me! You don't pay the money to mum. How can you love me?' he shouted with anger through the closed door.

These words, which came from the mouth of a ten-year old boy I had helped bring into this world, really destroyed me deep inside. I couldn't understand what I'd done that was so terrible to warrant such punishment. I didn't deserve to lose my only son.

Fortunately, through the passing of time things slowly improved. A new woman came into my life, I began seeing Steve again and when he was 16 he came to live with the two of us. In one way, it was like starting over again. We hadn't lived together for nearly seven years and during this time my boy had grown up into a young man. But now I'd finally been given the chance to be the father I had always started out to be.

Shortly after he joined us, my fiancée received a nursing position in Bermuda, where she remained for more than year while Steve and I lived together in our house in Bournemouth. We began splitting the day-to-day household chores of cooking, shopping, washing, ironing and cleaning, and between the two of us we made a good team. During that very precious time we also became the best of friends. We discovered how similar we were; he really was his father's son and there were so many things we could share.

Steve was at art college and I, too, had always been quite artistic, having owned one or two businesses in the past that had required a creative input. Consequently, every evening I was ready to give considered advice on whatever project he was working on, and this soon developed into a rewarding little routine for both of us. In fact, when I was his age I'd always intended to study art but an acquaintance with a hairdresser had led my life down a different path. Now it felt almost as if he were realizing my dream for me.

Then there was music, something we'd had in common right from the early days when I'd given him a toy drum kit on his fifth birthday. Seeing as I was still working as a percussionist, I helped my son to start making a bit of cash from our shared talent, and very soon every weekend evening we could be found at different pubs around the town, providing the live entertainment with our respective bands.

A year later, on finishing a foundation course at art college, Steve decided to travel for a while before starting university. Taking time off studies to travel wasn't something I'd heard of before, so it was an unexpected decision but one that I supported, and it ultimately became something almost akin to a habit. He was away for a couple of years on his first trip, then he returned to England and resumed his studies. But Brighton University had just incorporated an Australian exchange programme into their graphic design course, so he went away again for another six months. When he came back, he finished his degree and then worked for a year as a musician while qualifying to be an English teacher.

Nevertheless, he still had the travel bug and started to talk about his desire to visit Venezuela. As a father, this was much harder to accept because there was a big difference between Australia and Venezuela. I had recently seen a television documentary about this country that gave the impression of a land filled with violence and insecurity. I didn't want him to go but I couldn't forbid it. He was an adult now and I knew I had to let him make his own decisions.

I can still remember how I felt that day at the coach station, waving at his smiling face full of excitement at the start of another adventure. I was unable to hide my anxiety, I just couldn't bear the thought of losing my son again, and as the bus began pulling away I

96

began to cry.

To my immense relief, he returned a year later, having travelled through the south of the Caribbean before finding work in Venezuela in his new profession. He came back to live with us, got a job teaching at a language academy and started seeing a Colombian girl. This relationship eventually resulted in another trip to South America, which, again, was very worrying, although this time at least he wasn't backpacking around. This time he was living in the relative safety of a Colombian family home. Also, by then I'd begun to accept that my son was a traveller.

Throughout his travels he always kept in touch and I felt proud to have a son with the courage to fulfil all his dreams. I even joined him once and flew down to Key West to work with him for a month. It felt a bit strange being a 'guest' in my son's house, the complete reverse of life in England, but I could see how much he'd matured through his travels and felt very contented with the man he'd become. We shared a very special time there and many of his friends couldn't believe we were father and son when they met us out socializing together.

When he went to live in the Canary Islands, it was quite a relief in many respects. After South America, I felt so much more comfortable knowing he was in a safe part of the world. Of course I missed him, but my wife and I went out to visit him and the following summer he came home to work in England for a couple of months. It was wonderful to hear all about his new life there and at long last it looked like he was ready to settle down.

At the end of the summer, he returned to the islands and worked hard developing his career as an English teacher while also starting a new one as a salsa dance teacher. He rapidly became successful in his new vocation and during the Christmas holidays he proudly showed us a video of a television presentation of one of his classes and an interview with him. When he left us again, we felt sure he was returning to the place he wanted to be and was content with the life he was building for himself there.

Ten days later I received a phone call from his boss in Lanzarote. She told me that my son was in intensive care due to a car crash two days earlier, and although they'd received news from the hospital that he didn't have brain damage, he was still in a critical condition.

Ten hours later I was on my way to Lanzarote. Most Brits board a flight to the Canary Islands full of high spirits in anticipation of a great holiday. I boarded that same flight feeling nothing but apprehension. My son was at death's door in a foreign country and the only thing I could think, no matter what would happen in the near future, was that I had to be with him. I couldn't lose my son again.

I arrived late morning at Arrecife airport to be met by his boss and was at his bedside by early afternoon. Nothing could have prepared me for this moment. As I looked at the body lying there before me, I found it impossible to believe that it belonged to my son. His face was so swollen and disfigured that if he hadn't had a name-tag on his wrist, I would never have recognized him.

He certainly didn't recognize me and obviously had no idea where he was or what had happened to him. Sometimes he would talk, or even shout, though not in a comprehensible way. During his time in intensive care he 'returned' to many destinations he'd visited in the past, places where he'd been happy, where the memories were good. I suppose, in his mind, he just wanted to be anywhere that didn't involve the pain he was feeling at the moment.

Every morning, I would leave a flat full of all the memorabilia of his travels to make the 30-minute walk to the hospital, never knowing what I would encounter upon arrival. On my third or fourth day, I was shocked to find him tied to his bed and was informed that this had become necessary for his own safety. During the night, a nurse had heard shouting coming from his room, so she'd gone to investigate and found that Steve had climbed out of bed and was standing on his good leg with his left leg still strung up in traction. The moment he saw her he screamed, 'Get me a Cuba Libre and come and dance salsa with me!'

Obviously he needed to be restrained, but once I'd arrived they untied him and he remained that way until I left in the evening. Then I repeated the walk back to his flat wondering what could possibly happen the next day.

Those were the thoughts I imagined filled my father's head whenever he was alone, and every morning, the best part of the day, the best moment for me was the second he walked into my room.

'Hello, Pops! You're early!' I exclaimed when my favourite face appeared at the door to my room.

'Am I?' he replied with a little smile. 'I guess I must be getting used to all this walking. So, how are you this morning?'

'I'm OK, thanks. What about you? You look a bit tired, actually.'

'No, I'm all right. Just had a lot of changes to deal with recently, that's all. It's not easy for a man of my age to adapt to life in a bachelor pad again,' he explained. 'And hey, when did you become so damned organized? I've never seen such a tidy flat!'

'I don't know. That's the way I like it, I suppose. You know, "A place for everything and everything in its place."'

'Well, you'll probably have to spend a bit of time putting everything back in its *proper* place once you get out of here. I don't share your obsession with organization I'm afraid.'

'That's OK, Dad, don't worry about it. So, what have you got for me today?' I enquired, eyeing the bag he was holding in his left hand.

This was a routine we'd established very soon after my return from Gran Canaria. Every evening he would leave the hospital with a list of things to bring the following day. He always brought a flask of juice, some bananas to have with breakfast and maybe another book to read or some more cassettes to listen to. It was never anything that exciting, yet still a small consolation to me.

But today was special. Today I knew he also had a clean T-shirt for me, and I'm sure he must have seen the look of delight on my face when he took it out of his bag. It was one of my favourites, a T-shirt I had bought whilst travelling in South America, and as I struggled with the soiled one I'd been wearing for several days the memories flooded back. I was having trouble trying to untangle it from the tubes coming out of my right arm . . .

. . . but finally I managed to pull it over my head and dropped it on the floor in the corner of the mud hut. Then, on turning back again, I was shocked to find that the witch was disinfecting the razor-blade with a South American spirit called *aguardiente*, and instantly that ominous question began tormenting me once more: Why have I been brought here?

The unusual course of events that had culminated in my presence at this ceremony of witchcraft, or *brujería* as it was called here, in Venezuela, produced confused conclusions in my agitated mind. It truly felt as if I had walked onto the set of a Hollywood film about voodoo, since so many of the strange happenings I'd witnessed that day resembled the type of things I had only ever seen in such films.

The razor-blade-toting witch was a guy called Sálomon. I had met him the previous night at the waterfront plaza of Choroní, a small coastal village a few hours west of Caracas. After working for several months as an English teacher in a town inland, I'd decided to travel the coast for a while before returning to England. This village had featured in a television documentary I'd seen not long before catching my flight to Venezuela. Consequently, it had been on my list of places to visit and that night I'd gone to the plaza to listen to a group of drummers who had highlighted the presentation about this village. They were a bunch of local lads who regularly met to play Latin rhythms on conga drums, accompanied by dancing girls and forming Choroní's foremost tourist attraction.

While I was enjoying this spectacle, the young guy standing next to me started chatting about Latin American music. Our engaging conversation eventually led to an invitation for a drink at a bar nearby where he told me there was a DJ who played all the latest salsa releases. The offer of great music plus the opportunity to meet some more locals was too great to refuse, so I accepted.

It was an enjoyable evening with plenty of drinking and dancing, and my new friend seemed to be an interesting guy. During the course of conversation, we chatted about places, people and professions.

'I'm a *brujo*,' he said but my Spanish was too weak to understand.

'What does *brujo* mean?' I asked.

There was a brief discussion amongst a few people at the bar, then someone stepped forward and in English said, 'He's a witch.'

This was something I didn't take all that seriously because, well, he didn't look like a witch! In his early twenties and dressed in a Nike T-shirt, Levis and a pair of white trainers, he resembled every other

Venezuelan of his generation. I just assumed it was nothing more than a passing comment intended to impress or confuse a gringo tourist. To be honest, I was more than grateful to have met some natives who were prepared to 'fraternize with the enemy'. I'd been finding it very difficult to interact with the locals during my travels along the coast, and on previous trips this had been something very important to me. I'd always believed if you wanted to see that third dimension, the depth that makes a place real, you had to mix with the people who lived there. Now that I'd finally met some, I didn't mind if they had a bit of fun at my expense.

Towards the end of the evening, Sálomon invited me to visit him and his grandad for the weekend at their house further up the valley. I believed this would certainly be a good opportunity to broaden my understanding of Venezuela, so a time and a place were arranged and we met at nine the next morning to begin what would become a very long day.

We took a bus up a mountain road, travelling inland along the side of the river valley. It was a warm, bright, sunny morning and there were breathtaking views across this verdant vale that could be appreciated with the greatest of ease, since this 'bus' was actually an open-back lorry with passengers seated on bags of grain and enjoying a 360-degree panorama of the passing scenery. About ten miles up the road, Sálomon banged on the roof of the cab to let the driver know we'd reached our destination. Once he'd pulled over, we unloaded my backpack and then wandered down a dusty track towards a wooden house built on a small plateau at the edge of the river.

'That's my grandad's house,' he told me, though when we arrived we found no one was home so we left my backpack, locked inside the house, and set off for a walk down the river. It was a walk through my type of landscape: lush, jungle vegetation with citrus and palm groves, banana and breadfruit trees, climbing bougainvillaea, and all amidst a lattice of vines and bamboo. There were occasional breaks in the canopy overhead, causing the semi-darkness of the trail to be interspersed with bright pools of light and creating a wondrously exotic visual sensation.

About 20 minutes later, we came across a larger clearing with a small mud hut in the centre. I assumed it probably served as a goat stable or was used for some other agricultural purpose but Sálomon proudly declared, 'This is *my* house!'

'Pardon?' I replied, almost certain I'd misunderstood him.

'I live here, this is my house,' he repeated. 'I bought it last year for $1,000. And I also own this piece of land, from the river here to that rock over there.'

'Wow! That's great!' I exclaimed, trying to sound enthusiastic. His house really *was* nothing more than a mud hut. But as I thought it over a little, I eventually found myself feeling mildly impressed. I mean, here was a young man no older than me who possessed his own home and a small plot of land. What is more, he held the deeds to a piece of land situated amidst scenery of such overwhelming beauty that it was impossible not to feel at least a little awestruck.

He proceeded to give me a brief tour of his humble abode, which consisted of a one-roomed hut with no electricity or running water. It was furnished with a small wooden table and a chair in one corner, a hammock strung across another, and a bucket of water that appeared to serve as a washbasin and kitchen sink.

It was certainly like no home I had ever seen before, though what caught my eye were some strange patterns on the mud floor, seemingly made of candle wax and black and white powder. However, just as I was on the point of asking what they were, Sálomon set off again, out of the hut and across the clearing towards another path through the jungle. I immediately followed, having temporarily lost interest in these patterns and being far more concerned if I would be spending the night in his grandad's sturdy residence or on a bed of scorpions in Sálomon's cell.

The path he had taken was a more direct return route, and after a short walk through a thick palm jungle we were climbing the wooden steps to the veranda of his grandad's house. This time we were welcomed by the elderly gentleman, so I introduced myself as best I could with my limited Spanish and even though his dialect was a lot broader than Sálomon's, I concluded he was happy to have an English visitor in his home.

He subsequently ordered Sálomon to do something, a request he had to repeat before his grandson would comply. I hadn't understood a word, but I followed Sálomon to the end of the veranda, where he unlocked a door with a key he kept on a chain around his neck. Then, as the door slowly swung open, I began to realize that the previous night's revelation about his profession might have been closer to the truth than I had originally believed. It was a small windowless room, one that would normally be stored with house cleaning equipment, but here it was being used for a very different purpose.

Peering into this little closet, I could see that it was candlelit and a white sheet had been draped down the back wall and across part of the floor. Standing on this sheet between a forest of lighted candles were three small statues: a negro on the left, an indian on the right and in the centre a woman whom he told me was called 'The Queen of the South'. In front of these statues were a half-empty bottle of rum and a bottle of a cinnamon flavoured spirit called *canela*, and to the left of this ensemble I could see a small table cluttered with numerous photographs, photocopied documents and identity cards.

As I studied this extraordinary display, something about it felt strangely familiar. Then suddenly I realized it resembled what I'd seen in a film called *The Believers*, a film about a West Indian black magic belief known as *santería*. In South America the equivalent faith is called *brujería*. Sálomon was a *brujo*. He *was* a witch!

While I became mesmerized by this mysterious little exhibition, Sálomon began chanting some kind of 'brujerian' prayer. Then before I knew what was happening, he started pouring liquid from the bottle of *canela* over my head. As I felt it run down my neck, I panicked a little and tipped my head forwards, causing it to run straight into my eyes. I cried out in pain, feeling sure I was about to go blind, but Sálomon pulled my head back and began blowing on my face to evaporate the spirit. Amazingly, the pain died away very quickly and he resumed his chanting.

Once I was able to see properly again, he'd finished his prayer and was trying to persuade me to inhale from another, smaller bottle of spirit. Finding myself in such a bizarre situation, I couldn't help but suspect it was a drug of some kind, though I still went ahead and took a deep breath, more out of fear than anything else. Fortunately, I felt no subsequent change in my state of consciousness and then, from the aroma, I realized it was nothing more sinister than liquid incense.

After that somewhat surreal incident, the day progressed without further anomalies. We chatted with his grandad, had lunch together and then the old man insisted on showing me where he'd used to work as a shepherd. This involved another pleasant walk through more succulent scenery and by the time we returned to the house I was feeling completely at ease in their company.

An hour or so later, three men arrived looking for Sálomon. They appeared to be businessmen and started to discuss something with him, producing documents to support whatever it was they were trying to explain. Following a brief consultation with his grandad, the three men and I accompanied Sálomon to a local shop to buy two boxes of candles and a bottle of *aguardiente*. Then we returned to the house and the ceremony commenced.

The three men all stripped down to their boxer shorts and sat at the table on the veranda, looking very serious yet presenting an amusing view for a visiting foreigner unfamiliar with the traditions of *brujería*. Then followed another brief discussion of business, and Sálomon issued instructions, upon which the first man got up, walked over to the open-air shower at the edge of the veranda and began to wash himself very thoroughly. He repeated these ablutions twice more, scrubbing his body so aggressively that it was almost painful to watch. When he'd finished, he turned the water off and then stood completely still with his back to us, looking out across the valley.

Sálomon got up and took his position behind this man, an open bottle of rum in one hand and *canela* in the other. Then he started chanting and at the same time pouring rum over the man's head. After wasting a good hangover's worth of liquor, he wiped the excess rum off his shoulders with a practised flick of the wrist and repeated the whole process with the *canela*. Once this was over, the man had to stand still for another two minutes, then he went into the 'shrine' at the end of the veranda and shut himself inside to smoke a very large Cuban cigar. In the meantime, Sálomon repeated the same ritual with the second man, who was already waiting at the shower.

In this way, the ceremony proceeded until the third man emerged from the shrine and promptly vomited twice, except this wasn't part of the ritual, I think it was simply because he was a non-smoker. When he'd finished bringing up the contents of his stomach, he joined us at the table and I waited for someone to open the bottle of *aguardiente* so we could all toast a successful ceremony.

However, we sat there for what seemed like hours, the men all involved in a mundane conversation that I was unable to follow and the unopened bottle remained in the centre of the table. Then one of them made a comment directed towards me, at the same time pointing at my elbows. I quickly understood that he must have been saying something about my psoriasis but before I had the chance to attempt a response, Sálomon's grandad jumped up and began rummaging around in a cupboard close by. He quickly found what he was looking for and came back to the table holding a large coffee jar full of a brown liquid that looked a lot like water taken from a stagnant pond. He carefully opened this jar, passed it to me and told me to take a drink.

Although initially a bit confused, I soon realized it was intended as some kind of herbal remedy for psoriasis. As I held this jar up to the light, I could see that it contained an organic mix of leaves, twigs and roots . . . and a maggot swimming through the centre! Not having a particularly strong stomach, I felt sure that one small sip would leave me on the toilet for a week, but in my current situation it would have been very rude to refuse.

Five sets of eyes intently stared at me as I took a deep breath, brought the jar to my lips and swallowed two generous mouthfuls. Despite the old man's request for me to drink a little more, I felt I'd done enough to avoid offence and politely placed the jar back down on the table, unable to bring myself to look and see if it still contained the maggot.

After this rather disconcerting interlude, the men returned to their conversation while I sat there in ignorance. Eventually, Sálomon glanced at his watch, sprang up from his chair and started packing the candles, rum, *aguardiente* and a couple of small, rectangular, tobacco tins into his knapsack. Instructions were given and we all followed him down the steps of the veranda and through the jungle towards his mud hut. By this time night had fallen but the three men all walked barefoot, still dressed in nothing more than boxer shorts.

Once we'd arrived at the hut, Sálomon lit a few candles and we sat wherever we could while he set about clearing away the remains of the previous ceremony. He began scratching at the wax patterns on the floor, throwing the debris into a plastic bag and sweeping away the black and white powder. This seemed to take forever and he mumbled endlessly as he toiled away, making me feel quite bored and a little regretful I had come.

When the floor was clean, he positioned half a dozen fresh candles in the mud. Then he connected these candles with trails of black and white powder from the two small tins he'd packed earlier, producing a series of patterns that resembled astrological symbols. Next he started lighting the candles and he also asked me to take off my boots and socks. I briefly glanced around the hut and realized I was the only person not barefoot, so I promptly complied, keen to avoid any disruption the ceremony. When everything had been prepared, the three men stood in a line in front of him and he began chanting while I quietly slipped into the shadows of a corner and the *real* ceremony commenced.

As the chanting intensified, Sálomon did something that disturbed me a little. He took a razor-blade from his pocket, and this was the moment when I started to wonder why I'd been brought here.

The chanting continued to escalate, and after a short time he told me to remove my T-shirt. Again I acquiesced, backing further into the darkness as I fumbled with my clothing. Finally, I managed to pull it over my head and dropped it on the floor in the corner of the hut. Then, on turning back again, I was shocked to find that Sálomon was disinfecting the razor-blade with the *aguardiente*. As this horrifying discovery began to sink in, I also noticed a very large spider, possibly a tarantula, that was crawling down the wall on the far side of the hut. I told myself if the tarantula reached the floor, I would put my boots back on.

It did, so I did.

By then I was feeling extremely anxious about the whole situation. My head was awash with images from the film I'd recalled earlier that day and terrible conclusions invaded my mind. It was impossible not to consider the unusual course of events that had led to my present predicament. I was in a foreign country, in the middle of nowhere, surrounded by people I hardly knew and involved in a ceremony completely alien to my culture. My backpack, which contained all my belongings including my passport, ticket and traveller's cheques, was locked in a house some 15 minutes walk away through dense jungle in complete darkness. Absolutely no one knew I was here and everything that proved my existence had also been hidden away. As a human being, I was conditioned to accept the reality of the world with which I was presented, and in this 'world' I didn't even exist. Was I going to be sacrificed?

Seeing as I'd put my boots back on, I decided to put my T-shirt on as well, in the hope that I might feel a little safer fully dressed. This action resulted in an evil glance of disapproval from the witch, though he still continued chanting.

Then all of a sudden, he picked up the bottle of *aguardiente*, brought it to his lips, rapidly gulped down an astonishing amount and subsequently went into an alarmingly fiendish trance. His whole body contorted, his voice took on an unnerving animal-like quality, and this transition reached a climax when he raised the disinfected razor-blade to his mouth and started vigorously rubbing it up and down his outstretched tongue. He drank again, repeated the slicing action and continued growling his chant in an unreal voice as a river of blood poured down his chin and onto his chest. At this point I became stricken with terror.

He staggered over to the first man and anointed him on his forehead and shoulders with some of the blood pouring from his mouth. Then, using the razor-blade, he sliced the palm of the man's left hand and wiped it down his own chest, mixing their blood together. At the sight of this, I frantically began looking for something I could use to defend myself. All I could find was an empty rum bottle but I went ahead and picked it up anyway, unsure of my exact intentions.

The witch staggered over to the second man, administered the same ritual, and on to the third man, where it was repeated identically. Then I felt the fear mounting inside me and wondered if I was going to defecate in my shorts. He had turned around and was now moving towards me!

On impulse, I smashed the bottle against the wall of the hut and screamed, 'Get the fuck away!' whilst brandishing the broken bottle in front of me. This had absolutely no effect. He continued to approach, his twisted body limping, so I darted across to the opposite corner in an effort to escape his advances. While all of this was happening, the others were shouting things to try and calm me down but by then it was much too late. I was beyond pacification.

The witch turned and pursued me once more, in lethargic lurches, so I shot back to my original corner, begging him to leave me alone. Then finally, just as I was on the point of losing all hope, he seemed to accept my reluctance to be involved. His menacing approach came to a halt and he returned to the centre of the hut to continue with the ceremony.

As it reached its climax, about eight hours after commencing at the house that afternoon, the strange patterns on the floor suddenly burst into flames, burning down the trails and ending with two small explosions. This completely filled the tiny hut with smoke and it was only much later, on recollecting the events of that horrific night, that I realized the black powder he'd used to make the patterns must have been gunpowder.

Unable to breathe, everyone rushed outside and to my utter amazement the 'witch' had disappeared and Sálomon had returned. He briefly looked me up and down and then turned to the others to ask them what had happened. He obviously had no memory whatsoever of the ceremony but could tell from my appearance that I hadn't taken part. Amidst much laughter, they recounted my antics with the rum bottle as if it were the story of something funny that had happened at the local pub. Then we all made the midnight walk through the jungle and back to his grandad's house.

Upon arrival, I immediately told Sálomon that I needed to get something from my backpack. As soon as the door was unlocked, I dashed inside, grabbed it, bade farewell and rapidly retreated to the main road. I hiked for three hours that night along a meandering mountain roadway in complete darkness, carrying a very heavy backpack and an even heavier mind. I didn't feel truly safe again until I'd reached the village beach, where I spent what remained of the night simply glad to be alive.

'So, do you like the T-shirt then?' my father asked with a contented grin.

'Er . . . yeah, it brings back a few memories,' I mumbled.

'What, of your travels?'

'My travels? Er, yes, that's right, my travels.'

'I bet you're thinking about a bikini-clad bird lying beside you on a Caribbean beach,' he said with a suggestive wink.

'Well, something like that,' I replied. 'So, did you remember my fruit juice today?'

'Of course I did, son. How could I forget a thing like that?'

'Yeah, I know what you mean.'

9 *Driving Mr Devereaux*

My father picked up the dirty T-shirt and put it in his bag. Then he took his customary seat at my bedside and we began another routine hospital day together, something that now felt quite normal.

'So, Pops, what did you do last night?' I asked, as I always did.

'Well, I went home and called Lyn, then I cooked up a curry and watched a couple of films. You know, the usual,' he replied with a restrained smile that said so much more about how he really felt than any words he would actually allow past his lips.

'What did you watch? Anything good?' I enquired, trying to steer the conversation onto harmonious ground with a subject I knew he loved talking about.

'Just a couple of videos I borrowed from your school. One I'd seen before and a new one, but I can't remember what it was called,' he said, making no effort to develop the dialogue. 'What about you?'

'Nothing too exciting. I watched a football match on TV with Nick because his home team was playing – I think it was Manchester United – then we had a chat about work, travel, music, stuff like that. It's so good to finally have someone in the next bed who I can really talk to.'

'Yeah, I bet it is,' he commented, his eyes briefly glazing over. 'So where is he? They haven't moved him to another room, have they?'

'No, of course not. They've taken him down to do some X-rays but he should be back soon.'

Nick was my new room-mate. He'd arrived the previous afternoon and when they wheeled him into my room it had come as a big surprise to both of us. There was an incredible story of coincidence behind Nick and I sharing a hospital room, since our country of birth wasn't the only thing we had in common.

110

We'd first met in October the previous year when he came along-side me on a dual carriageway in his Mercedes and shouted at me to pull over. During the subsequent conversation, he explained that my car was still registered in his name because he had sold it without transferring the name on the registration document. It had been sold on a couple more times since then, making it difficult to track down, and obviously he wanted to rectify this oversight. Consequently, he took my phone number and promised to get in touch.

However, a couple of months passed and I still hadn't heard from him so I decided to try and make contact myself. Fortunately, one of my salsa students was a police officer, and on hearing of this problem he put my car registration number through the police computer to find the name and address of the registered owner. A week or so later, I managed to get the phone number but when I called no one was home and I had to leave a message on an answerphone.

I never received the return call. Later that very same day I had the accident that had put me where I was now. It was my father, just a few days after arriving, who answered the phone to a woman explaining that this registration problem couldn't be resolved at the moment because her husband was in hospital due to a car crash. This was very confusing for him, since he knew nothing of this problem, but he confirmed that his son was in hospital following a car crash. It took a moment for him to realize that they were talking about two different people in hospital as a result of two separate accidents. Then, as things became clearer, he also remembered chatting with an Englishman at the hospital that afternoon, a man who'd recently had a car crash. He realized he had already met the man she was talking about.

I didn't meet Nick again until a few weeks later. Continuing along the theme of coincidence, he was sent to the hospital on Gran Canaria at the same time I was there, except we were on different wards and our paths didn't cross. Nevertheless, when they flew him back to Lanzarote, he was allocated the bed next to mine and we began what developed into a lasting friendship.

In many ways, it was a great relief to have a room-mate with whom conversation was easy. Obviously, we shared the same native tongue, which eliminated any communication problems and was probably one

111

of the reasons why he'd been put into a room with me. But it was more than just this linguistic connection alone. We had so much in common, so much more than both being in hospital with a broken leg after accidents in vehicles that were both registered in the same name.

Nick was a tour guide and a very gifted conversationalist who really knew how to tell a story. There was also something about him I couldn't quite place that made me feel like I'd known him a long time. He'd travelled extensively and had lived in several countries, working in various fields before finally settling in Lanzarote ten years earlier and becoming a tour guide. Naturally we had a mutual love of travel, but what I liked most about him was his positive outlook on life. In spite of the terrible trauma he'd suffered and the lengthy convalescent struggle he was currently enduring, he always had a witty comment or a joke to make which would immediately be followed by the most infectious smile I've ever seen. I felt very lucky to be confined to a hospital room with him. He was the perfect remedy for my emotional recovery.

'Hey! It's the *Bongo Boys* back together again! So, what are you two up to? Planning a reunion concert?'

'Hello, Nick. Back already?' I said as my new room-mate wheeled himself through the door. 'That didn't take long.'

'Well, I've been here so long now that I get the VIP treatment. They don't keep *me* waiting in any long queues. And how are you today, Paul?' he asked my father with his usual excessive optimism.

'I'm all right I suppose, you know.'

'No, I don't. Come on, man, isn't it just wonderful being alive!' he declared. 'Though the other option only has limited appeal. And anyway, things could be worse. You could be in England!'

'Yes, I could be in England with my wife.'

'In England with the cold, the damp, the short days and constant rain,' Nick corrected. 'But no. You're *here*, in the Canary Islands, with your son, cheap booze, blue skies and beautiful *chicas*. And on top of all that, the Carnival!'

'Well, it's not exactly a holiday, Nick.'

'No, of course not, and it isn't a funeral either, so get rid of the long face and tell me what you got up to last night.'

'I watched a couple of videos.'

'No, I don't want to hear what you told your son. Tell me what you *really* did,' he demanded as a cheeky grin began breaking across his face. 'I'm sick of hearing gossip about gallstones, blocked catheters, gangrene and leaky bedpans. Give me some scandal! It doesn't have to be true, just make something up.'

Nick was able to raise the spirits of anyone within his proximity, and very soon my father's despondency had all but disappeared.

Late morning was usually punctuated with a visit from Doctor Ruiz for a short conversation about my impending operation. This doctor was another thing I shared with Nick and in this respect we were both very lucky: he was a true perfectionist. His manner was always very professional and serious, though never cold or uncaring, and he rarely smiled although even when he did, it was difficult to detect due to a large, groomed moustache that obscured his mouth.

He was also an exceedingly patient man and never failed to explain everything extremely carefully. Yet despite speaking English quite fluently, he would only converse with me in Spanish. This may have been through a perfectionist's need to appear faultless in the eyes of his patient (an English teacher) but he would always endeavour to limit his vocabulary to a lexicon he felt sure I could understand, no matter how time-consuming our consultations became.

After the usual pleasantries had been exchanged, he had a brief discussion with Nick and then joined my father at my bedside. He told us that, unfortunately, no date for my operation had been set yet because they were still waiting for a metal plate of the required length to arrive from Switzerland. However, he assured me that I wouldn't have to wait much longer and returned to his morning rounds.

When lunch arrived, my father would go down to the hospital café for a cup of tea and I was usually asleep again by the time he returned. Around mid-afternoon, formal visiting hours began, though I guess right from the start the doctors could see in my father's eyes that the terms 'visiting hours' simply didn't apply to him. Many visitors would arrive and there was always a varied mix of friends, colleagues and students, and in addition to these, hardly a day went by without receiving a visit from someone I considered as nothing more than an acquaintance, just someone I had a drink with occasionally. I guess this must be a cultural difference because all of my various room-mates also received numerous visitors. If you are hospitalized in England, only family and close friends come and visit. In Spain you can expect anyone from your priest to your postman.

Visiting hours drew to a close, friends left and dinner arrived. My father was always the last to leave and he ran through the list of things to bring the next day before going out and closing the door behind him. Then a little later, the nurse on the night shift arrived with evening medication.

'Hello, Nick,' she said on entering the room.

'Good evening, *Florence*,' he replied with an exaggerated, school-boy formality – an attempt at humour that was wasted on a Spaniard!

'Hello, Steve. Oh, what a lovely T-shirt!' she exclaimed.

'Yeah, well, at least it's clean, which is more than I can say for the rest of me.'

'Why? Didn't you have your bed bath this morning?'

'Of course I did, but what I'd really like is a shower.'

'Well, you know that's impossible at the moment, don't you?'

'Yes, I know,' I reluctantly agreed.

'I'll tell you what; we can wash your hair tomorrow morning too, OK?'

'Oh, thank you, that'll be nice,' I replied appreciatively, but in truth I didn't think it would be all that great. More than anything, all I wanted was to take a shower.

'Please, could I just go and take a shower?' I pleaded.

'I'm sorry, it's against the regulations,' she replied.

'Look, I've been travelling for nearly 80 hours without a wash, and as I'm sure you can see, I really need a shower.'

'I'm sorry but we can't let guests into the room without first seeing the confirmation slip,' replied the receptionist. 'Those are the rules and there's nothing I can do about it.'

Having made her point, she turned away and proceeded to check in some other new arrivals.

'OK then, I'll have to wait here!' I retorted and promptly walked over to a plush reception sofa, took off my hiking boots, lay down and went straight to sleep.

I was at the Winner's Circle time-share resort in Del Mar, a few miles north of San Diego. I had arrived that morning after travelling non-stop for over three days to spend two weeks with my parents, who, for some strange reason, still hadn't arrived from England.

When I'd entered just a few minutes earlier, I imagine the receptionist must have smelt me before seeing me and in one way her curtness was understandable: I did closely resemble a wandering, homeless vagrant. With long matted hair, filthy skin and a scruffy backpack; and dressed in a T-shirt, shorts and hiking boots, all deeply ingrained with dust and dirt, she couldn't contain her surprise when I claimed to have an apartment reserved for two weeks.

'What name would that be?' she sneered, looking distastefully at me down her nose.

'Mr. Devereaux,' I confidently replied, and her look of disdain was instantly replaced with an expression of utter incredulity the moment she found my name on the list. She immediately demanded to see the confirmation slip, which I politely explained was with my parents, who would be arriving presently. I even produced my passport and a photocopy of my birth certificate to dispel any doubts concerning my identity and to prove that I really was the son of the time-share owner. But this made no difference. The rules had to be obeyed, so I resigned myself to a wait in the reception on a comfortable sofa in full view of all the new arrivals.

The journey that had left me in this disgraceful state of personal hygiene had begun a few days earlier in Acapulco on the west coast of Mexico. I was there with my friend Scott, having travelled together through Central America. It had always been one of my dreams to visit Acapulco and see the cliff divers, something that had fascinated me since watching an Elvis Presley film set in this famed beach resort. Consequently, as soon as we arrived in Mexico City I started making plans for a trip to the Pacific Coast.

Even so, we were in the capital city of a country steeped in a rich cultural heritage, so we first spent a few days immersing ourselves in the history of what was once the most developed civilization in existence. It's a city of contradictions – colonial palaces alongside sprawling slums, confusing streets of deafening traffic interspersed with majestic peaceful parks, abundant wealth beside extreme poverty – and is peopled with over 20 million inhabitants, making it one of the most crowded metropolitan areas of the world.

The day after arriving we visited the historic centre of the city, the Zócalo. This immense plaza is home to the National Palace, built on the site of an Aztec palace, and the magnificent Metropolitan Cathedral. Then, in keeping with the theme of disparity, we managed to lose our way and subsequently spent a couple of hours wandering through a district that had been completely destroyed just two years earlier by a devastating earthquake that had led to over 10,000 deaths.

The next morning, we took a bus 30 miles north to visit the ruins of an ancient city. It was called Teotihuacan and had reached its zenith of influence in 500 AD, though its most impressive feature was the Pyramid of the Sun. We scaled this enormous, primeval structure, ate our packed lunch on its pinnacle in an atmosphere of peace and tranquility, and then returned to the turbulent, fume-laden streets of Mexico City.

We spent the afternoon at the Museum of Anthropology. I had always preferred art galleries to museums but this extensive exhibition of indian artefacts, housed in a spacious airy edifice in the city's largest park, the Chapultepec Forest, forced me to review my opinion. We stayed there until it closed and we still hadn't seen even half of the exhibits, although we did spend quite some time standing in silent awe before the gargantuan Aztec calendar stone.

Finally, we concluded our culture-filled day with an evening of Mariachi music played in the streets of the Garibaldi District by groups of musicians all dressed in traditional costume, complete with those characteristic, broad-brimmed, Mexican sombreros.

The following morning we got up early, packed our things and then struggled through suffocating crowds towards the nearest subway station, countless individuals bouncing off our backpacks as they bustled along the busy streets. We reached the station during the morning rush hour and successfully managed to slip through the turnstiles without attracting the attention of the Metro staff, despite a regulation that forbade travel during peak hours with any kind of oversized baggage. But when I tried to board the train, I discovered why this rule had been introduced.

As the doors slid open, a mass of Mexicans surged forward with all the politeness of a professional rugby team, and I only just managed to climb aboard at the last possible moment. By then the carriage was extremely full and even though my body was inside, the rucksack on my back was still beyond the imaginary line that divided 'inside' from 'outside'. Of course, the closing doors quickly replaced this line with solid metal, except, unlike the trains of the London Underground, they didn't re-open on encountering an obstruction. As a result of this unfortunate design defect, I had to spend a couple of minutes in acute nervous embarrassment, locked in the doorway until we reached the next station, hoping that the tunnel was wide enough to permit the safe passage of my protruding backpack.

Eventually, we arrived at the central bus station and made a 250-mile journey south to the Pacific Coast. It was an uneventful trip apart from two stops at military roadblocks en route, which I thought rather surprising since I'd believed we had left all indications of political instability behind us after passing through Central America. Then, as we reached our destination, I was very excited to finally be in a position to realize my life-long dream of watching men hurl them-selves off a 136-foot cliff into crashing surf.

The moment we arrived, we were pounced on by a hustler with a Hawaiian shirt and a waxed moustache who claimed to know the best place in town for two young gringos.

'Is nice hotel. I sure you like very much,' he said with a crooked smile.

'But is it cheap?' I asked.

'No worry, no worry, the manager he give good price for my friends. You come, is this way.'

We followed like lambs to the slaughter and, not surprisingly, at the end of a tiring walk through rancid smelling streets in a stifling heat, he led us to the doors of an establishment that we knew would be way beyond our budget. While feeling sure he had no concept of a backpacker's requirements, we still followed him along another confusing, protracted route to a 'cheaper place', again unsuitable. Then suddenly Scott remembered the name of a hotel recommended by a Swedish guy we'd met in Nicaragua. Our 'guide' claimed that no such residence existed (obviously he had no commission arrangement with the management) but after asking one or two passers-by for directions, we soon found Hotel Colimense.

It was in a perfect location, midway between the old town square and La Quebrada, where the cliff divers performed, and offered clean, economical rooms. We checked in, had refreshingly cool showers, changed our sweat-stained city clothes for more comfortable beach-wear and then went out to explore the environs.

The town itself was a little disappointing, rather more slummy and dirty than Hollywood had led me to imagine. La Quebrada, however, more than lived up to my expectations. I remember standing on the crowded cliff-top viewing platform alongside hordes of tourists armed with cameras and camcorders, and feeling a tingle of excitement run through my entire body. Then I watched in amazement as four young men threw themselves off the perilous jagged precipice into the narrow inlet below, timing their jump to coincide with the incoming waves that cushioned their impact and protected them from landing in the shallows. It was such a breathtaking performance that I returned to La Quebrada many more times during the week I spent in Acapulco.

The night-life didn't disappoint either. On Saturday evening we consulted our guidebook while consuming one or two tequilas, and then took a taxi to Midnite, the town's top nightclub. Upon arrival, we were greeted at the door by the manager, shown to a table and introduced to our waiter, who immediately went off to fulfil our drink requests leaving us completely overwhelmed by the upmarket atmos-phere. It really was quite a step up from what we'd experienced on our budget backpack travels in recent months. Several of the lustrous, smoked-glass tables had reserved cards placed on them, presumably for vacationing film stars and politicians, but the most impressive thing for two young bachelors was the large number of beautiful, youthful, single women.

In hindsight it was a sad reflection on the economic distinction between the West and the developing world. These impoverished local girls weren't here solely to enjoy a Saturday night out on the town. They also harboured a desire to become romantically involved with a rich tourist who would wine and dine them and possibly even, in the fullness of time, offer a 'passport out of Mexico'. Nevertheless, we were travellers, not tourists, and we certainly weren't rich, so we just danced with as many of these beautiful girls as our legs could stand.

Later that evening, a young lady offered to buy me a shot of tequila and asked if she could join me. We chatted for a while – her in broken English and me in bar-floor Spanish – until another girl joined us who was introduced as her sister. After quickly assessing the situation, I called Scott away from his group of dancing devotees to come and make up a foursome with my new friend and her sibling. It turned out to be the greatest favour I could have done him. I went home alone that night, whereas he disappeared with my friend's sister, not to be seen for a couple of days, and I couldn't help thinking that the schoolboy coaching I'd given him in the opposite gender might have been rather more successful than I had originally believed.

I didn't see him again until dawn was breaking on Tuesday, when he woke me from a drunken stupor on the floor of our hotel en suite bathroom. The previous few days had been quite difficult without my *amigo* to help me communicate with the locals, and on my final night in Acapulco I had returned to Midnite for one last dance with the Mexican *muchachas*. Unfortunately, conversation had been extremely limited and I had subsequently spent a lot more time drinking than would have been sensible before commencing a 2,000-mile journey north.

'Come on, Steve. It's time to wake up,' Scott softly said. 'You've got to get your bus to San Diego. Your parents will be there in a couple of days and they're expecting to see you.'

'What?' I murmured. 'Oh . . . hello . . . we're leaving today, aren't we?'

'No, listen, there's been a change of plan. I'm really sorry but I won't be coming with you. I'm going to stay on here and try and get a job in a hotel or something,' he explained.

'Wow . . . she must have been good. And hey, don't worry. You go ahead and do whatever you want. I mean, it isn't like we're still kids.'

'But I feel terrible. I left you on your own for two days. That's not how a best mate behaves.'

'No, don't be stupid, I'd have done the same. But thanks for coming back to say goodbye.'

Following a brief farewell (the excess of alcohol the previous night had rendered me incapable of a more sincere valediction) I stumbled through the dusty streets, successfully managing to carry a weighty backpack without falling over, and arrived at the station in the transitional stage between drunk and hung-over.

I quickly discovered I'd missed the seven o'clock bus by about five minutes, though this was probably a blessing in disguise. At least it gave me 55 minutes seated on a stationary bench with my head in my hands, trying to stop the world from spinning like a roulette wheel. Even though I desperately wanted to return to my bed at the hotel, I knew I had to endure this discomfort as my parents were expecting to meet me in California on Friday morning. Eventually, still feeling extremely delicate, I boarded a bus to the capital and had to ask the driver to stop on three occasions during the seven-hour journey to let me get off and throw up.

I arrived in Mexico City around mid-afternoon and took a taxi straight to the train station. I bought a first-class ticket for a train to Mexicali, a town on the American border, then left my backpack in a locker and went out to get something to eat. By the time I returned to the station I was starting to feel vaguely 'human' again. I'd survived the worst hangover of my life and now I just felt extremely tired. I collected my luggage from the locker and then strolled down the platform in anticipation of a good night's sleep in a comfortable first-class carriage.

My prediction proved to be somewhat wide of the mark.

Although I had a first-class ticket, this train didn't have a first-class section. It comprised only sleeper and second-class carriages. I must have walked the entire length of that train three or four times, showing my ticket to any guard I encountered in the hope of solving this mystery but each time being told to go back the way I had come. Finally, just as the whistle was blown to signal the train's departure, I realized I had no other option and quickly climbed into a very full second-class carriage.

I spent the next 13 hours standing in the doorway of what must have been one of the most crowded carriages on the train. Every single seat was packed with people – bags, cases, boxes and baskets wedged between their knees and those of the passengers seated opposite – and the aisle was a solid mass of bodies, some of which were standing on *four* legs. The entrance vestibule of this coach crammed with yokels and farmyard animals was also jam-packed, and as a result of boarding at the last minute I had only just managed to secure standing-room in an open doorway not equipped with the standard 'movable barrier' one usually closes after climbing aboard.

This resulted in further inconvenience. Once we'd got up to speed, I found myself gripping the door frame with a white-knuckled hand whenever we negotiated a curve in the track and the mass of vestibule passengers forced me through the open doorway, out into the chilly night air of a Mexican desert. We were also in complete darkness, so as I desperately held on to the train with one hand, my other arm was wrapped around my backpack in an effort to deter any would-be thieves.

It was a cold, sleepless night with no opportunity to eat, drink or even use the toilet; quite an ordeal to endure in the best of health, much less whilst recovering from a 'hangover made in hell'. And it's strange how, sometimes, in such an extreme situation you think little thoughts that are of no consequence. Throughout that entire night, the one absurd detail I couldn't clear from my mind was that I had paid about 15 times more than my fellow passengers had for this wonderful experience. Without a doubt, they were all travelling on *second-class* tickets.

In the morning we arrived in Guadalajara, where I was due to change trains. With aching limbs and suffering from sleep deprivation, I wandered along the platform simply saying nothing more than, 'Mexicali?' to any guard I came upon. After a few attempts I was pointed in the right direction, found the train and to my intense relief I discovered that this one had a first-class carriage.

I climbed aboard, stored my backpack on the overhead luggage rack, settled into a comfortable seat and fell asleep within seconds. I didn't sleep for long, though. About five minutes later I was rudely awoken by a lady who claimed that I was occupying her seat. Without saying a word, I reached into my pocket, pulled out my ticket and confidently showed it to her. Then, as I leaned over to look at the ticket she was holding in *her* hand, I realized my troubles were far from over. The two tickets were completely different, and mine didn't even have a seat number. I attempted an apology in Spanish, retrieved my luggage and returned to the platform to find someone in authority to help me solve this conundrum.

'No, *señor*, you train no go now. You train, it go at two of the afternoon,' the benevolent guard informed me.

'But do I have a seat on that train?' I asked in desperation.

'Is possible . . . *pero* . . . sometimes is . . . *¿cómo se dice?* . . .with many people,' he said with a Latin American shrug of the shoulders. Then he casually turned away and strolled back down the platform.

This wasn't the reply I'd been hoping to hear. Without a second thought, I marched out of the station and went in search of the only other cheap travel option available: on a bus I definitely stood a better chance of getting a seat. I didn't have to walk far and on reaching the bus station I went straight up to the counter and asked for a ticket to Tijuana.

'*Tijuana?*' repeated the ticket clerk, looking a little puzzled.

'*Sí, Tijuana*,' I confirmed.

Despite her apparent confusion, she acceded to my request and sold me a ticket for a bus that would arrive in Tijuana at eleven the following night. Regardless of all the hardships already endured, I managed to console myself with the fact that once I reached the border, my journey to San Diego would now be considerably shorter, since it was but a stone's throw from Tijuana.

However, as I wandered out into the bustling morning streets of Guadalajara to find somewhere to have some breakfast, I glanced back at the bus station and realized I had made yet another mistake. This bus terminal was unlike any I'd seen before. It was split into two halves, each with a separate entrance. Above one doorway was a sign that read 'First Class' and above the other, 'Second Class'. I'd just exited from the second-class terminal.

Immediately, I went into the first-class booking office and enquired about buses to Tijuana. To my dismay, I discovered that the price difference between first and second class was minimal, the complete reverse of train travel in Mexico. First class offered a 24-hour trip on an air-conditioned bus with a buffet service and videos at a price that was only about $1.50 more than the same journey second class. I tried to upgrade my ticket, though of course this was impossible, so at 11 o'clock that morning I boarded a dusty, yellow, ex-American school bus, half eaten away by rust, to begin a 36-hour journey to the border.

As I climbed aboard, my ticket was closely examined by one of the two drivers and he appeared to be rather perplexed. No one ever took a *second-class* bus all the way from Guadalajara to Tijuana. This service was used by people travelling no more than a few hours from one town to the next. Consequently, it stopped at virtually every urbanization along the way, making the journey 12 hours longer than a first-class passage.

Even so, by then I was past caring. As soon as I was aboard, I found a vacant double seat, made myself as comfortable as was possible on the primitive, undersized pew and went straight to sleep. I was so tired that neither the drone of the ancient diesel engine, the frequent stops, the clouds of dust pouring through the windows nor the cluck of chickens as they scurried up and down the aisle could keep me from my dreams.

That evening one of the drivers woke me up and told me that we had a rest stop for dinner. I followed him off the bus and into the roadside diner, where we joined his co-driver at a table in the corner to dine on tacos, rice and beans. During the meal we chatted within the restrictions of my limited Spanish, as I recounted the terrible ordeals of my disastrous journey so far.

About half an hour later, we re-boarded the bus and I received the first surprise of this leg of my journey. One of the drivers walked straight up the aisle to the back seat and asked all the passengers seated there to move. When this seat was empty, he retrieved a blanket from the overhead luggage rack, spread it out on the seat and called me over to come and make myself comfortable on my bed for the night.

Obviously, I slept very well that night and I was only woken once by a police stop-and-check inspection. As the policeman shuffled up the aisle of a half-empty bus, I fumbled with my money belt in an effort to find my passport. Yet when he reached the back seat, he gave it nothing more than a passing glance. Something else had caught his attention: my Walkman was lying on the seat at my side.

He asked if he could have a look at it, so I picked it up and handed it over somewhat reluctantly. During my travels through the USA, I'd heard numerous backpackers' horror stories of travel in Mexico and I was almost certain it wouldn't be returned. But as I watched him, I noticed he was caressing it almost lovingly. He had the intense excitement of a child with a new toy in his eyes, and I began to realize that certain technological advances such as personal stereos were not yet commonplace in rural Mexico.

'How much did it cost?' he enquired, more through innocent curiosity than the desire to actually purchase it. Once I had done the mental arithmetic of changing from pounds to dollars to *pesos*, I told him the approximate price in local currency. A look of complete shock spread across his face and he gently placed it back down on the seat at my side, then said goodbye with a respectful nod of the head and left me to return to my dreams.

The surprises didn't end there. The next morning I was again roused by one of the drivers, this time to serve me a breakfast of tacos, eggs and hot coffee! Apparently, I'd been in such a deep sleep that I hadn't woken up when the bus had pulled over for a breakfast rest stop half an hour earlier. Now we were about to get under way again and he didn't want me to go hungry. In addition to his kindness, he even refused the offer of payment for this service. I knew the first-class bus provided such luxuries as air-conditioning, a buffet service and videos but I didn't remember anything about breakfast in bed.

Soon the bus once again became very crowded and just as I had discovered on second-class trains, provincial Mexicans often travelled with a variety of livestock – the aisle was filled with domestic fowl, squealing piglets and one or two lively goats. At least this provided an entertainment of sorts with which to pass the time, seeing as by then the batteries in my Walkman had run out.

Later that day, during a chat over lunch with the drivers, I was told that we wouldn't reach Tijuana until about two the following morning. This surprised me a little because in Guadalajara the timetable had indicated an 11pm arrival. Also, it left me unsure of the best course of action on reaching the border town. Nevertheless, this journey hadn't exactly gone to plan, so I decided I would just have to see what occurred once we arrived.

A few hours later we stopped outside a small town in northern Mexico for our evening-meal rest stop. It was at a bus station without a restaurant and I was beginning to feel the pangs of hunger, so I strolled into town to get some dinner. I guess I must have wandered further than intended or got a bit lost in unfamiliar surroundings after dark, and subsequently had to rush back, feeling worried that the bus might leave without me. Much to my relief, when I reached the station it was still there but as soon as I climbed aboard I found that both of the drivers and half of the passengers were missing. Then one of those remaining explained that the drivers had refused to leave without the gringo and had dispatched search parties with strict instructions to scour the streets for him.

As a result of their concern, I had to spend the next 20 minutes in extreme discomfort while those still present made it obvious they weren't happy with the delay I had unintentionally caused. Eventually, the other passengers returned with the drivers, who appeared to be genuinely relieved to see that I was back on board, and we set off on the final leg of our journey.

We arrived in Tijuana in the early hours of the morning and I decided it would be well worth finding a cheap hotel to have a much-needed shower and a couple of hours sleep before crossing the border into San Diego. However, as with every other part of this journey, even *that* wasn't going to be easy. The bus terminal in Tijuana was at the airport, quite some distance from town and nowhere near any cheap hotels.

I thanked my genial drivers, got off the bus and was immediately subjected to a severe drug search by the border police. I guess it was to be expected, considering the geography of the location, but it was the last thing I needed at the end of such a gruelling journey. During this obligatory invasion of privacy, one of the officers spoke to me in English so I took the opportunity to ask him about the accommodation in town. He told me I could take a taxi there for about $10 and get a hotel room for around $5, or I could wait here for three hours and catch a local bus for 25 cents. To a backpacker, a decision like that is easy. My plans for a hot shower and a short nap instantly disappeared.

Consequently, after nearly 70 hours on the road, I began a three-hour wait in a drab, dilapidated bus terminal, fighting the desire to sleep through fear of having my backpack stolen. At one point I did doze off for a minute or two but was quickly awakened by a police officer who demanded to see my identity documents. I produced my passport and told him my travel plans, which seemed to satisfy his curiosity, although he gravely stated that people were not permitted to sleep in the bus station.

It took a few minutes for me to understand what had just happened. My appearance must have been considerably worse than I'd imagined because this policeman had perceived me to be a homeless drifter, trying to scrounge a night's sleep inside.

At daybreak I began the search for a bus to town and to my delight I discovered I could take a Greyhound bus directly from the station to San Diego. Finally, things seemed to be getting a bit easier and I didn't have any great desire to see Tijuana, anyway. By then I'd seen more than enough dirty Mexican towns.

After a short drive, we reached the border crossing at around seven o'clock but had to wait in the rain for nearly an hour until the immigration office opened. Once the officers had arrived, I was bombarded with questions as one of them thumbed through my passport.

'What were you doing in Nicaragua?' he demanded in a brisk manner.

'I was just passing through,' I replied, resisting the temptation to say I'd been selling M-16s to the Sandinistas. I had previously spent long enough in the USA to learn that English humour wasn't a thing that Americans could readily understand. My replies appeared to be satisfactory and I was granted permission to stay in the country for up to six months.

Next I was faced with a customs officer who wasn't at all interested in my activities in Central America. He seemed more concerned whether I had any fresh fruit or vegetables about my person. I replied that I didn't and was permitted to stroll back to the bus, wondering if he hadn't had time for breakfast before starting his morning shift.

At long last, I was back in the US of A – back in the developed world, the modern world, the clean world – and the contrast after such a lengthy period in Latin America was a dramatic one. Despite being my first time in this particular part of California, I'd been surrounded by squalor for so long that these sanitized environs felt strangely familiar. In one sense, it was quite reassuring at the end of such a tough trip, though in another way it only served to exaggerate the appalling state of my appearance. Somehow, I felt even dirtier than I had in Mexico.

I took the bus to the Greyhound station in San Diego and from there a city bus to the airport, where I planned to meet my parents. My journey had reached its conclusion.

At the airport, I telephoned my sister to find out what flight they would be arriving on and she told me they'd flown into Los Angeles the previous night. Apparently, unable to get tickets to San Diego, they had flown to LA and would be travelling down to Del Mar that morning. She suggested that I go straight to the time-share resort and meet them there, so she gave me the address and I took a bus back to the city and then another one up to my ultimate destination.

And here I was: a 'tramp' sleeping on a sofa in the reception of the Winner's Circle resort on the morning of checking in day.

When my parents eventually arrived, they walked straight past me and up to the reception desk, unable to recognize the dirty, dishevelled features of their own son. The receptionist had to point out that there was a 'man' waiting for them, and she also had a security guard at her side, ready to throw me out the second they denied my acquaintance. However, her manner completely changed on seeing us exchanging hugs and kisses, and she had the keys to our apartment in her hand before we'd even reached the reception desk.

'I knew he was waiting for you, so I had everything ready,' she said self-consciously.

'Yeah, even the security guard,' I mumbled under my breath.

The moment we opened the door to our apartment, I went straight to the bathroom, stripped off and had the best shower of my life. As I revelled in the relief of soap working its magic over my soiled torso, I remember looking down towards my feet and being amazed by the colour of the dirty water running off my body. It was such a shocking sight that I promised myself, right there and then, that I would never again go so long without having a shower.

The moment the nurse handed me my medication, I took the prescribed pill and as I revelled in the relief of a pain-killing capsule working its magic over my tender torso, I remember thinking that sometimes in life you can find you've made a promise that is simply impossible to keep.

10 *Beautiful Island*

My father arrived, as he always did, shortly after breakfast and bed bath, and we began our usual daily routine. However, this particular morning was enlivened a little when Doctor Ruiz paid his customary visit.

'Good morning, Steve. How are you today?' he asked on entering my room, and as I turned to face him I felt there might actually be a smile hidden somewhere under his moustache.

'I'm OK, doctor, and you?'

'Fine, thank you, and I have some good news,' he said in his now familiar formal manner. 'Finally, I can put an end to all this waiting. The metal plate arrived from Switzerland today, so I've scheduled the operation for the end of this week, on Friday morning.'

'Oh yes! That's great! Thank you, doctor, thank you.'

'Of course, you must understand that we cannot guarantee the operation date because there may be an emergency, though I'm fairly confident we'll be able to proceed without any problems.'

'Yes, I understand, but that's still very good news, thank you.'

'OK, I'll see both of you tomorrow morning, as usual,' he said, briefly glancing from me to my father, and then he turned and left.

My father watched the door close and then spun round with an animated excitement that had been absent for quite some time. 'Yes, yes, yes!' he exclaimed, nodding emphatically and punching the air before him with two clenched fists. 'At last we can start thinking about getting out of here and going home!'

'Wow! . . . Going home,' I echoed. 'That sounds *so* good.' During the past few weeks I had felt an enormous distance between me and everything real, yet the sound of those two words suddenly brought me much closer to the journey home.

129

While we were still celebrating the good news, another visitor appeared at the door. It was Carmen, one of the nurses at the hospital, though I still thought of her as a 'salsa student' because she and her daughter had joined my classes from the very first week. She was a petite lady with silky auburn hair and a little-girl smile who had quickly displayed a capacity to learn and soon established herself as a core member of our group of *salseros*.

Even so, our relationship had changed somewhat over the past few weeks. Now she wasn't attending my classes; she was attending to me. On the weekend of my accident, she had been working in the intensive-care unit and had taken care of me for a few days without even realizing who I was. In fact, she wasn't the first person who'd been unable to recognize me and it was only on the Thursday after my crash, when she went to the Rincon del Majo for the salsa class, that she received the bad news. The following morning, the moment she arrived at work she went straight to intensive care to look at the name on my wristband. She knew the name. She knew the patient. She knew there wouldn't be any more salsa classes.

'Good morning, Steve. How are you today?' she asked with a radiant smile that somehow fitted so perfectly with my own positive mood that morning.

'I'm great! What about you?' I replied, leaving her a little confused at my enthusiasm.

'Yes, I'm fine, thank you. So, have you seen the doctor today?'

'I sure have, and guess what! He's going to operate on Friday morning!'

'Oh, that's wonderful news, you and your father must be very pleased, and I have some more good news for you. Would you like to go out on the balcony today?'

'What?' I asked, feeling sure I had misunderstood her because I knew it would be impossible to wheel my bed outside. Nevertheless, she proceeded to explain exactly how this *would* be possible. Apparently, the hospital owned an unusual type of wheelchair that could be better described as a 'wheelbed', and she'd been granted special permission to use this expensive apparatus for recreational purposes. Consequently, she told me she would come back when her shift finished and take me outside.

Early that afternoon, Carmen and my father carefully lifted me off my bed and onto a strange looking piece of equipment. Then a couple of minutes later they wheeled me through some double swing-doors and out onto the sun-drenched balcony.

'Wow! This is fantastic!' I exclaimed, squinting in the bright glare of a cloudless sky. Until that moment I hadn't realized how much I'd missed the open air, the sounds of the streets, a view more varied than the four walls of my room. 'Look! You can see the Gran Hotel from here, and the football stadium. God, this is great! This is *really* great.'

As the three of us sat there, contemplating a panorama of the sea and city to one side and sepia volcanic cones to the other, we began talking about all the wonderful things Lanzarote has to offer the visitor. It wasn't my father's first time on the island. He'd visited me the previous year in addition to taking a holiday here several years earlier, so he was quite familiar with Lanzarote.

'Yes, it really is a beautiful island,' he said.

'Well, I could think of worse places to go on holiday,' I replied.

'No, I wasn't talking about that. I know there are plenty of nice beaches, which you need in a tourist resort, but there's so much more here. I mean, there's the Volcanoes National Park, which is a great place to visit, and that artist, César Manrique, certainly left his mark, so there's plenty of culture too. Yes, beaches, volcanoes, culture; it really is a beautiful island.'

Beaches, volcanoes, culture. It didn't take me long to fall in love with this island. It really was a beautiful island.

It's the largest in a group of eight, said to be the most isolated part of the world, being more than 2,500 miles from the nearest continental land mass. The locals call it the Big Island, since its name, Hawaii, is also the collective name of the group. I had chosen this destination on the recommendation of a Swiss guy who had travelled with me across the USA several months earlier. We'd driven from Los Angeles to Miami, a 3,000-mile journey that had taken twelve days to complete, and he'd told me many stories of his experiences on the Big Island.

My original plan had been to spend a month there, hitchhiking around the island and camping on the state beaches, and when I arrived that was exactly what I did. I landed in the capital on the wet side of the island and began travelling north up the lush Hamakua Coast. Never in my life had I seen such a strikingly scenic landscape. Luxuriant rainforests laced with streams and waterfalls, and edged with steep, rugged cliffs and unfrequented beaches. I camped in several different places, all overflowing with exuberant foliage, and spent my days swimming, sunbathing, fishing and trekking through the jungle.

It's an island populated with a myriad of ethnic minorities – Japanese, Filipinos, Chinese, Koreans, Puerto Ricans, Samoans – and shortly after arriving I found my own nationality to be very popular amongst the native Hawaiians. These islands were originally discovered in 1778 by an Englishman called Captain Cook, although he also died there, killed by natives when a misunderstanding developed into a fight. Many years later, in 1843, Hawaii actually became British, albeit for just six months as Queen Victoria wasn't happy with her naval commander's decision and subsequently restored Hawaiian independence. Then in 1898 Hawaii was annexed to the USA, an arrogation that wasn't favoured by the native Hawaiian population who would rather the islands had become a British territory. This feeling amongst the locals continued through to modern times and when Hawaii eventually achieved statehood, they chose a state flag consisting of the Union Jack in the top left corner and red, white and blue stripes filling the remaining area. Consequently, a British visitor is always well received by native Hawaiians.

On becoming aware of the elevated status of an Englishman in these islands, I decided to put this information to good use. Whenever I started hitchhiking, I first draped a Union Jack the size of a large handkerchief over the top of my backpack and I never had to wait long before someone stopped and offered me a ride. In this way, I continued my travels up the verdant Hamakua Coast, and then across the northern tip of the island to the arid Kohala Coast – the dry side of the island.

Yes, it was dry . . . and hot! I was astonished by the dramatic contrast in vegetation from one side of the island to the other: from jungle to desert in less than 30 minutes. I was later told that the unique location and landscape of this island produce 20 distinct climates, which is quite amazing since only 22 exist on this planet. A change in climate produces a change in vegetation, so any short drive on the Big Island always takes you to a completely new terrain.

I camped in the desert at Spencer Beach County Park for a few days on a coastline edged with water that clear, turquoise colour you get with a white sand bottom. Then I headed south to Kailua-Kona, the tourist capital of the island, and it was there that my plans began to change.

I spent the afternoon wandering the streets of a town so tailored for tourism that the locals describe it as 'Disneyland without the rides'. Then I continued hitching south with the intention of finding some-where to camp. My second ride was from a very helpful guy called Tom, who first took me to the County Office to renew my camping permit and then down to the town of Captain Cook, named after the famous explorer as it was the place where he ultimately met his end.

I had read about a youth hostel in this town but when we arrived I found they charged an outrageous $14 just to pitch a tent for the night. This was a bit rich for my budget, seeing as I was surviving on $10 a day mainly because camping on state beaches only cost a dollar a night, thus making accommodation a minimal expense. Unfortunately, on this part of the island there weren't any state beaches with camping facilities and this left me in a difficult situation.

As I was pondering my predicament, Tom came to my rescue and offered to let me stay at his place for a couple of nights. He seemed pretty trustworthy and straightforward, and a few nights in a proper bed sounded quite tempting. So we drove back to Kailua-Kona, where he had an apartment, and then a little later we went out for a pizza.

During the course of conversation that evening he told me that his wife had just left him and that he'd never lived alone before. This helped me understand one thing about him because, despite being ten years my senior and by no means pathetic in appearance, he somehow came across as a man who needed someone to look after him. Now I understood why he was keen to have a flatmate for a few days.

I also learned that he worked in construction as a carpenter, and I told him about the construction work I'd done in Florida as a painter.

'Well, there's plenty of work here, if you're looking for a job,' he said.

'That sounds quite tempting. I wouldn't mind spending a bit longer on this island and the extra cash would always come in useful.'

'You'll make good money here as well because the pay is much better in the islands than on the mainland,' he added.

'So, how would I go about finding a job here?'

'Well, if you like, tomorrow morning you can drive me into work and then take the car to go round all the construction sites. I can show you where they are on a map and I'm pretty sure you should be able to find something without too much difficulty.'

'OK, great. Tomorrow I'll get myself a job!'

However, there was something I hadn't revealed to Tom that was worrying me. While on the mainland, I had been working illegally. I didn't have permission for employment in the USA; I only had a tourist visa. Of course, I hadn't been alone in this respect. Many of my friends had been in a similar situation and understandably we often chatted about the methods of deception we used to prevent detection. We all lived in constant fear of capture by immigration officers and subsequent deportation, and there were always a few stories of other travellers' misfortunes circulating amongst the backpacking fraternity. For us, 'immigration' was a four-letter word.

My current situation was rather different to what it had been in Florida and California. Now I was travelling alone in a place visited by very few backpackers, so there wasn't anyone else here I could ask for advice. There was no way of finding out how travellers got illegal employment on Hawaii and, more importantly, no way of knowing what lies I could tell without arousing suspicion.

The next morning, I followed Tom's advice and set off to make a circuit of the construction sites in Kailua-Kona. At the first one, the foreman said he might be able to use me the following week but he had nothing for me at the moment. At the second I was told I could start right away . . . provided I had a haircut first! I was quite proud of my long ponytail and certainly wasn't prepared to sacrifice it for a job, so I declined his offer and continued on my way. At the next few sites there were no vacant positions, but at the fifth or sixth one the fore-man said they needed someone to help lay insulation and while I had no experience in this particular undertaking, he assured me it wasn't difficult. He told me to come back in an hour to start work – with no need to visit a hairdresser beforehand.

I went back to Tom's apartment to change my shorts for a pair of old jeans, a mode of dress that the foreman had advised would be more suitable for the job in hand, and then returned to be introduced to my new workmates.

It was quite a small team, less than a dozen guys, but consisted of a much broader cross-section of characters than I'd previously encoun-tered in construction. There were two bosses, Don and Gordon, who were the owners of building site yet they chose to work alongside the rest of the crew. Don, the elder of the two, was a small, bright-eyed, white-haired man who had worked for most of his life as an airline pilot before going into partnership with Gordon. Despite his advanced years, he had certain mannerisms that indicated a mass of stored-up energy and he seemed to take great pleasure in continually nominating himself for the nastiest, dirtiest, most unpleasant tasks on site. Con-sequently, he quickly earned my deepest respect, a feeling that was evidently shared by all who worked with him.

The foreman was a guy called Jim, who immediately took to my English sense of humour and our professional relationship was soon surpassed by a social one, a friendship that, even today, is still very much alive. I was introduced to Kenny, a pot-bellied carpenter who could be a bit of a tearaway at times and had a firm grip that made me feel somewhere in his youth he'd been told a man was measured by the strength of his handshake. There was Bill, who was about the same age as me and shared similar interests, so we quickly cultivated a friendship that also crossed over into our social lives. Cliff was a thin, balding, sad-faced man and as the only electrician in our team, he tended to keep to himself; as did the two plumbers, who also preferred to work as an isolated unit. And last but not least, there was Monico, an undersized, ageing, Filipino guy who seemed most at ease when in the company of Don, a man whose conversational skills more than made up for his own natural reticence.

135

On my first day I was put to work with Gordon, one of the owners, and it wasn't long before he asked me how it came about that an Englishman could work in America.

'Well,' I said, preparing to recite my well-rehearsed story. 'My mother worked over here as a nanny in New York when she was nineteen. She fell in love with a guy there and they eventually got married in England, so I was born with dual nationality.'

'Really?' said Gordon. 'That must be great for you. So, did you go to New York and visit any of your relatives?'

'Er, yeah,' I lied, not expecting to be asked about my extended family. 'I met a couple of uncles but I was only there for a few weeks and I didn't have time to find everyone.'

In the past I had never been very good at lying, nor had the inclination to experiment with deceit, yet now it seemed to be working so easily. If I'd tried the same lie in Los Angeles, the boss would've simply laughed at me and said it was the tenth time that day he had heard such a story. But here it was different. On this island there weren't hordes of backpackers seeking employment without papers, so to Gordon it had sounded quite believable. Indeed, it was probably the first time he'd ever heard such a story and I realized right then that it was going to be easy here. Working illegally on the Big Island was not going to be a problem.

At the end of the week, I was called into the office to fill out my tax forms. I'd been in the same situation in the past and did exactly what I had done back then: I used my parents' telephone number with the area code as my tax number. That way I was sure I'd be able to remember the number if I ever needed to reproduce it. Everything appeared satisfactory to those in command and I strolled out of the office feeling very contented. In fact, things couldn't have been better. I had a stable job with first-rate pay, Tom was more than happy to provide me with accommodation for the duration of my stay, and above all else, my worries of immigration and deportation had as good as disappeared.

About a week later I was working with Jim, the foreman. During the morning we chatted about many different things – life in England, life in Hawaii, my travels, his family – and the topic of conversation eventually moved on to the building under construction.

'So, what's it going to be when it's finished?' I asked.

'Well, it's a small block of offices,' he replied.

'Yeah, I know, but what will be here? More lawyers, estate agents, that kind of thing?'

'No, nothing like that. The whole building is going to be used by government officials. I think they're planning to fill it with customs and immigration staff.'

The new immigration offices. I was working *illegally* building the new immigration offices! I couldn't believe it.

In spite of this set back, I stayed with the job and saw it through to completion . . . without deportation. Nevertheless, during the final few weeks I did receive one or two strange looks from my workmates when I always disappeared into the toilet upon the arrival of immigration officers, dropping by to check on the progress of their new premises. I would remain there, hidden away until they left, afraid that if one of them asked me a question, my accent would betray my origins and a situation like that would almost certainly end in disaster.

But I didn't get caught. I worked there for nearly five months, postponing my departure three times because the desire to stay was simply overpowering. I found my job immensely rewarding through continually learning new skills, and it was an added bonus to be working alongside people who tried so hard to make me feel at least a little special, being the only Englishman on site. The island gradually strengthened its hold over me as I began to perceive it more and more as the paradise I'd been dreaming of during my childhood beach-boy days, and on top of all this I had become romantically involved with a young lady in town.

I first met Christie a few weeks after starting work. Although originally from Montana on the mainland, she'd been living on this island for a little over a year and was able to open my eyes to the charms of Hawaii from a female perspective. Over the following months, our relationship steadily developed and once I'd helped Tom become proficient at housekeeping I decided to move in with her.

She lived in a comfortable, two-bedroomed apartment in a small block on a sweeping avenue of banyan trees, and she shared it with

137

Tina and Kito, a young couple she'd known for several months. Tina was English but her family had moved to the Big Island when she was still a child, and Kito was a native Hawaiian who also happened to be one of the best surfers on the island. As a result, there were half a dozen expensive surfboards in the flat, all donated by sponsors, and soon after moving in he gave me an open invite to use any of them whenever I wanted. This came as a wonderful surprise, seeing as surfing had always fascinated me, and I was very excited to have been presented with the opportunity to learn, particularly considering the context of location: learning to surf in Hawaii!

Late one afternoon, I arrived home from work to an empty apartment and decided it was time to take up his offer. I was ready to begin my education in the art of riding waves. I got changed, grabbed a towel and was then faced with the difficult decision of surfboard selection. As I surveyed Kito's varied collection, I noticed one that was decorated with an aesthetically pleasing, colourful design. As an artist, my choice had been made. I seized my selected board and headed off to the beach.

It was only a short walk and on arrival I was pleased to discover that the waves were good that day. I could see quite a number of guys out there, all cutting back and forth in the breaking surf with a graceful ease that filled me with confidence. I excitedly kicked off my trainers, discarded my T-shirt and towel and then started to make for the water's edge, but I hadn't got very far before a raucous greeting stopped me in my tracks.

'Hey! Nice board, dude!'

I turned to my left and saw a group of lads sitting on the sand, surrounded by an assortment of surfboards.

'Yeah, er, it's a nice colour,' I replied. 'You know, a really cool design.' I didn't want to get into a heavy debate about surfboards because I was already out of my depth and I hadn't even reached the sea yet.

I turned back and continued on my way but just before entering the water, I suddenly remembered a very important detail: I first needed to attach the safety cord to my right ankle. This little device, whilst designed to prevent the loss of one's surfboard in crashing breakers, also ensures that should you fall off when catching a wave, the board shoots away and then springs back and hits you in the head.

At last I was ready to go. I charged into the water with the macho bravado I had seen displayed by numerous surfers and began paddling out to the point break, at the same time feeling that the lads back on the beach were still watching me. I was a strong swimmer and an experienced bodysurfer, so it didn't take me long to position myself correctly and time my approach with that of a respectable, though not oversized, incoming wave. Then, as I felt the board beneath me lift on its surging power, I made the quick and intricate move to an upright stance and immediately remembered another important detail: I didn't know how to surf! In less than a second, the board slipped away, throwing me backwards into the crashing surf, then it shot up into the air and sprang back at me making noticeable contact with my cranium.

When I told Kito this story, later that day, he instantly burst out laughing.

'Don't you understand what happened?' he asked.

'No, what do you mean?'

'Didn't you realize what those guys were thinking? As soon as they saw a surfboard covered with sponsors' stickers, they all figured you had to be a top competition surfer!'

'What? They thought I could surf?'

'Surf! They were all expecting to see some shit hot wave riding! God-damn! It must have been such a surprise to see that you weren't shit hot . . . just shit.'

Trying to learn how to surf wasn't the only thing I did on Hawaii. I travelled all over the island, saw the most active volcano in the world, witnessed molten lava pouring into the sea, and I even skied on the snow-capped volcano Mauna Kea. I learned much about the Hawaiian people and their culture, went on several camping trips, made many new friends, enjoyed lots of parties, worked really hard and played even harder. I saved a whole heap of money and had a whole heap of fun but eventually I knew it was time to move on.

My girlfriend Christie had decided to accompany me all the way to Australia via Fiji and New Zealand, so our final week on the Big Island involved a series of leaving parties. The guys at the construction site, Christie's colleagues, our mutual friends and also our two flatmates all wanted to give us a good send-off. Finally, we took a flight to Honolulu, where we'd given ourselves three days to arrange the visas required for a visit to Australia, and here was where my new-found ability to lie really developed into a class of its own.

As soon as we arrived we went straight to the Australian Embassy, filled out application forms and were told to phone after two the following afternoon to see if our passports were ready for collection. Christie made this call and was told that *her* visa had been processed but they needed to speak to me. This, however, came as no surprise.

Despite only having permission to stay in the country for up to six months, I had arrived in the USA over eight months earlier. Conse-quently, before submitting my passport I'd removed the I-94 Record of Departure card that stated the date by which I was obliged to leave. It was a little trick I'd learned from other backpackers the previous year when I'd been in a similar situation and it had worked without any problems back then.

'Mr. Devereaux, we can't seem to find an I-94 immigration card in your passport,' announced an official-sounding voice on the other end of the telephone line.

'Yes, I know. I think I lost it one night because I always had to take my passport with me when I went out to bars and discos, seeing as it's the only form of identification they'll accept,' I replied, using the same excuse that had been deemed acceptable a year earlier.

'But you don't have an entrance stamp in your passport either.'

This was something I wasn't aware of. I'd entered the USA at the border crossing in Tijuana and had followed all the usual immigration procedures.

'I don't know anything about that,' I replied, beginning to feel a bit nervous.

'Exactly where and when did you enter the USA?' he asked very formally.

'I crossed the border at Tijuana on . . . er . . . on Christmas Eve,' I replied, choosing a date at random that kept me within the six-month limit.

'And what were you doing before you entered the USA?'

140

'I was travelling through Central America and the Caribbean,' I replied more confidently, since this was actually true.

'I see, and how long have you been travelling, Mr. Devereaux?'

He'd asked me a question that was much harder to deflect because I knew he could find the answer right there, in the passport in his hands.

'Let me see . . . er . . . about a year and a half,' I replied somewhat hesitantly.

'A year and a half!' was his astonished response, followed by the big question, 'Have you been working in the USA, Mr. Devereaux?'

'No, of course not!'

'So how have you been financing this trip?' he asked suspiciously.

Now I was struggling. He'd caught me by surprise with that one.

'Well . . . my dad sends me money.'

'And what does your father do for a living?' asked the experienced embassy official, presumably running through a list of standard questions.

'He's in exhibition design,' I lied quite creatively. My father actually worked as a painter and decorator but he'd recently branched out into stand fitting for exhibitions.

'How much does your father earn a year?' was the next question on his list.

'I'm not too sure. About sixty grand, I think. But that's sterling, you know, £60,000,' I replied with a smile, thinking how happy my father would be if that really were the truth.

'I see, and why do you want to go to Australia?'

Obviously, I wanted to go there to travel around a bit and work illegally to pay for my travels. But I couldn't tell *him* that. I had to come up with a more acceptable reason.

'I'm going with my American girlfriend, my fiancée, for a little holiday before we get married,' I declared, and had to endure the pain of a sharp kick in the shins from Christie whilst consenting to come to the Embassy at four o'clock to talk a bit more.

I guess the word 'panic' would best describe my feelings at that moment, but we put our heads together and started planning a course of action. Clearly an engagement ring was required, though this was quickly taken care of at a minimal cost of $6.95. More importantly, we needed to be sure we could answer any possible questions about each other's habits, quirks and family history in case we were interrogated separately to ascertain the validity of my story.

We arrived at the Embassy feeling very well prepared. I hadn't gone quite as far as memorizing the colour of Christie's toothbrush or the name of her face-cream, but I was confident I could answer any questions that might arise. We'd even invented a creative itinerary of wedding plans.

Christie walked up to the desk first, said her name and was given her passport. That was no surprise. Then I followed, announced my presence and waited for the imminent request for an interview. The clerk looked down her list, picked up a passport and handed it to me. Feeling very confused, I nervously thumbed through it until there, on page 17, I found an Australian visa. Incredibly, it appeared they had believed me. I could go to Australia!

Still numb with excited confusion, we drove to the airport, where we dropped off the rental car and checked in for our flight to the South Pacific Republic of Fiji. It was a strange moment for me. I felt happy and sad at the same time; happy to be going somewhere new, to be moving on, yet also sad to be leaving somewhere that was so special to me. I was leaving Hawaii, an island that had been my home for nearly half a year, a place that had given me so much pleasure. It really was a beautiful island.

'Yes, it really is a beautiful island,' I agreed.

'Anyway, Stevie, I suppose we should go back inside now,' my father said.

'Er, yeah, OK. I guess it's time to be moving on.' Then they wheeled me back to my room, helped me onto my bed and I thanked Carmen for her kindness before settling down to another afternoon in hospital.

11 *Toilet Bag*

'It was good to finally see Quentin here this evening, wasn't it?' I said to my father as the last of my visitors left.

'Quentin? Yeah, he's a nice lad.'

'Yes, I know, but I was surprised he didn't come a bit sooner. I mean, it's been over a month since my accident and that's the first time I've seen him. And he didn't really seem to be himself today. He was a lot quieter than normal, you know, a bit subdued.'

'Look, Steve, you've got to understand that your accident was quite a shock for him too.'

'Why? What do you mean?'

'Well, it was Quentin who found you. He was the first person to see you after you'd had the crash. He was the first one to come up here to the hospital.'

'What? *Quentin* found me?' I asked in disbelief.

'That's right. He came to intensive care the day after your crash.'

Until then we'd never actually talked about who had found me. In fact, I hadn't even thought about it much. I guess I'd just assumed that when I hadn't turned up at work on the Monday after my accident, my boss must have eventually realized something serious had happened and subsequently called the hospital.

Quentin was a colleague who had joined the staff of our language school at the start of that academic year, so I had only known him a short time. As my father had said, he was a nice guy but if I'm honest when we first met I hadn't anticipated having much more than a professional relationship with him. He wasn't typical of the type of person I would usually mix with socially and in many ways we were very different people. Yet there was something about him that was difficult not to find appealing.

As an Irishman, he had many of the idiosyncrasies endemic to someone of this nationality and he had no difficulty making friends. However, I got the impression he'd had an unsettled upbringing and even though he rarely talked about his family, somehow I suspected there might have been a need for some kind of reconciliation. He was also a bit of a drifter and had been travelling around for quite some time, though I wasn't too sure exactly how long.

Nevertheless, he was a lively character with a wicked sense of humour and more importantly, when prepared to expose his soft underbelly, it was easy to see he had a big heart. He'd even become one of my salsa students, despite not being a fan of Latin music or dance, and had attended the classes right from day one. Indeed, it was his unfailing support of my salsa classes that had ultimately led to him being the person who had found me.

On the night of my accident, a Friday, I was planning to go to the cinema with Quentin after the meeting at a hotel in Costa Teguise about more dance classes. Of course, that evening I never contacted him and he just assumed that something had come up or maybe I'd bumped into someone. But the following night, when he arrived at the Rincon del Majo for the salsa class and discovered I wasn't there, he knew something was wrong. He knew I would never miss my dance class.

So great were his convictions that he went straight to my flat but found nobody was home and that my car was also missing. His next thought was to phone a couple of mutual friends but no one had seen or heard from me for over 24 hours and this heightened his anxiety enough to warrant a call to the hospital. During that conversation he was unable to give my full name, only knowing me as Steve, but was told they had a young man in intensive care who loosely fitted his description; a man who had been in a car crash the previous night although nobody had enquired about him yet. Consequently, they asked if he could come and try to identify this man, so he hailed a taxi and made the short journey to the hospital.

Upon arrival, he was taken straight to the intensive-care unit and asked if I was the man he was looking for. He wasn't sure; he couldn't be sure. It wasn't easy to identify the owner of the bruised, swollen, disfigured face before his eyes. How could anyone identify that?

'I . . . I don't know,' he mumbled. 'I just don't know. It might, but–wait a minute! Can I have a look at his knees? I know he's got psoriasis there. I saw it when we were at the beach.'

The nurse acceded to his request and lifted the bedclothes to reveal two easily identifiable, flaky, knobbly knees. He knew who it was – he'd solved the mystery – although he also understood that he now had the uncomfortable responsibility of breaking the bad news to everybody else. I'm sure there were better ways he could have spent a Saturday night.

'So, I guess after that he wasn't too keen to come back and see you right away,' my father explained. 'I imagine he wanted to wait until, you know, until your face looked a bit more . . . normal.'

'Yeah, I understand. It must have been quite an unpleasant experience for him, and I reckon he's a lot more sensitive than most people think when they first meet him.'

'Well, I don't know him nearly as well as you do, Steve, but I still think he's a good lad.'

At that moment our conversation was interrupted by the arrival of a nurse with some news that didn't exactly fill me with joy.

'What did she say?' my father asked. 'Have I got to leave now?'

'No, it's not that, and I'd rather you stayed a little longer, really.'

'Why? What's up?'

'She said they've got to do that 'toilet' treatment again; that thing they did when I was on Gran Canaria.'

'What *thing*? I don't know what you mean.'

'She said they've got to give me an *enema*!'

'Oh, right, I understand. Shall I wait outside while she, er, does the business?'

'If you don't mind. Nick's out on the balcony having a cigarette, so why not go out and have a chat with him?'

'OK, I'll see you in a minute then.'

It was such a relief to know that my father would be with me this time. I had received the same disagreeable treatment about ten days earlier and I could still remember the excruciating pain of intense stomach cramps shortly after it had been administered.

My memory hadn't misled me and less than a minute after the nurse had left I was screaming for my father to bring me a bedpan. He immediately entered the room with the necessary container in hand, having chosen to wait outside the door rather than join Nick on the balcony. He also seemed surprisingly well prepared for the task and attended to my needs with a caring efficiency I had never previously seen him exhibit. I began to realize that he, too, must have learned a great deal through the experiences of my hospitalization.

Once the unpleasantness was over and my father felt sufficiently comfortable to leave me, he said goodbye and I settled down for what I hoped would be a good night's sleep. Unfortunately, this was not to be the case.

At some point during the early hours of the morning, I was dragged out of a deep sleep to find three nurses around my bed attempting to change my sheets and clean my private parts. It appeared that my earlier performance had been insufficient for the treatment I'd been given and there had been an unplanned repeat performance while I was asleep. By this time I had become accustomed to group participation in my daily personal hygiene, but this was different. This was so much worse, so much more humiliating. I could feel my face turning bright red . . .

. . . even before he started to open my toilet bag, and this distress was intensified by my concern that he would perceive my obvious embarrassment as suspicious. In desperation, I looked over to Scott, who was undergoing a similar examination of his personal effects by another customs officer, though in reality there was nothing he could do to help.

By coincidence, that embarrassing day was also my anniversary. It was October 7th 1987 and on the same day, exactly one year earlier, I'd left England on a flight bound for San Francisco. Now I was in El Salvador, Central America, trying to cross the border into Guatemala, and until that moment everything had gone fairly smoothly.

The previous day we had successfully managed to leave Nicaragua, which was quite an achievement since it had been our second attempt. We'd made an early start and bussed to the border crossing, where

146

formalities on the Nicaraguan side had unexpectedly progressed without the customary tribulations of life in this country. Then we continued our journey north, travelling in the back of a truck through four miles of *no man's land* to the Honduran border. At immigration we got our passports stamped, paid the $3.50 'entrance fee' to the country and then went to customs for the obligatory bag search. Once we'd fulfilled all the legal requirements for admission to Honduras, we wandered into the border town and began looking for somewhere to have some breakfast.

After spending the past two weeks in Nicaragua, a socialist country suffering the effects of American economic embargoes, it was a pleasant change to see shops that actually had shelves stacked with merchandise. Admittedly, it was more expensive here, but at least there were things on which we could spend some of our money. In Nicaragua this had been a big problem.

After breakfast we taxied to the nearby town of San Carlos. From there, two bus rides were necessary to complete our journey across this country along the Pan American Highway, a route that connects Alaska to Argentina apart from a small yet significant missing link: the Darién Gap. Surprisingly, the second bus was quite comfortable and was equipped with reclining seats and primitive air-conditioning, thus affording us a pleasant trip through the mountainous Honduran countryside.

As I gazed through the bus window at an almost unchanging landscape, I started to understand a joke I'd been told at some point earlier on our travels through Central America. A Honduran is asked what his country looks like, so he takes a piece of paper, screws it up into a ball, then opens it out loosely and replies, 'It looks like that!'

It was true. Honduras seemed to be full of nothing but crisp and pointy mountains.

We arrived at the border of El Salvador late that afternoon and experienced what had been our quickest border crossing so far. This may have been aided by our 'bribes' to the immigration and customs officers in the form of British coins. It seemed they were all avid coin collectors and not many Brits passed through this particular crossing. So our brief visit to Honduras was over. A visit of just six and a half hours that had been spent almost exclusively travelling on this country's public transport.

From the border we took a bus to San Miguel. We arrived after nightfall with no connecting bus to the capital until the next day, so we checked into a cheap hotel. It had certainly been a unique way to spend the final day of my first year away – travelling many miles, crossing two borders, using three different currencies – and also very thought-provoking. I found border towns immensely intriguing due to the nature of their geography: a bridge between two nations yet a true part of neither.

But I realized this was something that could also be said about me. I'd been travelling for so long now that I knew the land of my birth could never again be the home it had previously been. I'd begun to feel like a man with no country at all.

Later that evening, we went out for a stroll around San Miguel in search of somewhere to dine. In many ways, it was quite American-ized and we saw one or two familiar department stores and fast food restaurants, though we could also sense a very sinister atmosphere of tension.

As we wandered up and down the dark and dusty streets, alive with rats, we suddenly became aware that the street we were in was completely deserted. Then we noticed that every doorway was shielded by waist-high barricades of sandbags and the whitewashed stucco walls were peppered with bullet-holes.

For a moment I felt a strange need to explore further – that unexplainable desire to do something that common-sense tells you is wrong – but the human instinct of self-preservation soon took control. We quickly realized it wasn't a good neighbourhood to be in after dark, so we headed back the way we had come and found a cheap place to have dinner in a somewhat safer locality.

We awoke early the next morning, feeling refreshed and ready for the journey to Guatemala City. For me, it was a special day and as I showered and dressed I thought about all the adventures of the first year of my travels and how these experiences had changed me. Just one year earlier, I'd set out on a trip that I'd perceived as a *break* from my studies. Now I understood it was the complete reverse. Travel was a unique form of education not on offer at colleges or universities, yet something that held a value beyond any certificate or diploma.

We caught the six o'clock bus to San Salvador, an unremarkable trip apart from a luggage search at a military roadblock along the way, and arrived around mid-morning. It was a fast city with a menacing military presence evident from countless machine-gun-toting soldiers on every street corner, and we both felt truly glad we'd avoided a nocturnal arrival the previous day. We only stayed long enough for a quick breakfast before getting tickets for a direct bus all the way through to Guatemala City.

This service only had one scheduled stop at the border crossing. At this particular checkpoint there was no town astride two nations, just a couple of buildings in a dusty, barren, mountainous setting which housed the government officials who processed passing travellers.

As the bus pulled into the car park and came to a stop, we decided there was no point in rushing. By then we'd experienced enough Latin American border crossings to know that two Englishmen could never compete with Latinos when it came to queuing technique – there was a distinct cultural difference in that respect.

We first let the other passengers hustle past us down the aisle. Then we wandered off the bus, bought a couple of cold cokes from a street vendor and sat on a wall, waiting for the 'immigration scrum' to subside. Finally, when only a few people remained in the queue, we strolled over to join them and got our passports stamped.

As a result of our tardiness, by the time we'd returned to the car park all our fellow passengers' luggage had already been searched by customs and everyone was back on board. Outside the bus there were two customs officers standing next to two backpacks, waiting for the gringos to arrive so they could search the remaining luggage.

Once we had reached them, one officer started wading through my dirty laundry, souvenirs and other bits and pieces while the other officer began examining the contents of Scott's backpack. Meanwhile, a busload of Central Americans sat with their faces pressed against the windows, all trying to sneak a look at what the two gringos were carrying. Also, many street vendors soon gathered around us, keen to see what our strange-looking bags contained.

As the officer continued to rummage through my belongings, I suddenly found myself in a state of extreme agitation. I could feel my face turning bright red, even before he started to open my toilet bag, and this distress was intensified by my concern that he would perceive my obvious embarrassment as suspicious. But my nervousness wasn't due to any sense of foreboding. It was simply because, in addition to the usual soap, shampoo, deodorant and razors, I knew my bag also contained some other more 'personal' items.

I anxiously watched as he slowly unzipped the bag and put his hand inside to sift through the contents. Then a few seconds later, he looked up at me with a wide grin revealing a gold-capped tooth.

'No problem, no problem,' he said with a little laugh and pulled out a couple of condoms to show his colleague. However, it wasn't only his workmate who could see them. He held them up high enough so that some 60 or 70 onlookers could all feast their eyes upon my preferred brand of birth control.

As I stood there, my face glowing like the setting sun, I looked around me at the large group of smiling spectators and felt I would rather have been anywhere else in the world right then than there.

Suddenly, the officer working on Scott's backpack let out a wild shriek of excitement and immediately looked up with an even wider grin. Then he extracted a string of some ten or twelve condoms from Scott's toilet bag and proceeded to wave them around his head in triumph.

'You guys won't get AIDS!' he roared and having made his point he eventually put them back where he'd found them.

That was the end of the bag search. They'd had their fun and I'm sure they told this story over a few beers at the local *cantina* that night. But it wasn't over for us. We had to get back on the bus, enduring numerous knowing grins from many of the passengers and feeling completely overcome with embarrassment.

I was completely overcome with embarrassment. Despite being a full-grown man, I felt like a toddler who hadn't yet mastered toilet training. The nurses were very professional and understanding, and I'm sure it wasn't the first time they'd had to deal with such a situation. But this did little to reduce my sense of humiliation. It was the first time something like this had ever happened to me, and I fervently hoped it was going to be the last.

12 *Ski Hat*

'Bloody hell, Pops, you look rough! What happened?' I exclaimed when my father's haggard face appeared at the door to my room.

'Well, that's what a night of Carnival does to a man of my age,' he replied in a husky voice.

Of course! Isolated from the outside world in my 'party-free' hospital environment, I had almost forgotten that the rest of the island was revelling in the joys of the biggest celebration of the year; a time when the streets are crowded with multitudes of merry people dancing till dawn, fuelled by Cuba Libre and driven by salsa and merengue bands.

'Did you have a good time?' I asked while trying to suppress the tinge of envy I felt through my inability to have been there with him.

'Yeah, it was fantastic! I started off at Sammy's flat for a few drinks and a bit of a party. Then I went to that concert you'd recommended, that Cuban woman, Celia Cruz.'

'You saw her!' I shouted in genuine delight. 'Oh, that's great, I'm really glad you went. So, did you go with Sammy and the rest of the gang?'

'No, I lost all of them pretty soon after we'd left her flat. The streets were absolutely heaving and I ended up with a group of local lads.'

'Really? And how did you cope with the language barrier?'

'With difficulty,' he sighed. 'I mean, French flows along softly, Italian dances around a bit, but Spanish . . . Spanish is kind of mad.'

'Yeah, I suppose it is.'

'No, you don't get it. I asked one of these lads what his name was, you know, *"¿Cómo te llamas?"* and he said "Wanker!"'

'What?'

'He told me his name was *Wanker*. I spent the evening with Wanker and his buddies.'

'And how did you manage to pull that one off?' enquired my room-mate with his characteristic little-boy giggle.

'Yeah, very funny Nick, and a good morning to you, too,' replied my father, realizing he'd overlooked customary pleasantries.

'No, wait a minute,' I interrupted, still struggling to understand this mysteriously crude appellation. 'Are you sure he said Wanker?'

'Yeah, definitely.'

'Ahhhh! I get it! His name was Juan Carlos but a lot of people shorten it to Juan Ca'.'

'What? Like calling someone Dick instead of Richard?' asked Nick.

'Yeah, right, something like that,' I chuckled. 'But the thing is, to an English-speaking person Juan Ca' sounds a lot like wanker. So you spent the evening with Juan Carlos and his *amigos*, not with a wanker. There are no wankers here, Dad.'

'Are you sure about that?' asked Nick.

'What?'

'Well, are you sure there are no *wankers* on this island?'

'Sorry? Oh yeah, well maybe one. And he's the nephew of a doctor at this hospital, isn't he?'

'That's the spirit!'

'Anyway, what did you do when he said he was called Wanker?' I asked my father.

'I said, *"Me llamo El Zorro"*,' he replied, proudly demonstrating another Spanish phrase he'd managed to commit to memory.

'Zorro! You wore my costume!'

Carnival in the Canaries not only involves music, dancing and Cuba Libre. There's one more vital ingredient: fancy dress. Everyone goes to a lot of trouble and expense to create elaborate costumes, and on Carnival nights if you're not in fancy dress the locals simply assume you're a tourist – or a *guiri*, as visitors to the islands are 'affectionately' called by Canarians.

In England, the big night for fancy dress is, of course, New Year's Eve. I had spent the previous Christmas holidays at home with my family, and when selecting an outfit for the New Year's Eve party at the salsa club I'd decided to make a costume that could also be worn in Carnival. The choice was easy. It had been the big movie of the year and fitted perfectly with my Latino image. I was going to be 'El Zorro'.

I spent almost an entire day going round second-hand shops, trying to find the materials I needed. Then I spent the next day sat at my mother's sewing-machine and the end result was a mask, a cape and a belt almost identical to those worn by Antonio Banderas in the film. I was quite proud of my efforts, which were well received at the New Year's Eve party, but that was only a trial run for the 'main event': Carnival. I knew it would be a popular choice of costume amongst the Spaniards and I had hoped to be one of the most authentic Zorros on the streets of Arrecife that year. However, even though my accident had denied me this opportunity, I couldn't let all my hard work go to waste. Consequently, I had told my father where the costume was kept in my flat and had insisted that he wore it.

'Of course I wore it!' he exclaimed. 'And it was brilliant! I must admit, I did have a bit of trouble getting the belt to fit my waist but once I'd sorted that out it was great.'

'Oh, I'm so glad,' I said. 'After all the hard work it took to make it, I feel a lot better knowing that someone got to use it.'

'Yes, you certainly did a good job there, son,' he commented. 'It must be said that when *you* make a costume, you really do make one.'

'Are you really going to make one?'

'Yeah, of course I am,' I replied. 'Why not? It'll be a laugh.'

'But won't you feel too embarrassed to wear it?' asked Christie.

'No, of course not. As long as I have a couple of drinks first, I'll be all right.'

I was in the process of organizing the materials I had gathered to make a hat. On this occasion it wasn't a complete costume because we were going to a 'hat party', so this was all I required. We'd received an invitation to this party a few days earlier from some friends who lived close by, and on hearing the theme of the party it hadn't taken me long to come up with an idea. This idea was, perhaps, a little extreme but I'd always been proud of my English sense of humour and the longer I spent away from home, the more extreme it became.

That morning I'd woken up early with the intention of going skiing but unfavourable weather conditions had kept me inside. Not wanting to waste the day, I had spent the morning writing letters and in the afternoon I'd decided it was time to start work on my party hat.

Scheduled for Saturday night, this party would mark the anniversary of our arrival in Queenstown six weeks earlier. Our first week in New Zealand had been spent in Auckland. We'd flown there from Fiji and despite knowing beforehand that we were arriving at the start of winter in the southern hemisphere, we initially found the dramatic change in climate came as quite a shock.

But this wasn't the *only* surprise New Zealand had in store for me. For an Englishman who hadn't seen his homeland in more than a year and a half, it felt like a true home from home, albeit my grandparents' home. Just as we were coming in to land, the pilot of our plane (a British aviator) had made an announcement over the intercom, 'We're arriving in Auckland, New Zealand, so please put your watches back 50 years.'

He was right. The ambience, architecture and streets of this city were so similar to those of my father's youth that I truly believed I'd discovered time travel.

After a quick lunch – pie and chips with mushy peas seemed to be the extent of any menu on offer – we began organizing accommodation.

'Well, Steve, they don't got that many hostels listed here in the guidebook,' said Christie, 'but I reckon we should be able to get a bed at one of 'em.'

'Yeah, but I was thinking of something else, actually.'

'Hey, Steve, there's no way I'm gonna sleep in a tent here! It's too god-damned cold.'

'No, don't be silly. I was thinking about that lad we met on Fiji. You remember, Terry, the bloke from America who gave us the phone number of some people he knows here.'

'Ah yeah, that's right!' she drawled. 'Said he stayed with a couple a really cool guys. Reckoned they'd be happy to let us have a room.

So whaddaya waitin' for? Call 'em up already!'

I complied with Christie's request, called the number we'd been given and subsequently spoke to a Kiwi named Andrew. It was a brief conversation and I'd hardly had time to finish explaining how we'd got his number before he offered us a bed for the night. He gave us directions to his house, which wasn't far from the city centre and was also a residence he shared with a friend called Barry. We had already been told that both of them had a wide experience of backpacking, particularly in Latin America, and this helped us understand a strange slogan we saw spray-painted across the wall of the front garden when we eventually found their house. It was a two-foot vertical white line followed by the words, '¡No Lo Hagas!' – White Lines, Don't Do It! Obviously, this had been inspired by the combination of travels in cocaine-producing countries and a love of Hip Hop, Grandmaster Flash in particular.

We spent the next few days shopping around for ski clothing and accessories whilst trying to acclimatize to the change from subtropical to subzero, and our hosts showed us the best of Auckland's night-life in addition to giving much-valued advice on the purchase of cheap tickets to the South Island. Then, once we had everything organized, Andrew drove us to the airport and we took a flight to Queenstown.

We flew via Christchurch, the second-largest city in the country, and along the way we enjoyed some spectacular views of the Southern Alps, a magnificent spine of mountains that run almost the entire length of the island. In Christchurch we changed planes and boarded a small, 16-seater propjet to continue our journey. Then after another brief stop by a lake in the shadow of Mount Cook, New Zealand's highest mountain, we finally reached our destination.

Upon arrival, we were surprised (and relieved) to find it was a little warmer than it had been in Auckland. We took a bus to the town centre and got a room at the Pinewood Lodge, a rustic alpine retreat that served as the local youth hostel. Then we went out to have a look around the town.

Queenstown once went by the name of 'Fit for a Queen', and it was easy to understand why. It's a picturesque resort situated on the shores of the enormous, S-shaped Lake Wakatipu, and was founded during the gold rush of the 1860s, although the principle industry of the present day is tourism. As we wandered through the streets of the compact pedestrian centre, I was intrigued by its contradictory complexion of a small-town feel alongside an air of cosmopolitanism that is only usually associated with larger cities.

The majority of visitors to Queenstown come in pursuit of outdoor activities – hiking, mountaineering, white-water rafting – and just minutes from the town centre is Kawarau Bridge, the birthplace of bungy jumping. This internationally famous, adrenaline-rush sport was originally conceived by a Kiwi on returning from a trip through Papua New Guinea. He'd got his idea from a ritual in this country that involves adolescent boys throwing themselves off tree-top platforms in the jungle with nothing more than a vine tied around their ankles, a ceremony that signifies their initiation into adulthood. But we hadn't come here to indulge in such pastimes. Our primary interest lay in the mountains, where there were two ski fields that offered the best skiing in Australasia on fine powder snow and in a landscape of breathtaking vistas.

Our plan was to spend the whole ski season here, so on our second day we bought ski equipment and lift passes. Then later that day, we also had an amazing piece of luck and moved into a flat very close to the edge of the lake. We shared this flat with two other tenants: an amiable guy from Auckland called Andy who was also down for the ski season, and a lively lady from London called Sharon who was working at a nightclub just outside town. It was a comfortable flat, ideally located, and offered fantastic views of the lake and mountains, a panorama that could be enjoyed through French windows from the privacy of our bedroom.

The following day we awoke early to a morning that was bright and blue. We had a quick breakfast, gathered together our ski gear and were out at the roadside hitching before nine. About half an hour later, we got a ride to The Remarkables ski field with a couple of Aussie lads and began the first of many days of skiing. Life quickly slipped into a routine of early mornings followed by a day on the slopes, and evenings spent relaxing in front of the television with an occasional 'day off' due to bad weather or the need to rest aching limbs.

To break up this routine a bit, we usually went out socially at the weekend. There were one or two good pubs in town and after more than a year of life in America, it was a real treat to go to a tavern where they served beer in pint glasses. But Queenstown was small and the social life rather limited, so we'd eagerly accepted an invitation to the party. By then we were quite keen for a change, and my own enthusiasm was obvious when, three days before this party, I started work on the hat I intended to wear that night.

Over the next few days, progress on the hat proceeded to schedule and on the day of the party all it required was a coat of paint. Even so, the design was pretty outrageous and as night fell there was one more thing I needed: I definitely required some Dutch courage. I went to an off-licence, bought two bottles of wine and a case of beer, and then returned to the flat for some dinner. Over the meal we finished both bottles of wine and one or two beers before I'd reached a sufficient level of alcohol-induced confidence to actually wear my creation. Then I donned my delightful headgear, collected together the rest of beers and we set off to find the party.

It was a short walk through a residential neighbourhood and I managed to resist the temptation to remove my 'ski hat', despite passing an elderly couple out walking their dog. Then came the moment to enter our friends' house. It was time to join the party.

I'll never forget the shrieks of laughter induced by my dramatic entrance when the door finally swung open. This was followed by a word shouted by several party guests, a name that would haunt me throughout the coming weeks.

'*Dickhead*!'

Yes, Dickhead. Sitting on top of my head was a bright pink penis about two feet tall, complete with bulbous testicles. I'd come to the party as a 'dickhead'.

Once the initial impact died down, the party progressed through a session of drinking games to the judging of the hat competition. It was quite an international affair with entries made by backpackers from all over the world and an intense feeling of national rivalry. However, English humour was ultimately declared the winner and I proudly received the 'rosette' for first place.

After celebrating this momentous victory, my memory of that night's revelries is a little hazy but the following day I was to receive plenty of reminders.

One of the girls at the party worked at the photo processing shop in town and she had spent the entire evening shooting several rolls of snapshots. The next morning, she developed them at work and put them together on a large display board in the shop window, offering to sell reprints to any interested customers. About a third of these photos featured a very drunk man wearing a very large penis on top of his head.

That afternoon, we went out for a stroll in the crisp mountain air to try and clear our hangovers. During the course of our walk through town we happened to pass the photo shop and I must admit to feeling a certain amount of national pride when I first saw this display board. The English are famous for their unique sense of humour – their willingness to ridicule themselves in the presence of others – and from Benny Hill through to Mr Bean, we've been entertaining people from all over the world for many years now. I believe this is what separates us from the rest of the English-speaking world. It's our sense of humour that makes us English, not our beer, our pop music or our fanatical football fans.

It's also something that gives me great pleasure on a personal level. There must be hundreds of my ex-students around the globe who would all agree that it's impossible to get through an hour in Steve's classroom without at least one or two displays of English humour. Consequently, when I saw these photos I realized I had every right to feel proud of my experimentation with self-humiliation. My intention had been to provide everyone with a source of amusement for the evening, and from this photographic evidence I concluded I'd been successful. But the consequences aren't always what you think they're going to be.

'Hey, Dickhead!' someone shouted from across the street.

I was still recognizable without my phallic appendage.

These cries continued throughout the rest of my stay in Queenstown, no matter where I was or what I was doing. Whether I was walking around town, drinking in a pub, skiing down a mountain or even going up one in a chair-lift, several times a day I would receive that same address.

And it didn't end once I'd left the 'scene of the crime'. Following a two-month stay there, we hitchhiked for several days, passing through Christchurch, Wellington and Rotorua, and all the way back up to Auckland, putting many miles between us and The Hat Party. Yet a couple of days after arriving in New Zealand's largest city, we walked into a pub with our friends Andrew and Barry, and as we made our way through the crowds towards the bar the babble of voices suddenly became overpowered by that familiar greeting, 'Hey, Dickhead!'

I thought it had to end there. I assumed that when I boarded a plane and left New Zealand I would leave my epithet behind me as well. But it wasn't to be so. It followed me across the ocean to Australia with still time for one more friendly salutation.

On my first day in Sydney I was walking along the main street of hostels in King's Cross – the heart of backpacker land – and through the open window of a passing car I heard someone scream, 'Hey, Dickhead!'

That was many years ago and I can laugh about it now, though at the time I was starting to become a little worried. Would I spend the rest of my life, no matter where I was in the world, being known as Dickhead?

Luckily my concern proved unnecessary but this story isn't quite complete without recounting what happened the evening after The Hat Party. On the Sunday morning, I had woken up on my bed, still fully clothed with the cardboard brim of the hat around my neck. The rest had disappeared; someone must have literally ripped it off at the party. That evening, we were in the flat watching late night TV when Sharon arrived home from work. As she walked through the door, I sensed that something had happened because her eyes were glittering with excitement and she had a naughty grin on her face.

'What's up?' I asked inquisitively.

'You won't believe what I just saw!' she exclaimed with a giggle. 'I'd just finished work at the club and was waiting for a taxi under the door canopy, trying to keep out of the rain. A taxi pulled up and as I crossed the pavement to open the door, I saw something floating down

160

the stream of water in the gutter. It was all shrivelled and pink, and as it passed me I realized it was your penis!'

So my penis drowned on a rainy Sunday night, somewhere on the outskirts of Queenstown.

'So, did my costume survive a night of Carnival?' I asked my father.

'Yeah, don't worry about that. Everything's still intact and I've put it all back in the drawer in your bedroom. I made sure nothing got damaged or ripped off.'

'Oh good, thanks. It's just that after all that hard work, I wouldn't mind using it at some time in the future. It's something I wouldn't want to lose.'

'Yeah, I know what you mean.'

13 *Own Goal*

I was enveloped in a darkness of infinite depth and the bitter night air cut right through me, making my bones feel brittle and numbing my hands and feet. My parka was zipped to the top of the snorkel hood, leaving me with little more than a keyhole field of vision, and although it wasn't raining, the air was like cold soup, soaking the fur-lined hood and filling my nostrils with a rank smell that stifled me. I had no idea of my whereabouts but was in dire need of warmth and the company of adults to help me through this inhospitable wintry night. The obscurity denied me any sense of direction, though I perceived I was on some kind of a roadway and started to walk forwards, my legs almost paralysed in the biting cold. My progress was very laboured and as I limped up a gentle incline, I glanced ahead and suddenly my heart skipped a beat. There, in the distance, I could just make out a faint glow. My pulse began to race – light meant people, warmth, safety – and my pace started to quicken. This lumin-escence slowly intensified as I neared the brow of a small hill. Then on reaching the end of my climb, I came to an abrupt stop. Below me I could see the flashing lights of the emergency services, and illumin-ated in the headlights of several vehicles was a mêlée of men around the tangled wreck of a car. But it wasn't this shocking image that had brought me to a halt. Behind me I could hear the sound of a voice softly calling my name. It compelled me to turn and go back into the murky, chilling darkness from which I was just on the point of escaping. I heard my name repeated a second time, then a third, and my stride rapidly lengthened with the hope this familiar voice had inspired in me. I felt sure I knew him; certain he would save me from this daunting nightmare. I could almost see his face and on hearing my name called once more, I broke into a run, extending my right hand before me. Finally, just as I reached him he took my hand in his and filled me with the warmth and security I so desperately needed.

'Hey, Stevie,' my father softly whispered, and as my vision gradually cleared I found him at my bedside, my right hand gently clasped in his. 'Don't worry, everything went all right. You just need to get some rest.'

The circumstances of my current situation slowly began to return. That morning I'd had an operation to rebuild my left leg, and now my father was sitting with me while I recovered from the general anaesthetic. I fell in and out of sleep over the next few hours, limiting conversation, but by early afternoon I was feeling more responsive. Eventually, a nurse arrived and wheeled me down to radiology to take some post-op X-rays, and a little later Doctor Ruiz paid a visit to see how my recovery was progressing.

'Good afternoon, Steve,' he said brightly on entering my room.

I turned to face him and as soon as I saw his familiar visage I was instantly put at ease. This time I was certain his moustache was obscuring a smile. My father's synopsis of the operation had been correct. Everything *had* gone all right.

'How are you feeling?' he asked as he walked round to the left side of my bed to examine the leg he'd operated on that morning.

'I'm OK, thanks. Still a bit sleepy, but I'm alright.'

'Good, good. It always takes some time to get over the anaesthetic, so don't worry, everything appears to be normal,' he assured me. 'Are you in any pain?'

'No, really, I'm fine.'

'Well, if you start to feel uncomfortable, just call one of the nurses.'

'Yes, OK.'

'So, would you like to see what your leg looks like?' he asked, and started to remove an X-ray from a white plastic sleeve that had been tucked under his arm. I looked towards my father on the other side of the bed but he didn't need to say a word. His eyes told me not to worry.

When I turned back again, Doctor Ruiz was already holding the X-ray up to the window for us to see, and in his habitual professional manner he began to explain precisely what he'd done. However, as soon as I saw this X-ray I was unable to concentrate on his detailed description. Even though I had known long before that day what the operation would involve, the image before my eyes still took me by surprise.

Along the outer edge of my thighbone I could see a metal plate that stretched from my hip to a few inches above my knee. The top end of this plate was attached to the bone by a large pin that had been drilled deep into the hip joint, and down its length were more than a dozen screws of differing lengths depending on the thickness and fractures of the bone into which they had been embedded. I was so engrossed in this fascinating image that I missed my father's joke the first time round.

'I said he forgot to countersink one of those screws,' he repeated, always ready to offer advice on DIY.

But at that moment I wasn't interested in humour. The X-ray had my undivided attention and I just couldn't stop gazing at all that metal inside my leg. As I stared . . .

                              . . . at the screen of the X-ray machine, I could see a piece of metal inside my backpack that was distinctly foreign to me, yet also something that was very easily recognizable. Gradually, a few of the passengers nearby became interested in the surprising image on view, but this was the least of my concerns. The most important thing right then was that I was certain this piece of metal simply didn't belong to me.

I was just outside a Venezuelan town called Santo Domingo, close to the Colombian border, at a small airport run by the National Guard. While the majority of aircraft here were used for military purposes, there were also a few small commercial jets that offered short-haul flights to internal destinations and neighbouring countries. I had come here to take a flight to the Colombian capital, Bogotá.

I had been in Venezuela for about four months, working as an English teacher in a town called Mérida. It's in the south of the country, over 400 miles from the coast, and is situated on an alluvial terrace 5,000 feet above sea level, surrounded by cliffs and plantations and within sight of Venezuela's highest mountain, Pico Bolívar. It's a pretty little town and still retains some old colonial buildings, which contrast with many modern edifices including those of the University of the Andes.

Before coming to this town I'd read that this university had around 40,000 students from all over South America, so I had assumed that a native-speaking English teacher would probably be able to secure employment there. My prediction had proved correct and I'd found a job without too much difficulty at a language school called Venusa – a name derived from the combination of 'Venezuela' and 'USA' – in addition to acquiring a significant number of private students.

When I first arrived, I stayed at a backpackers' hostel just a few minutes walk from the start of the world's alleged highest and longest cable-car (though it was no longer in working order). This hostel was called Posada Las Heroinas and was owned by Tom Evenou, a friendly Swiss guy, himself an ex-backpacker, and his Venezuelan wife Raquel. By this stage of life I'd spent a total of around three and a half years travelling and had acquired a wide experience of back-packers' hostels all over the world. Tom's definitely featured among the best.

In general, this type of accommodation can be loosely classified into three groups. There are traditional establishments, such as those of the Youth Hostel Association, an organization that was founded long before the concept of a 'backpacker' came into existence. These are run according to a strict code of rules including cleaning duties, no daytime occupancy, no alcohol on the premises and lights out by 10pm – not the kind of environment a modern-day backpacker can appreciate.

There are others that operate as nothing more than a money-making venture started by a businessman who noticed the emergence of a new market for budget-priced accommodation in his or her region. In these, the management's knowledge of a backpacker's needs is virtually non-existent, the atmosphere is impersonal and tariffs are levied on any and every service and facility available.

Finally, there are those hostels, few and far between, that are owned by ex-backpackers who see it as a way of settling down while still remaining in a travel environment. Here the owners have a very clear understanding of their guests requirements, can anticipate what questions might be asked, what problems may arise, and due to their past lives are ultimately perceived more as friends than proprietors. Posada Las Heroinas fell comfortably into the third category.

During my first few days there I met a Brazilian resident named Joâo. It wasn't difficult to cultivate a friendship with him. We both enjoyed foreign travel, music, films and black humour, and there was something about him I couldn't quite define, like the memory of someone I'd met somewhere else and then lost track of. After growing up in Brazil, he'd lived in England for about five years and had come to Mérida as part of a degree in Latin American Studies he was taking at a university in London. A requirement of his course was to spend a year in South American to study Spanish, a language he spoke almost as well as his native Portuguese.

Joâo had been living at the hostel for several months and although he enjoyed its friendly, sociable atmosphere, he was keen to return to a more independent and private lifestyle. Unlike the majority of guests at the Posada, I was planning to remain in Mérida for at least half a year, so a couple of weeks after becoming acquainted we decided to look for a flat together. A few weeks later, we moved into a very large two-bedroomed apartment in a tower block not far from the centre of town. It was a great location, close to all the amenities, and also had magnificent views of the nearby snow-capped mountains.

And it wasn't long before we found that sharing a flat turned out to be advantageous to both of us. As an English teacher, my timetable involved early mornings and late evenings, since most of my students could only attend class outside normal work or university hours. Joâo, on the other hand, had a very relaxed routine, having already mastered the subject he was here to study. But he was also a master chef and had worked in this profession for several years before starting his degree. As a consequence, every evening I would come home to find a delicious South American meal prepared and waiting, and after dining I would wash the dishes (a chore that I happen to enjoy immensely) while Joâo relaxed with a drink and a good book, thus making the whole arrangement mutually beneficial.

The social life in town was another plus point of my life in Mérida. I soon had a circle of friends of mixed nationalities – Venezuelans, Colombians, Americans and even several fellow countrymen who were studying at the university – and we regularly met up for a drink at one of the many bars in town. But the best thing for me socially was something that stems from a piece of Venezuelan trivia I've never been able to forget: Venezuela has won Miss World more times than any other country. It's a fact that was very easy to believe if you were actually living there, and I suppose, on average, I fell hopelessly and madly in love about 30 times a day.

And no day in Venezuela was ever like the preceding one. I quickly learned that it was impossible to establish any sense of a routine in a country whose inhabitants all lived by their own baffling set of rules and whose government appeared to have no idea what set of rules it would be better for everyone to live by. Consequently, my own life was far from perfect.

Shortly after arriving, I had gone out to change some traveller's cheques and had spent over an hour wandering the streets until I eventually found the only bank in town that accepted American Express cheques. This hadn't been particularly surprising because I'd had similar experiences in other parts of the developing world, and the 45-minute wait in a queue of only five people was also nothing out of the ordinary. Once I'd reached the counter and handed over two $50 cheques and my passport, I wasn't even unduly perturbed by the amount of form-filling and photocopying that was required to process this simple transaction. It was when the clerk gave me the Venezuelan money that I started to become a little disconcerted.

Just as I was about to pocket the pile of notes and coins he'd placed on the counter in front if me, he made a gesture to indicate that our business wasn't complete. He carefully explained that I needed to take a 100-*bolívar* coin to the cashier at a desk on the opposite side of the bank and get some change. I followed his instructions, waited in another queue, 'bought' a bag of one-*bolívar* coins and returned to the original clerk. Then I patiently watched while he counted out the entire bag and handed me the one *bolívar* (0.4 pence) that I was still owed!

Another day I was walking to work because the bus drivers were on strike, and on passing the engineering faculty of the university I felt an uncomfortable burning sensation in my nose. Later that day, I mentioned this to Joâo and he explained that it was probably due to the canisters of tear gas used by the police to quell the student riots that had happened that morning. Apparently, the students had become enraged when the municipal bus company had suspended their travel concessions, and they'd set fire to four buses. This had resulted in the bus drivers taking industrial action and the students had taken to the streets and rioted since there weren't any buses to take them to university and they couldn't afford taxis.

Rioting was all the rage in Venezuela that year. A couple of weeks later I couldn't even get to work because the streets had been closed off in an effort to contain further student riots. This time they were rioting in sympathy with students who'd rioted in Caracas two days earlier, a demonstration that had been sparked off by the shooting dead of a student during riots in the capital the previous week, except I never found out what those riots were about.

Pot-banging was another popular form of public protest. Early one evening, I was awakened from a *siesta* by what sounded like someone starting a car with a broken exhaust manifold. I went to investigate and from the living-room window I saw that virtually every balcony of the surrounding apartment blocks was crowded with people beating on innumerable pots and pans. In addition to this deafening racket, those still indoors were repeatedly turning all the lights on and off, throwing strobe-effect lighting across the whole neighbourhood.

This lasted for about an hour and the next day someone told me the entire town had participated in this demonstration. They went on to explain that in the more affluent parts the servants had been commissioned to do the pot-banging, and one creative entrepreneur had even marketed a cassette-recording of this unsociable din, thus leaving his customers with nothing more to do than move their stereo speakers to the balcony.

On this occasion the population was protesting about utilities provided by the water and electricity companies, both of which services were sporadic at the best of times. But the kitchenware was brought out onto the balconies several more times during my stay there due to a variety of grievances.

One of these problems was petrol. Venezuela was a country where milk (imported from the USA) cost 55 *bolívares* a litre, whereas the equivalent quantity of petrol cost a measly six *bolívares*. Yet when the government raised the state-enforced fixed price of petrol by one *bolívar*, it provoked a very violent pot-banging session and the resultant minimal increase in bus fares led to more student riots. Oil was a big issue in a country that produced almost nothing else.

I had come to Mérida with the simple intention of working hard for several months to save enough money for further travels. But in spite of a very busy timetable, I soon discovered that even *this* wasn't going to be possible. When I'd arrived in Venezuela the exchange rate had been around 100 *bolívares* to the American dollar, but not long after I started work the local currency began a dramatic and rapid fall in value.

As in many third-world and developing countries, US dollars were in demand here. This had forced the president of the Banking Council (a man who incidentally owned a bank and therefore had a more than vested interest) to introduce a radical system for distributing dollars to banks throughout the country. Five times a day, each bank had to make aggressive bids for dollars at whatever price they thought would be competitive and the Central Bank would sell to the highest bidders. This resulted in some banks over-bidding and subsequently selling their dollars at a loss, while others would under-bid and receive none. But the unfortunate outcome for the Venezuelan *bolívar* was that it started to behave like an 'elephant tranquilizer' on the international currency market and in a matter of weeks it had halved in value.

One more frustration in life was caused by my visa situation. As always, I was working without the required papers and on a tourist visa you were only permitted to stay in the country for up to 60 days. This meant I had to leave Venezuela at regular two-month intervals to renew my visa, and the nearest neighbour was Colombia.

The first time this had become necessary I'd gone to Cúcuta, the closest border town to Mérida. It was an arduous journey that began with a five-hour bus ride to a town called San Cristóbal. During this trip I was seated next to a young Swiss guy whose opening gambit was, 'I am travelling for one month now and I want to go to Colombia to try the real cocaine!' With him as my only 'companion', I slept through most of this journey.

From San Cristóbal I took another bus to San Antonio, just over an hour away. I had my passport stamped at the immigration office in this town and then walked across the international bridge into Cúcuta, Colombia. I first got an entrance stamp before having a cup of coffee at a nearby café, then I returned to the Colombian immigration office, claiming I needed to go back to Venezuela to retrieve a camera I'd left in my hotel room. The officer perceived this as an acceptable excuse for leaving his country before the ink had even dried on the entrance stamp in my passport, and permitted me to return to Venezuela, begetting a visa valid for another 60 days.

However, this laborious journey had taken a complete day, most of which had been spent on buses. Consequently, when my visa was once again about to expire, I'd decided against repeating the Cúcuta trip and instead had chosen to fly to Bogotá for a weekend stopover.

'Did you get your ticket to Bogotá?' asked Joâo, whilst serving me an ample helping of a South American stew called *sancocho*.

'Yeah, I sorted it out this morning. I'll be leaving on Thursday afternoon.'

'What time is your flight?'

'Well, the *flight* leaves early Friday morning.'

'What? You just said you're going on Thursday.'

'Yes, I know, but the cheap flights don't go from here. I've got to take one from an airport just outside Santo Domingo,' I explained.

'Santo Domingo? Where's that?'

'It's a little bit south of San Antonio.'

'Close to *Cúcuta* you mean.'

'Yeah, well, not far I suppose,' I reluctantly agreed.

'*Ay, mi madre!*' he exclaimed. 'You English will do anything to save a bit of money. You need to go to Colombia, you decide to fly, and to get a cheap ticket you go to an airport that's a stone's throw from the Colombian border!'

'But I saved almost $45,' I interjected.

'Forty-five dollars! Is that all? Mind you, the way things are going with the *bolívar*, it was probably a wise decision. And you'll need that money in Bogotá because once you start meeting those Colombian *chicas . . . mamasitas*, all of them!'

'*Mamasitas*?'

'Yes, Steve, *mamasitas*. You're gonna have a good time in Bogotá, believe me. Those girls love the gringos!'

I left Mérida on Thursday afternoon and bussed to San Cristóbal, where I arrived early evening and managed to find a room at a cheap hotel close to the bus station. This was in June 1994, the year of the World Cup in America, and that night Colombia was playing against the United States. Living in a Latin American country during this very special time in the football calendar, it was impossible not to get caught up in the excitement of this unique sports event. As a result, I found myself not only watching many matches but also getting involved in lengthy discussions about each team's performance when the full-time whistle was blown. Even though this was completely out of character for me, the combination of geography and timing had ultimately led to this unexpected new-found passion.

As soon as I'd checked in and left my backpack in my room, I went straight down to the hotel lounge and joined the other guests watching the game on a tiny black and white portable television. This was the night of that ill-fated, historic match when the unlucky Colombian, Escobar, scored an own goal that led to an unbelievable victory for the USA. On returning to his homeland he was killed for his mistake, gunned down outside a nightclub in Medellín, and his assassin was reputed to have shouted, 'Goal!' each time he pulled the trigger. Nevertheless, it was a bad night for all Latin Americans. There could be nothing worse than being beaten by their rich, overbearing, northern neighbours at a game for which Latinos were world famous.

After this depressing match I went out to try and lift my spirits with a good meal at a small bar close by where they served fried chicken. It appeared to be quite busy, so I assumed the food was palatable, but on entering I could sense an atmosphere of depression. I also noticed that a television in the corner was broadcasting the after-match opinions of various football experts, and before I'd even had a chance to get my

171

bearings I was interrogated by a group of three men seated at a table near the door.

'Are you American?' one of them growled.

'No, no, I'm not a gringo,' I quickly replied. 'I'm English.'

'Ah, English! That's OK,' he said in a much friendlier voice. 'Please, sit down and join us.'

I followed his orders, more out of politeness than the desire to make new friends, and a cold beer was thrust into my hand as a reward. He then proceeded to order food and more beers for all of us, and I started to realize that his generosity was inspired by the simple fact that I *wasn't* American.

These three men had an eclectic mix of linguistic abilities. One could speak a little English, one could write a little and the other could understand a little, if I spoke very slowly and limited my use of vocabulary. At that time my Spanish was far from fluent, so this produced an unusual but interesting evening of communication. We ate fried chicken over a rather depressing 'discussion' about Colombia's tragic misfortune, then despite my attempts to leave with the excuse of an early morning flight to catch, the cold beers continued to arrive.

Eventually, our table was virtually full of beer bottles. It appeared that the custom in this part of Venezuela was to pay at the end of the evening, when you'd finished drinking, and your bill was calculated by simply counting the number of empty bottles on your table. Due to the macho tendency of Latin American men, the amount of respect you received from your peers was directly proportional to the number of empty bottles on the table before you. By the time I managed to leave, we had amassed a small forest of them and my generous hosts wouldn't even let me pay my share of the bill. Finally, I was permitted to bid these new friends farewell and staggered back to my hotel in the early hours.

The next morning I awoke at five, feeling the worse for wear, packed up my things and set off to catch the early morning bus to Santo Domingo. I didn't have far to travel and got off the bus about a mile before it reached town, at the closest stop to the airport. Then I began hiking along the road that led to my destination, though just a few minutes later I was picked up by a flight attendant who dropped me off in front of the main entrance.

I had arrived with an English punctuality and decided I had more than enough time to smoke a cigarette outside before checking in. This airport was owned by the National Guard, so a soldier was stationed in front of the entrance and it wasn't long before he strolled over to ask for a cigarette. He stayed with me for a brief chat and, obviously, the topic on everyone's lips that morning was the disastrous football match the night before. As I'd found in the bar the previous evening, this Venezuelan soldier was deeply disappointed by Colombia's defeat at the hands of the United States, as were a great many of his compatriots. Consequently, I quickly made it clear he understood I was *English*, not American.

When we'd finished our cigarettes, I told him I had to go inside to check in for my flight to Bogotá and he kindly held the door open for me. It was a very small airport terminal and as you entered you were faced with the machine that X-rayed your luggage. A woman with five or six suitcases had entered just before me, so this obliging soldier told me to leave my backpack in front of the machine, explaining that he would pass it through for me. I thanked him for his help and walked past the metal detector to the other side, where I stood and waited facing the screen of the X-ray machine.

Once all of the lady's suitcases had been examined, the image of my backpack appeared on this screen. But even though I recognized this image immediately, I still couldn't believe my eyes. This familiar shape was overshadowed by an item inside that was very *unfamiliar*.

In the top pocket of my backpack I could clearly make out the image of a pistol!

I instantly went into a state of panic but before I could make sense of anything, a soldier blew a whistle, my backpack slid out of the machine onto the rack in front of me and an officer appeared at my side. He was a short, paunchy man with a forbidding countenance that was arrogant or something else I couldn't quite place. Following a swift contact of the eyes, he bent down, opened the top pocket of my backpack and reached inside. Then he pulled out the pistol and, caressing this weapon in both hands, he turned to me, stony-faced, and started barking words in Spanish.

Due to my nervousness, my comprehension was severely impaired, although the basic gist seemed to be that it was illegal to travel with firearms. Then, gradually, I began to comprehend the gravity of this situation. I began to realize it was going to cost me a substantial bribe to prevent incarceration.

Just at that moment, I heard a peal of wild laughter come from the other side of the X-ray machine. This rapturous outburst seemed somewhat out of keeping with the current state of affairs and as I leaned over to take a look, I saw my friendly soldier with his colleagues, all in fits of laughter. The officer at my side gave me a gentle pat on the back, then walked towards my '*amigo*', returned the pistol to its rightful owner and strolled away with an amused grin that improved his appearance significantly.

As I gathered my things together and checked in for the flight to Bogotá, I felt quite perplexed by recent events. My head was filled with thoughts of an unlucky Colombian footballer in the USA, also about to take a flight to the same destination; a man whose life had been thrown into complete disarray due to a simple mistake he'd made on a football pitch; an error that had left not only his countrymen but most of Latin American in a general mood of despondency.

Yet on arriving at this airport I'd met one of these disheartened Latinos: a Venezuelan soldier who had subsequently used me as a pawn in a clever little hoax designed to lift the spirits of those around him. He knew I wasn't American, so his actions hadn't been an attempt to seek some kind of personal retribution. He had simply realized that the best way to combat the acute depression that had descended on South America that morning was to make a joke.

'Don't you get it? He forgot to countersink one of those screws,' said my father, repeating his joke once more.

'Yeah, Dad, I get it. It's just that I was thinking about something else,' I explained.

'Come on, son. There's no need to take everything so seriously.'

'No, I don't suppose there is.'

No, of course there wasn't. Here was a man whose life had been thrown into complete disarray due to events beyond his control, yet he still managed to find humour in all the craziness going on around him. He knew the X-ray wasn't amusing for me, so his comment hadn't been an attempt to seek some kind of personal gratification. He had simply realized that the best way to combat the acute consternation that had filled me that afternoon was to make a joke.

14 *Mountain Blues*

I awoke with the echoes of the dream still in my ears, except this time I was alone; my father wasn't holding my hand. However, I no longer felt the panic deep in my gut that had brought me out in a cold sweat the first few times I'd had this dream. It had become such a frequent occurrence that I'd begun to look upon it as nothing more than another hardship to be endured whilst recovering from the trauma of my accident. In fact, I couldn't even remember when it had first started happening. That memory was hidden somewhere deep in the darkness of post-traumatic delirium, though I was certain it had been with me since I'd regained lucidity.

But all of that was in the past and now my thoughts were firmly focused on the future. Three days earlier I had taken my first big step on the road back to a normal life. Five weeks after my left leg had been shattered in a car crash, it had finally been rebuilt and now I was ready to try and bring that leg back to life again.

I knew this wasn't going to be easy. Almost 40 days had passed and during this time I'd hardly been able to use a single muscle in a leg that had constantly been stretched horizontally by hospital traction. It was going to be a tough battle, yet I drew comfort from the knowledge that I wouldn't have to fight it alone. My father would be with me.

'Hiya, Stevie, how are you doing?' he asked as he breezed into the room.

'Good morning, Pops. I'm fine. What about you?'

'I'm OK, thanks. So, are you all alone this morning?' he enquired with a glance at the empty bed to my right.

'What? Oh yeah, they've taken Nick somewhere to do some tests. I'm not too sure exactly what. I wasn't really paying attention when he left. But anyway, what's all that stuff you've got there?' I asked, having noticed his arms were full of rather more than the customary paraphernalia.

'Well, I bumped into that doctor friend of yours down in the foyer. What's his name?'

'Manel?'

'Manel! That's the fella. He told me that he runs the physiotherapy department here and now that you've had your operation, he explained a few things we can do before you begin your official rehabilitation.'

I listened attentively while my father enthusiastically described his recent acquisition of the rudiments of physiotherapy, simultaneously finding myself looking at him through the eyes of an outsider. This man was so much more than just another 'hospital visitor'. Since the day of his arrival, he had been taking responsibility for an ever-increasing list of duties. Whether it was simply getting drinks or medication whenever the need arose, ensuring that IV tubes were free of bubbles, emptying bedpans and urine bottles, or restraining me during my 'crazy period', he'd always helped out and more often than not, without even being asked to do so. He had virtually become an unpaid member of the hospital staff and now that my leg had been rebuilt, he was ready to step into the shoes of a physiotherapist – my own personal physiotherapist.

'So, do you want to make a start?' he asked. 'Manel recommended we should try and do it twice a day, so I figured we could have one session in the morning when I arrive, then another one in that quiet time after lunch. What do you reckon?'

'Yeah, OK. I haven't got any other plans.'

The first stage involved a gentle massage to warm up the muscles. Then he took a hand towel, rolled it up into a long sausage-like shape and began slipping it under the knee joint. Once it was half way through, he brought the two ends together and grasped them in his right hand above the knee, producing a sling that would force the joint to bend when he raised his hand.

'Manel said this would probably hurt a bit because you haven't bent you leg for quite a while, so you're gonna have to let me know how much pain you're in.'

177

'All right, er, why don't we use a scale of one to ten? As you lift your hand, I'll call out a number.'

'OK, good idea. Here we go then,' he announced and slowly raised his hand.

Manel was right; it did hurt. Even though my pain threshold had become significantly higher through the experiences of hospitalization, we reached an eight on our scale surprisingly quickly and my father lowered his hand again.

'Wow! This is not going to be easy,' I confessed. 'But let's have another go. I'm ready.' Once more my father began gently raising his hand. 'Six– sev, ah– eight– ow! Nine! Yes, that's a nine.'

'Bloody hell, Steve! For a minute there I thought you'd got one of the nurses to give you a 'servicing' and you were giving her marks out of ten,' hollered Nick as he wheeled himself into the room. 'I was gonna wait outside, except we don't get too much excitement around here so I thought I'd come in and watch. Anyway, what in God's name *are* you guys doing?'

'A bit of physiotherapy,' explained my father.

'Well, that's another word for it. So what's with the towel and all those numbers?'

'We're trying to get Steve's knee joint working again and the numbers are so I know how much pain he's in.'

'Oh, right, I understand. Not quite as . . . *exciting* as I'd hoped. But don't mind me, you guys carry on.'

The final stage of the treatment was much more enjoyable. My father picked up a tube of Deep Heat cream, applied some down the length of my thigh and started to massage my leg. After years of playing congas and bongos, he had very strong fingers and was able to work each muscle into a state of extreme relaxation.

'How does that feel?' he asked, while continuing with a massaging rhythm of relief.

'Aaah, that's great,' I replied. 'Yeah– just there– aaah!'

'Aaah!'

'Are yer awright, mate?' came a voice through the darkness.

'Yeah, don't worry. Just giving my legs a bit of a massage,' I

178

replied.

'Oh, right, I guess it were a tough one for yer, weren' it?' he said. 'Maybe yer should try an' get yerself in better shape. But no, that's a bit unfair cuz yer made it up 'ere, didn' yer? Not everyone could a dun it. Reckon that's sumfink ter be proud of, init?'

'Yeah, cheers, and I'm certainly suffering for it now.'

'Well, don't worry, we dun the 'ard bit. It's all dahnhill t'morra. So jus' get yerself a good night's sleep an' we'll see yer at sunrise.'

I wasn't sure which of them had given this generous boost to my morale because they both spoke with cockney accents, though I was certain Mick and Les weren't suffering as much as I was. They were physical education teachers, so the past few days had probably been little more than a gentle stroll for the two of them. Even so, I did feel a limited sense of achievement. I *had* made it all the way up here, though I also knew I couldn't have done it without their help and support.

We were 7,400 feet above sea level, at the top of Jamaica, the Blue Mountain Peak, and in spite of the pain I was glad I had come. I'd arrived in Jamaica only four days earlier, yet so much had happened in that short space of time that it felt more like four weeks. I'd flown to Kingston from Miami, and after almost a year in the United States, I remember feeling a tense, nervous excitement in the pit of my stomach as the plane skimmed over this Caribbean island. I knew it was going to be a big change from the familiarity of America.

I don't know if it was a result of my nervousness, but I managed to make a short series of blunders the moment I arrived. My first mistake was at the immigration desk, where I was required to hand over my passport together with the immigration card I had been given on the plane. Unfortunately, I hadn't answered every question on this card as I was still unsure where I would be staying on the island. Consequently, I explained to the officer dealing with this oversight that I first needed to speak to someone at Tourist Information before I could supply an address in Jamaica. While making sure I understood that all official documents should always be completed in full, he agreed to overlook this discrepancy and allowed me to pass through.

I collected my backpack and went in search of the required

information but the 'laid-back' layout of this airport immediately gave rise to my next mistake. Unlike most international airport terminals, where the only route of exit is through customs, here they'd stationed the customs officers at a desk to one side of the arrivals lounge. With my recent chastisement still fresh in mind, I marched straight over to the Tourist Information desk but I hadn't even asked for assistance before a customs officer tapped me on the shoulder. I turned round and came face to face with a stocky man with a bullet-shaped bald head who told me it was a serious offence to try and leave the airport without first clearing customs. Following more apologies on my part, I fulfilled all the required formalities and then managed to get the address of a campsite just outside Kingston.

My next priority was changing money and even *this* simple trans-action resulted in further embarrassment. I found that the only place to cash a traveller's cheque was at the exchange bureau situated next to immigration . . . on the *other* side of the customs desk! Luckily, I was given special permission to pass back through customs to buy some local currency. Then, finally, I could leave the airport and begin to explore Jamaica – the land of reggae, rum and reefer.

Jamaica is the third largest island in the Caribbean and has a sombre history rooted in the sugar-plantation economy of the slave era, a memory kept alive in the lyrics of many reggae songs. It's a very densely populated, poverty-stricken country, and this was at a time when it was struggling to escape dependency and debt through the development of tourism, an industry that had replaced agriculture as the island's principle source of income. However, during the bus ride from the airport to the city centre, I discovered that their biggest advertising campaign was being mounted within the country itself. As the bus bounced along a pot-holed highway, we continually passed billboards plastered with slogans that were basically begging the native population to be nice to tourists!

When I arrived in downtown Kingston late that afternoon, I found this city neither welcoming nor beautiful. I quickly got a local bus and made a short but tedious 12-mile journey inland to Jack's Hill, a small settlement in the mountains just beyond the city limits. I got off the bus on the far side of this village and then still had to hike a little further before reaching a campsite hidden away in an idyllic, peaceful, jungle setting that couldn't have been more in contrast to the noisy, intimidating squalor I'd left behind me.

The following day I awoke to a blue Caribbean morning filled with all the promise of excitement and adventure. But my positive mood didn't last for long. As soon as I began preparing some breakfast I discovered that someone had stolen my Swiss Army knife! After recalling my exact movements since arrival, I assumed this must have happened on the bus from the airport to the city centre, when the driver had told me to leave my backpack at the front of the crowded bus. The loss of this knife was a major problem; without it I couldn't open tins and bottles or peel and chop vegetables. It was an essential tool for someone travelling on a shoestring budget and I realized I would have to go back into Kingston and buy a replacement.

With a rumbling stomach, I gathered together a guidebook, a map and my money-belt, and started hiking down the mountain to catch a bus. Adding to my frustration, the bus service was very infrequent and I continued hiking for over an hour before one eventually came along. I used this time productively, though, and abated my anger by persuading myself to look upon this trip as a cultural excursion. As soon as I reached the city, I went straight to the National Gallery and spent the rest of the morning in a calming environment of Jamaican contemporary art.

On leaving the gallery I had lunch at an economical street stall that offered jerk pork and chicken with breadfruit, while consulting my guidebook to find the best part of the city for shopping. For the purchase I needed to make, I concluded it would probably be best to head towards the centre of downtown, an area of high-rise hotels and office blocks in addition to many shops that catered for tourists. As I gradually got closer to the centre, I also discovered the streets there to be patrolled by an urban underclass of hustlers, street vendors and beggars. It was a vicinity where you could feel a seething tension simmering below the surface.

My young white face soon began to attract an uncomfortable amount of attention and at one point I felt sure I was being followed by a decidedly dirty, unsavoury looking character (and I mean 'dirty' in the way that some kids always look, even after they've just had a bath). I turned down a side-street, perhaps a little unwisely under the circumstances, but quickly doubled back in an effort to foil my pursuer. Just as I reached the corner again, this man was on the point of turning down the side-street and from his surprised expression when he almost bumped into me, I realized my earlier suspicions had been justified.

Once more filled with the apprehension that had marked my arrival in Jamaica the previous day, I entered the first suitable shop I came across and bought a new knife, too nervous to go through the back-packer protocol of shopping around for the best deal in town. Then I returned to the bus station, found one that was heading my way and retreated to the safety of my mountain hideaway.

In keeping with the earlier theme of frustration, the bus route I had taken terminated quite some distance short of the campsite, forcing me to hike uphill through the steaming, tropical heat. I arrived feeling weak and soaked with sweat, a damp T-shirt plastered to my back, and once I had drunk two full bottles of water I took a refreshingly cool shower and retired to my tent for a *siesta*.

Later that afternoon, I crawled outside again and met two new arrivals who were pitching their tent next to mine. 'Awright, mate?' one of them asked.

'Yeah, fine thanks. I've, er, just woken up, actually.'

'Just woken up!' he exclaimed. 'Blimey! Are yer a really late riser or 'ave yer got a young lady in there we ain't seen yet?'

'No, I'm all alone. It's just that I've had a very harassing day, that's all,' I explained.

'Oh, right. Well, this little fella 'ere is Les, an' my name is Mick,' he said, extending his right hand towards me.

They were a few years older than me, around their mid-twenties, and said they were from north London, where they taught physical education at a secondary school. They went on to explain that they always took a holiday together each year, without the distraction of girlfriends, to indulge in some serious hiking. After a short time, I also got the impression they enjoyed the temporary freedom of a female-less environment that allowed them to revert to the schoolboy humour they spent their working lives trying to control.

The next morning, I took a trek with them through the jungle to a valley a couple of hours away, where we bathed in the fast-flowing crystal-clear waters of a surging mountain river. Then in the evening we went to a rustic bar close by to end the day with a chat over a couple of cold beers.

Despite enjoying our little excursion that morning, these two guys wanted more than just a 'good walk'. They told me that they were planning a hike to the Blue Mountain Peak, the highest point on the island, and invited me to join them on this trek. Always keen for new experiences, it was an offer I readily accepted and we made plans to leave the following morning.

The next day, I set about preparing for our hike and, fortunately, I discovered that I was able to leave a lot of unnecessary possessions in a hut at the campsite, thus making my backpack considerably lighter. Even so, I had never done anything close to the planned expedition and although I didn't consider myself unfit, I wasn't a sports teacher either.

We set off around mid-morning and began a three-mile hike east to a small town called Papine, skirting the suburban sprawl of Kingston. Even though it was a fairly level route, for me it was quite a tough hike. As we trudged along a winding, rugged, mountain road, I soon became extremely uncomfortable due to the old-fashioned, external-frame rucksack that was violently bouncing up and down on my back. In addition to this burden, the morning was also marred by an incident that helped me better understand the billboards I'd seen upon arrival in Kingston.

It happened when we were passing below a large house set back from the road on a picturesque, landscaped terrace. Just as we were approaching the driveway to this house, a group of kids appeared in the garden above us and started hurling large stones and rocks at the three white-faced tourists below them. The weight of our backpacks made a rapid escape impossible and we had to creep along, taking cover in the shadow of the embankment at the side of the mountain road, trying to keep out of view of these adolescent thugs.

When we later retold this story to some locals, they said that this house belonged to Rita Marley and before his death the famous reggae singer had used it as his country retreat. It would be wonderful if I could tell friends that I went to Jamaica and got stoned with Bob Marley. Unhappily, the truth is very different. I went to Jamaica and 'got stoned' by Bob Marley's servants' kids.

By the time we reached Papine, I felt weak and nauseous and was about to give up. But Mick took one look at me and simply recommended that I ate some fruit and drank some milk. Much to my surprise, this dietary intake worked wonders and after a moment's respite I was ready to continue with the trip, feeling considerably refreshed.

From Papine we took a bus through 10 miles of breadfruit, Spanish lime and mango trees to a village called Mavis Bank, the place where the Blue Mountain trail began. Then it was time to start the *real* trek.

In the heat of the midday sun, we began climbing Jamaica's highest peak in a group of mountains that had been formed by the uplifting of a limestone plateau. The first part wasn't too difficult, a pleasant walk through undulating fields, but once we had begun the ascent I soon found myself struggling. I still hadn't got used to my uncomfortable backpack and was also having difficulty breathing due to a cold I'd picked up in Atlantis (the water park in Miami, not the mythical submarine city!) If I hadn't been with Mick and Les, I would definitely have turned back. But they gave plenty of encouragement, patiently waiting whenever I needed a rest and offering invaluable advice on hiking technique and limiting my intake of fluids. 'Take small swigs frequently. Don't down 'alf a bottle in one go!' cautioned Les.

Eventually, after hiking six miles through a landscape I remember as nothing more than the dirt track a few feet before me, we reached Whitfield Hall, a mountain lodge at an altitude of 5,000 feet. We pitched our tents, showered and changed, and then spent the evening relaxing in front of an open fire in the gaslit lounge of this charming wooden chalet, the perfect environment to recuperate from the rigours of such a challenging climb.

After an early night and a very good sleep, we set off at nine the next morning to ascend the final 2,400 feet to the peak. We still had a further seven miles to cover, though by then I was beginning to find it a little easier and managed to enjoy the passing scenery.

This part of the trek was through an area planted with bushes full of beans that would be picked and ground to produce the internationally renowned Blue Mountain Coffee. Despite claims that a lot on sale was not the genuine article, I realized that the TV commercials for this coffee were definitely authentic. As I looked around me at a sumptuous mist rising through steep, green-ridged mountains, the only thing missing was the soundtrack.

Finally, about four hours later we reached the Blue Mountain Peak and all the problems and pains of the climb were instantly forgotten the moment I saw the incredible view on offer from this unique location. It felt like I was on top of the world. In every direction the ground fell away in ripples of steep ridges covered with coffee bushes, clouds sitting in the deep vales between them, and these mountains continued to fall away until land eventually met sea. Never in my life had I seen such a sight.

We pitched our tents, had a late lunch and relaxed as the mountains around us gradually turned a red-gold colour in the last slanting rays of the sun. Then nightfall brought another surprise when Jamaica turned its lights on. Kingston was a distant, glittering, orange mass, and along the coastline each settlement was a Christmas tree of lights. Even in the mountains I could see the flicker of lanterns in isolated cabins. It was like being in an aeroplane during a nocturnal take-off or landing but without the restrictions of a window-seat view. I first gazed in one direction and then in another, consulting my map to find the names of the numerous towns, villages and hamlets that were all clearly visible through the darkness of a Jamaican night.

At the end of a second day of rigorous physical activity, we once again turned in early that evening. Also we planned to wake up in time for sunrise the next morning, so an early night was necessary. Before getting into my sleeping bag, I gave my legs a much-needed massage in the knowledge that the worst of it was over. As Les had said, it would all be 'dahnhill t'morra'.

Due to the altitude, it was quite a cold night without the necessary comforts for such temperatures, but exhaustion quickly took control and I soon fell into a deep sleep. The only disappointment was that we were unable to see the sun rise the following morning. We awoke to find ourselves enshrouded in a canopy of clouds, so I returned to my tent to try and get a bit more rest.

Unfortunately, my sleeping bag had absorbed the thick condensation of the clouds, making it quite damp and therefore removing the possibility of further sleep. As I lay there waiting for the warmth of the morning sun, I filled the time with thoughts of what I'd achieved. It was the first time I had ever done anything like this. On the backpacking circuit, everyone tries to do something different but you always wind up doing the same damn thing as everybody else. Yet this time I'd met a couple of guys who had shown me a completely new experience, and although it had been far from easy, it had given me an insight into my limitations and what I was capable of doing if I really pushed myself.

More than that, it had helped me understand how the support of another person could extend those limitations so much further. I knew without a doubt that I wouldn't have been there, if it hadn't been for Mick and Les. Through their constant encouragement and support, they had shown me I was capable of doing something I would never have even considered, had I been alone.

Sometimes a person needs to do something alone to gain the sense of achievement that comes with independence, and it's a wonderful feeling whenever it happens. However, sometimes in life you can find yourself in an almost impossible situation and even though you know you can't do it alone, you start to think you might just be able to succeed if someone else were there to give you that extra push. I had that person with me at that exact moment, except I don't think he ever realized how much my success depended on his constant encouragement and support.

'Thanks, Dad,' I said as he pulled the bedcovers back up. 'That feels so much better.'

15 *Bordering on Insanity*

'Well, you're looking pretty content with life,' my father said once the last of my visitors had taken leave of me.

'And I've got good reason to, haven't I?'

'Yep, you sure have,' he agreed. 'Only one more week to go then.'

'That's what the man said.'

'And when's he going to take the stitches out?' he asked, despite being at my side earlier that day when Doctor Ruiz had told us the good news.

'The day after tomorrow,' I replied, giving him the reassurance it appeared he needed. 'Then I can start thinking about getting out of this bed.'

'You most certainly can. And I'm sure we'll have you walking on crutches in no time at all, and it won't be much longer before we get your leg to bend to 45 degrees as well. Then, as the doctor said, we're out of here. We're going home!'

It made me feel so good to see that the happy, positive man I'd known my whole life had finally returned. His eyes once again had their mischievous sparkle and his naughty moustached smile had never looked so appealing.

'So, I guess it's time for me to leave,' he said when a nurse arrived with the evening meal.

'Yeah, OK, and what are you doing tonight?'

'The usual: a phone call home and a bit of food, then I'll watch a couple of videos and have a few drinks.'

'Well, don't drink too much whisky 'cause we've got a lot of work to do tomorrow, and don't forget to give my love to mum and Nikki when you speak to them.'

'No, of course not, son,' he assured me. 'Right then, I'll leave you to enjoy your meal.'

'What have I got tonight?' I enquired as the nurse placed a tray on the table at the end of my bed. My father lifted the lid and then looked up at me, grinning brightly.

'More good news. It isn't fish!'

For some strange reason, Canarian hospital catering almost always provided evening meals that were a fish-based menu. This was a dish that did little to delight my taste buds and even though the kitchen had long since been informed of my dietary preferences, the aquatic recipes had continued to arrive. Fortunately, that evening I had the unexpected pleasure of dining on Spanish omelette, a local dish that I quite enjoy.

While Nick and I shared our customary after-dinner conversation, a nurse arrived with a mobile phone. This was something that was becoming quite embarrassing because, unlike most people, I didn't own a mobile phone so family and friends had to call the hospital desk and the phone would be brought to my room. Consequently, I received more calls on the hospital mobile than any other patient did, and it had reached the point where the nurses had started referring to themselves as my 'secretaries'. The nurse handed me the phone, which I took with a self-conscious smile wondering whose voice would greet me this time.

'Hello, Steve. It's Gisela. How are you?' asked the voice of a woman in Spanish.

'I'm OK, thanks, and how are you?' I reciprocated, whilst trying to remember which of my Canarian friends the name and voice belonged to.

'Fine, thanks, but I only heard about your accident last weekend and I couldn't get the phone number of the hospital from your mother until today.'

'Oh, really?' I said, still unsure to whom I was actually speaking. Then suddenly I thought of a question that might help me solve this mystery. 'Where are you?'

'I'm at home, in Bournemouth,' she replied.

Now I understood my mistake. She didn't live here; she was one of my Bournemouth friends. Gisela was a Venezuelan lady, married to an Englishman, and we had met several years earlier when I started working as a disc jockey at the salsa club. Having solved the mystery, I was able to continue with the conversation feeling far more relaxed and knowing what people and places we had in common and what things we could talk about.

After returning the phone to one of the nurses, I turned to Nick and said, 'That was a weird one. I was talking to a woman and I didn't know who it was!'

'What do you mean? An old flame called you up and you couldn't even remember her name?'

'No, it was a friend who's got a Spanish name and we were talking in Spanish, so I assumed it was someone from here.'

'And who was it?'

'It was a Venezuelan friend who lives in England, but at first I couldn't work out who I was talking to.'

'So what did you say?'

'Well, suddenly I realized who she was . . .

. . . but it was really embarrassing!'

'Why?'

'Well, once I realized who he was I screamed, "*The Sweaty Sock*!"'

'The Sweaty Sock?' repeated Scott.

'Yeah, I met him when we were in Key West and I never got to know his name, but he was Scottish so I always called him the Sweaty Sock.'

'But why the Sweaty Sock?' asked Scott, still confused.

'You know, sweaty sock – Jock.'

'And what did he say when you called him a sweaty sock?'

'He just laughed, and he still lent me some money so I don't think I offended him too much.'

'You've got some money!' he exclaimed. 'Great! That means we can check in.'

'*Correctamundo, compadre*!'

In reality, it wasn't such a big deal. He had only lent me the equivalent of around $5, but that was more than enough to see us

189

through until the banks opened the next morning. After the terrible day we'd had, a chance meeting with a face from the past had been like a dream come true. The Sweaty Sock had certainly solved all our immediate problems by simply opening his wallet.

We were in Managua, the capital of Nicaragua, outside a *pensión* that was the Central American equivalent of a backpackers' hostel. However, that evening we had expected to be much further north, in Honduras or El Salvador, except things hadn't exactly gone to plan.

We had been in Nicaragua for about ten days and despite much advice in Costa Rica to fly over this socialist republic in a state of civil war, we'd initially found that the overland option had been a good choice. Admittedly, it was a country with many problems, though we also discovered it to be filled with a warm and friendly people who displayed such a sweet naivety about life in the developed world that they made their country seem like a land so innocent it still had dew on it.

Our problems had begun when we tried to leave. We'd planned a route using a guidebook that was only a few years old but things changed extremely rapidly in this part of the world. And this was something we learned the moment we crossed the border from Costa Rica. Our guidebook stated that the official exchange rate at the end of the 46-year Somoza regime was 15 Nicaraguan *córdobas* to the US dollar. Yet now, only eight years later, it had risen to an astonishing 8,500 to the dollar, and just before crossing the border we'd even been offered 14,000 by black-market moneychangers. This meant that once we had changed 60 American dollars into *córdobas* – a necessary requirement to enter the country – we'd struggled to fit over half a million in 1,000 notes (the largest denomination available) into each of our backpacks. Nevertheless, we did walk away feeling like high rollers at the Monte Carlo Casino.

From the border we travelled by taxi to the capital and were dropped off in a gloomy suburb, almost in darkness because so few streetlights were functional. It was rather confusing to be left in a residential neighbourhood with no point of reference to help us get our bearings, though it was something we should have expected seeing as Managua had become a city of suburbs.

In 1972 a devastating earthquake destroyed about 80% of the city centre, and under the dictator Somoza it remained as a pile of rubble, leaving Managua to sprawl around its own corpse. As a result, what were once residential districts had now become centres of business and commerce. Many houses had been converted into shops, offices, restaurants and hotels, but the extreme poverty of a nation on the point of bankruptcy had prevented these businesses from stretching to the expense of shopfronts, placards or neon signs.

Eventually, after a few minutes of confusion wondering how we were supposed to distinguish a hotel from a house, we asked a passer-by for help. To our surprise, he said that the 'private residence' right behind us was a hotel: the taxi driver had left us in front of suitable accommodation. We went inside and were told there was a twin room available at what appeared to be a very reasonable price, except they demanded payment in US dollars! The receptionist went on to explain that this was standard practice at every hotel in the city, so despite longing to lighten the load of our backpacks a little by spending some of our 'Monopoly' money, we each paid the $2 tariff and retired to our room for an early night.

The following morning we went out to explore the city and immediately I felt the foreignness of the place. Even though it was the capital of the largest country in Central America and home to a quarter of its population, Managua seemed to be almost deserted. There was very little traffic, and most of it was either military or public – East German IFA trucks full of soldiers and an occasional dilapidated bus, crammed almost to bursting-point with people hanging off from every available handhold. The few private vehicles that did pass us by all puttered along in clouds of smoke and were in such a state of disrepair that, in any country in the West, they would have only been considered usable in a demolition derby at the banger races.

The streets also lacked the traditional Latin American assemblage of impoverished hustlers and touts, vocally offering their services. In fact, there weren't even many commercial billboards. The only fresh paint in the city seemed to be the Dracula-cloak black and red political graffiti of the FSLN, the *Frente Sandinista*, which was spray-painted on any and every vertical surface.

We decided to visit the ancient ruins, which, in Managua, involved a stroll through the city centre, where the only structures left standing had been a cathedral and one or two government buildings. We had a late breakfast of cakes and Coca-Cola in *Parque Central*, seated on a crumbling wall in front of this cathedral and next to an unusual monument. It was unusual for two reasons: firstly, it was the only statue we'd seen so far that didn't feature a martyr holding a gun, and secondly, it appeared to be an art nouveau interpretation of a gigantic roll of toilet paper. This was something I thought quite appropriate in a country where this basic commodity was so scarce.

Early that afternoon, we boarded a train and made a 30-mile journey south-east to Granada. This city, nicknamed La Gran Sultana in reference to its Moorish namesake in Spain, was the oldest Spanish settlement in Nicaragua, originally founded by the *conquistadores* in 1524. It was a picturesque town situated on the north-west shores of Lake Nicaragua, and we found it came as a welcome relief to be in such pleasant surroundings after the 'twilight-zone' ambience of the capital.

From there we had considered travelling east, down the San Juan River, to visit the small town of Bluefields on the Caribbean Coast. Unfortunately, this required special government permission, which had become increasingly difficult to obtain due to the *contras* occasionally shooting at the ferry as it travelled through dense jungle down to the coast. In addition to this, we were somewhat reluctant to push our luck in that part of the world, since the memories of our previous visit to the Mosquito Coast in Costa Rica were still with us. Instead, we found accommodation at a hotel just off the central plaza, and after a few hours wandering the streets of a town with a distinctly colonial character, we decided to sample the nightlife.

On entering the local disco, we soon discovered that gringos almost instantly became the centre of attention amongst young Nicaraguans. Scott had to take the driving seat in communication in their native tongue, although one or two could speak English at a fairly competent level, so I wasn't completely excluded. It was an enjoyable evening that ended sooner than we had anticipated when the disco promptly closed at 10.30pm. But at least this made it easy for us to return home before the 11 o'clock curfew strictly enforced by the proprietor of our hotel.

The next morning we were woken by a young lad we'd met at the disco who had come to give us a guided tour of the town. We quickly got washed and dressed, and at the end of a more 'educational' circuit of the city, we saw him off to school, not before promising to write down the lyrics of the songs on a cassette of sixties American rock he'd left with us. As we parted company, I couldn't help finding it strange that a boy four or five years our junior should be so passionate about the music of our parents' record collections.

That evening we had yet another early night, then the following morning we made a four-hour boat trip to Omatepe, an island in the centre of Lake Nicaragua that had been formed by the eruptions of two volcanoes. After disembarking, we walked a mile and a half from the wharf to the village (it was an undeveloped island with no public transport) and got a cheap room at a homely little hotel that catered for the small number of visitors to Omatepe.

Once we'd settled in, we went to the hotel restaurant for dinner and met two Belgian guys, Johan and Manfred, who were over here on a voluntary aid programme. We all dined together, exchanging travel stories over the meal in the customary manner of backpackers becoming acquainted. Then during after-dinner drinks, Johan began reciting a fascinating encyclopaedia of information he had acquired about Nicaragua.

Two months earlier, this country had celebrated the eighth anniversary of the birth of *Nicaragua Libre*: the day the Sandinistas had marched into Managua forcing the utterly corrupt sleaze-ball Anastasio Somoza to flee to Paraguay, where he lived the life of a rich swine until somebody shot a bazooka through the window of his Mercedes limousine. His downfall had begun as a direct result of the earthquake in 1972, when almost all of the international aid that flooded into the country had gone directly into his pockets while thousands of his countrymen suffered and died. This had led to a steady build up of resentment and opposition that, seven years later, ended in revolution.

The government of the new Nicaragua was left without a penny in the national treasury and in possession of countless abandoned estates, making up over half the arable land of the country. Those landowners who had chosen to stay were permitted to keep their estates, but the remaining land was nationalized and turned into farming cooperatives managed along lines not dissimilar to those of the Soviet Union. This alarmed the US government, who had supported Somoza right up to the bitter end, and as soon as Ronald Reagan had taken office he suspended all US aid to the country and allocated $10 million for the formation and organization of the CIA trained *contras*.

Over the next few years, American intervention escalated. During the early eighties there had been an intensification of activity, particularly in the northern provinces along the Honduran border. This had resulted in a dramatic increase in the number of civilian deaths in this area, subsequently necessitating a programme of relocation for those peasants in the most dangerous areas. The previous year President Reagan had even approved a further $100 million-worth of *contra* aid, despite an International Court of Justice ruling that US aid to the counter-revolutionary forces was a violation of international law.

Johan went on to explain that the entire country, not only the north, was suffering due to US intervention, and the economic blockade had produced acute shortages in a never-ending list of essential commodities. A shipload of farming equipment sent by Oxfam America had been prevented from reaching the country, as had a shipment of Dutch cranes. IBM had been forced to withdraw all service facilities, thus compelling an already impoverished nation to change, at great expense, to another brand of computer. Even basic necessities such as beans were in short supply, which, in a Latin American country, was like not being able to find spaghetti in Italy!

It was a truly depressing collection of facts, and as I lay in bed that night I started to realize, for the first time on my travels, that I was in a place completely alien to anywhere I'd previously been. Until then I had only travelled through five countries on my world trip, my first journey outside Europe, and even though some of my experiences in the Caribbean and Costa Rica had been a tad out of the ordinary, they were nothing like this. Here it felt too different to even believe it was true. It was as if I were in the middle of a pulp-fiction spy story set in an imaginary socialist banana republic during an armed uprising. For the first time in my life, I began to feel totally cut off from the *real* world.

The next morning we were woken at dawn by the Belgians with an invitation to join them on a hike up one of the volcanoes. We breakfasted together on that classic Latin American menu of rice and beans, and then went to meet the guide they'd hired for this excursion. It was an enjoyable trek and I also noticed I'd learned a considerable amount about hiking through my experiences in Jamaica, though this time we didn't reach the 5,000-foot summit and chose to turn back at the line of clouds enveloping this peak. The descent was rather more tricky and both Manfred and Scott had one or two falls on the slippery smooth volcanic rock, but we still managed to return to the village before sunset without any serious injuries.

Early that evening we were told that a *fiesta* in the neighbouring village was just about to begin, so after dinner Johan and I decided to try and find it while the others stayed at the hotel to rest their weary limbs. We walked through the darkness for a mile or so until we happened upon a friendly local who gave us clear directions, then a little later we stumbled into the dimly lit, dusty village square, where we were readily invited to join the festivities.

It was a distinctly low-key affair, nothing like the hot Latin party I'd been anticipating, and the men seemed to outnumber women by about two to one. I thought this to be quite strange for a country in the middle of a civil war, but it wasn't the most unusual thing about this party. A quick recce revealed that there was no beer, spirits or alcohol of any description available, which was more than strange, it was almost unbelievable at a function organized by Latin Americans!

The lack of enlivening liquor and enough ladies to go round was an unfortunate combination. It had produced a *fiesta* that consisted of a large circle of men, patiently standing around a group of couples conservatively dancing to some very uninspiring salsa, all waiting for their chance to dance. However, just as Scott and I had found at the disco in Granada, it wasn't long before a small contingent of younger party-goers pounced on the two gringos and began bombarding us with questions about life in the outside world.

My Spanish was nowhere near adequate for such a task, but Johan seemed more than willing to take the role of 'tutor'. Unable to follow the conversation, I sat and watched their youthful faces, wide-eyed with excitement, while he told them about such unimaginable things as supermarket shelves stacked with food, record shops with all the latest releases, and teenagers, no older than themselves, with TVs and VCRs in their bedrooms and 50cc Hondas in the garage outside.

At one point I was briefly included in the discourse when one of them asked Johan to translate something for me. 'I think he must be quite impressed by your long hair and earrings,' he said.

'Why? What do you mean?'

'Well, he just told me to tell you that he thinks you look like John Lennon!'

'Oh, right, thanks . . . *gracias*,' I replied with a thumbs up gesture, although I would rather he'd compared me to a pop idol of my own generation than one from that of my parents.

The *fiesta* fizzled out very soon after ten so we said goodbye to our group of adolescent admirers and made our way back to the hotel. The following morning, Scott and I left our Belgian buddies to return to their duties and went down to the wharf to take the ferry back to the mainland. It was quite crowded, even by Nicaraguan standards, and we spent the entire crossing sitting on the roof of the wheel-house, which afforded good views but offered little protection from the fierce sunrays beating down overhead.

About half way across, the pilot made a sudden, dramatic U-turn, initially leaving both of us very confused. Then a few moments later I spotted the reason for his rapid change of course: he'd decided to chase a shark! Lake Nicaragua is not only the largest lake in Central America but also the only place on this planet where you can find freshwater sharks, so I guess our pilot didn't want his passengers to miss out on the opportunity of seeing one.

Upon arrival in Granada, we walked – or more correctly, *I* walked and due to his severe sunburn, *Scott* limped – up to the train station and we travelled back to Managua. On reaching the capital, we took a taxi straight to an establishment called Chepito's, having been told by Johan that it was the only hotel in the city that accepted local currency. We checked in, had refreshing showers and changed our clothes, and then went out for dinner at a 'restaurant' in the front room of the house opposite our accommodation. It had an economical menu (only 30 pence a head) including a soft drink and the additional surprise of a fried fly in your scrambled eggs.

In this eatery we were seated with an Australian lad who told us he had travelled down from the USA through Mexico, Guatemala, El Salvador and Honduras. It sounded like quite an impressive trip and was also one that we were about to commence along a reverse route, but what amazed me most was that he had managed to get this far, travelling alone, with a knowledge of Spanish that was even weaker than mine. Anything he said in this language was always pronounced with a broad Aussie twang, and whenever he didn't know the correct Spanish word (or words) in any given phrase, he would simply use the English equivalents in their place. Consequently, on being served with a plate of scrambled eggs and rice, he turned to the waitress, with a beaming white-toothed smile, and bellowed, 'Greycious, mate!'

The next day was spent in the capital, preparing for our journey north to the border. We went out to do some shopping and actually found a supermarket, the first we'd encountered since arriving in the country a week earlier. Scott was in desperate need of some shampoo, a product this retailer didn't have in stock at that time, but we were advised to try the Oriental Market, the largest market-place in the city.

Once we found it, we wandered for hours through the cavernous market sheds, past government-allotted stalls with government-fixed prices, all with very little merchandise on sale. In between these sheds, illegal vendors had set up rickety tables adorned with meagre mixes of over-ripe fruit and petite piles of rice and maize. There were others with crude kitchen utensils sculpted from scrap metal, and still others piled with old clothes and rags (though it was difficult to tell one from the other).

All of a sudden, Scott lost his patience and stormed off, leaving me in a state of confusion. Then as I looked around me, my bewilderment became even more intense. He had left me in front of a small man with thin hair and a pale face who was seated on the ground behind a pile of old screws, washers and 2-foot lengths of electrical cable. I stood there for quite some time, completely dumbfounded by his incomprehensible selection of 'products', until Scott finally returned with a bottle of shampoo tightly clasped in both hands.

That evening we dined at the 'fly food' restaurant across the street and then went to the cinema to see the latest Tom Cruise film to have reached Nicaragua. It was one that had probably been screened in the US several years earlier and had made such a poor impact that they hadn't even bothered to send it across the Atlantic. After the film we strolled back to Chepito's along deserted streets, silent save for the occasional roar of a distant bus or the barking of a stray dog. Then as we reached our accommodation, we decided to end the evening with a few beers at the local *cantina*.

We'd only just bought drinks and found some seats when suddenly I had to rush to the toilet, almost doubled up with acute stomach cramps. I nearly didn't make it there in time and my shorts hadn't even reached the floor before I was hit with a violent attack of 'Montezuma's revenge'. The subsequent feeling of relief was almost worth the discomfort that had preceded it . . . until I looked for the toilet paper! This was another product in very short supply and I sat there for a few long, silent, anxious minutes, wondering how I could overcome this complication.

Fortunately, I'm nothing if not resourceful. I retrieved my Spanish phrase book from the back pocket of my shorts and started pulling out pages from the appendix. Sadly, this was an insufficient amount for the job in hand so, not wanting to sacrifice a prized possession, I realized I would have to complete my ablutions with the only other material available. I opened my wallet, pulled out a wad of *córdobas* and began wiping my bottom on the face of Augusto César Sandino, Nicaragua's first national hero. In reality, due to the devalued currency of a nation with 500% inflation, this treacherous act of 'treason' cost no more than a couple of pence, considerably less than a visit to a public toilet in the UK.

We started our second week in Nicaragua with a three-hour train ride to León, the first town on a route we'd mapped out to the northern border. Upon arrival we initially had trouble finding a hotel with a twin room available, but on entering the reception of Hotel América we were told they had exactly what we needed. The surprise came when we enquired about the price. It cost an extortionate $3.25, almost three times more than we'd paid anywhere else apart from our first night in the capital. It wasn't until we saw this room that we understood why. It was large and clean, equipped with a spluttering air-conditioner, and had an en suite bathroom complete with half a roll of toilet paper and a soiled, threadbare hand towel – five-star luxury by Nicaraguan standards.

León was an interesting town filled with monuments to the revolution, walls of Sandinista murals and buildings that were riddled with bullet holes. The architecture was decidedly colonial and there were numerous Spanish-style houses with red-tile roofs, whitewashed stucco walls and thick wooden doors.

We decided to spend the afternoon wandering its cobbled streets but we got off to a very slow start. We'd hardly walked more than a couple of blocks before we were stopped by a group of soldiers for an identity check. I still hadn't adapted to the Nicaraguan way of life and had forgotten to take my passport with me, but they let Scott run back and fetch it while I waited with them in silence.

Eventually, he returned and we were permitted to continue on our way, so we went to find the largest cathedral in Central America. It had mistakenly been built in this town due to a geographical mix up made by the Catholic Church in Spain. They had thought they were building this immense edifice of worship in León, a large town in Mexico, except a breakdown in communication had resulted in it being built in León, a small town in a little-known, obscure, Central American country.

When we arrived we discovered that it *was* extremely large for a building in this part of the world, though architecturally quite ugly. Even so, it did have one redeeming feature: the tomb of the dead poet Rubén Dario, known as 'The Prince of Spanish-American Literature'. Poetry was Nicaragua's most beloved of the arts and everyone here was considered a poet until proved otherwise, so I accepted that it wasn't through the eyes that one should try and see the beauty of this building.

The following morning we'd planned to take a train to Chinandega, the next town on our route north. Unfortunately, the trains weren't running that day so we went back to the town centre to find alternative transport. After lunch we took a two-hour bus trip on an over-packed, rust-ridden vehicle, so full that we were forced to stand in the stairwell with Scott hanging out of an open doorway. It was our first experience of bus travel in Nicaragua but, unbeknown to us at that time, we were to become far more familiar with this form of transport the following day.

Although smaller than León, Chinandega seemed to be rather more lively with fewer memories of the revolution and a greater emphasis on fun. Once we'd organized accommodation, a short walk revealed three discos, two record shops and an above average number of bars for a Nicaraguan town of its size. The abundance of entertainment venues produced the prospect of a lively final night in this country, since we planned to cross the border into Honduras the next day and needed to spend the remains of our local currency before leaving. It was impossible to change Nicaraguan *córdobas* back into American dollars, or into any other currency for that matter.

We started the evening with a pleasant meal at the hotel restaurant. Then seeing as we'd decided the best way to lighten our wallets would be through severe exposure to the night-life, we went out to one of the nightclubs we had seen earlier that day. It was fairly crowded for a Thursday night and the music wasn't too bad, but as we'd repeatedly found in this country, it had the atmosphere of a 'school disco'.

The Nicaraguan government enforced a two-year military service that commenced on reaching the age of sixteen. Those fortunate enough to survive this obligatory tour of duty, tended to go on and start families almost immediately, thus forfeiting those fun-filled years of carefree clubbing. As a result, the clientele of virtually every Nicaraguan disco was made up of innocent adolescents, the boys grouped to one side and the girls to the other, all whispering, giggling and pointing whilst trying to drum up the courage to ask someone for a dance.

Nevertheless, I was amazed to find that these young lads were very passionate about break-dancing, a thing that had only recently reached this part of the world. I had spent my teens as a choreographer and dancer in a break-dance crew, so I decided to see if I could still put together a few of the old moves. I impressed myself as much as I did the locals, which amplified our 'celebrity' status as gringos quite considerably and I decided to celebrate with a round of drinks for my fellow back-spinning body-poppers.

On reaching the bar, I was told that the disco had sold out of beer but this didn't come as any great surprise. It was such a common occurrence here that Scott and I had begun to consider the name of Nicaragua's national brew as very appropriate. It was called 'Cerveza Victoria' and reminded us of our schoolboy English literature classes when we'd studied the George Orwell classic *Nineteen Eighty-Four*, a novel about a totalitarian state where the only ale available was called 'Victory Beer'. However, our new friends solved this problem by ordering a popular local cocktail: a mix of rum and coke with a slice of lemon – a drink *they* called *Nica Libre*.

We had little time to enjoy our brief moment of 'fame' because *this* disco closed at ten, and we reluctantly returned to our hotel feeling as if we were in a country governed by over-protective parents. This feeling was intensified on reaching our accommodation, when we had to ring the bell to get someone to open the door, seeing as all the other residents had already gone to bed.

After another early night, we awoke at daybreak, packed up and took a two-hour ride in a sweaty, overcrowded, rust-bucket of a bus to the border town. And it was quite a gruelling journey. We spent the entire trip standing in the aisle, our bodies tightly pressed against those of other passengers not lucky enough to get seats, but at least our European stature permitted a view over their heads of the passing scenery.

Along the way we saw many road-signs punctured with bullet holes and I began to notice a distinct difference in the architecture of peasants' homes in the northern provinces. In this part of the country they were built along the principle of a 'sandwich': walls made of concrete from ground level to waist height, then wood for the remaining sections up to a tin roof. It was an economical yet clever design that prevented the *contras* from setting fire to the roofs or shooting the occupants through the walls as they lay sleeping.

Upon arrival in Sometillo, a village about two miles from the border with Honduras, we asked the bus driver which way we needed to go in order to cross this border. Despite appearing a little confused, he simply raised his left hand and pointed straight ahead, and in reality directions weren't really necessary because Sometillo was nothing more than a one-street town. We climbed off the bus, shouldered our backpacks and started walking down this dusty street.

It was a warm, clear, sunny morning; the perfect day for a stroll in the countryside. First we passed by a row of houses with old men sitting on the steps and women moving in and out of doorways, happily returning their friendly greetings of, '*Buenos días*'. Then the village quickly gave way to countryside and we continued hiking on, past scraggy palms and an occasional pig snoozing in the shade, chatting about the special time we'd spent in this troubled country. Our visit hadn't been without problems due to the many shortages and government restrictions, and this had left me unable to characterize Nicaragua. I couldn't decide if it was a 'Colombia' anaesthetized by communism or a 'Czechoslovakia' spiced up with salsa bands.

As we reminisced about all the characters we'd met along the way, we suddenly became aware that we were no longer alone. We came to an abrupt halt because our path was being blocked some 20 yards ahead by four soldiers in full combat gear, all with AK-47s levelled at our heads. A few moments later, several more soldiers appeared out of the brush to our left and right, also in camouflage fatigues and with weapons in hand, and a brief glance over my shoulder revealed we'd been completely surrounded.

This was such an unexpected and shocking state of affairs that we just stood there, frozen in our tracks, with absolutely no idea of what we were supposed to do. Following several lengthy seconds of silence, Scott slowly turned to me with a look of distracted abandon on his face while the soldier closest to him nervously fingered his gun.

'W– what do we do now?' he whispered.

'I don't– I don't know,' I replied, 'but I think it comes down to a simple choice really: get busy living or get busy dying. I mean, I think we'd better try and make friends with these blokes.'

'Yeah . . . er . . . OK. *Buenos días*,' he mumbled in a faltering voice.

'*Buenos días*,' replied one of the soldiers, a spade-bearded man with a shrewd grin.

'We're on our way to Honduras,' explained Scott, his confidence building a little and also affording me a limited sense of relief that he'd managed to find the courage to try and take control of the situation.

'But the border crossing is closed,' replied the soldier.

'Oh, I see, and what time does it open?' asked Scott, briefly glancing at his watch.

'It's been closed for five years. You're in a military war zone!'

'A war zone!' repeated Scott, unsure if he had understood this soldier's surprising revelation.

'Yes, a war zone. Civilians are not permitted to enter this area.'

'Really! Bloody hell! We didn't know. So where *can* we cross the border?'

'It's only open in one town, a place called Somoto.'

'Where's that?'

'About 50 kilometres east of here.'

'How can we get there from here?'

'You can't! The whole area between here and there is a war zone,' replied the soldier with another shrewd smile.

'So what can we do?' asked Scott in desperation.

'You have to go back to Managua and take the Pan American Highway.'

'But we thought *this* was the Pan American Highway.'

'This?' laughed the soldier. 'No, this little country road isn't the Pan American Highway.'

This was the moment when we realized that, in addition to being outdated, our guidebook also had an incorrect map. No wonder the bus driver and villagers had appeared surprised to see us hiking out of town in a northerly direction. It was just a pity they'd neglected to mention we were entering an area where the counter-revolutionary forces had been so active that the government had evacuated all civilians.

Scott briefly translated the pertinent details of our predicament to me and then turned back to the soldier to apologize for our faux pas. After accepting the apology, this soldier said something that made all of his 'comrades' instantly burst out laughing.

'What did he say?' I asked, becoming nervous due to this unexpected display of frivolity.

'He said we were lucky they found us,' replied Scott.

'Why?'

'Because you're wearing khaki shorts and you've got a khaki backpack. These guys are Sandinistas but if the *contras* had found us, it might have ended a bit differently.'

We bade them farewell and started back the way we had come, although two soldiers were assigned to escort us as far as the village. Then we walked past the same elderly residents, all still seated on their doorsteps, and received the same friendly greetings of, '*Buenos días*,' though I couldn't help feeling that they, too, had somehow been a party to the *contra* joke. Next we boarded the same bus that had brought us here some 20 minutes earlier and began the journey back to the capital. In Chinandega we changed to another equally dilapidated bus, and on reaching León we discovered we'd arrived 15 minutes late for the last train to Managua, which meant taking yet another bus. The air in this one was like steam but every window was closed, making the smell unbearable, and by the time we had reached the capital I was dizzy and soaked with sweat.

During this arduous journey, we had both agreed that once we reached Managua we would go straight to the airport and fly to Guatemala City. If there weren't any flights that evening we would simply sleep at the airport – a thing I'd done a few times in the past without any problems – and take the first flight the next morning. We just couldn't face another bus ride in Nicaragua.

When we eventually arrived in the capital we were very tired and hungry. That day should have been our last in this country so we'd only had sufficient funds for bus fares and had subsequently gone for several hours without food or drink. But even though we'd spent all our Nicaraguan *córdobas*, I had a few dollars in cash and we used some of these to pay for a taxi to Augusto C Sandino Airport.

By the time we reached the airport it was just after seven in the evening and we soon discovered that the next flight to Guatemala City didn't leave until five the following afternoon. Our frustration was increased when we learned that it cost a staggering $135. Then to end the 'perfect' day, we were also informed that the airport was about to close for the night, thus making it impossible for us to sleep there.

This was as much as Scott could stand and on seeing the intense look of despair on his face, I realized it was my turn to take control. I told him we could use the few remaining dollars I had in cash to take a taxi to Chepito's, where I felt sure they would accept a passport as a deposit until we changed some money at a bank the next day. My plan appeared to calm him down, so we went outside and hailed a taxi.

In a matter of seconds, a cab pulled up in front of us and Scott leaned through the open window to tell the driver where we were going and that we wanted to pay with American dollars. We offered him $2, which was all I had left in single dollar bills but was also more than generous seeing as dollars were worth a fortune on the black market. He immediately refused our offer and asked for $5, an exorbitant amount of money for the distance we wanted to travel. I tried to bargain with him but he wouldn't give in and by then I, too, had reached my breaking point. I told him exactly what I thought of him, picked up my backpack and stormed off.

As I stomped down the road I could hear him behind me, revving his engine, and a moment later he pulled up alongside me. But despite expecting a torrent of verbal abuse in Spanish, I was surprised to hear him offer a price of $4, then $3 and ultimately $2.

A ten-minute taxi ride took us to Chepito's and we prepared to face the final hurdle: negotiating a night's accommodation. On reaching the steps to the entrance, I recognized a familiar face and told Scott to wait while I said hello to someone I knew. Luckily, the Sweaty Sock remembered me from Key West, and once I'd explained our predicament he instantly opened his wallet. Finally, something had gone in our favour that day. We had enough money to pay for a room and a meal, and then a refreshing shower was all we required in preparation for a good night's sleep.

The next morning we went out to change some money but, unfortunately, a $50 bill was the smallest denomination I had left in cash. This was significantly more than we needed to change so we first went to the Managua Intercontinental Hotel – an ugly pyramid of 'wedding-cake' architecture that had gone wrong. In the reception, we successfully managed split the fifty into two twenties and a ten, and then went in search of a bank.

At the first one we tried, they told us if we wanted to change American dollars we needed to go to another that was a couple of blocks away. At that bank we were instructed to go to one in the Plaza España, and things started to become a little urgent because all banks closed at eleven on Saturdays. On finding this one we were told to go to yet another, the only bank in the city that had a machine for checking if dollar bills were authentic. In the end, we were able to change a $10 bill and returned to Chepito's to pay our debts and go to the airport.

Nevertheless, during a brief chat with the Sweaty Sock we learned that he'd entered Nicaragua from Honduras, just a few days earlier, at the border crossing in Somoto. He said that this checkpoint was definitely open and his obvious conviction that we would have no problems crossing there forced us to reconsider our plans. Despite our horrendous bus journeys the previous day, budget took precedence over comfort and we knew a bus ticket was what we would be buying. But this presented a new problem. To travel overland we needed to change some more money and by then the banks had already closed. Consequently, the only option available was to try and change dollars on the black market. Nothing was easy in Nicaragua.

Our friends at Chepito's told us we would find illegal money-changers at the Oriental Market, so we took a bus there and began looking for a suitable 'accomplice'. After a short time we saw a guy who was selling lottery tickets and agreed that he could be a possible candidate. His teeth were bad, he needed a shave, his clothes looked like they came from Oxfam and he had fistfuls of banknotes.

We strolled over and initiated a conversation with him but rapidly sensed that something wasn't right and made a hasty retreat. However, he quickly followed us and once he'd caught up he said that he *was* a moneychanger. This came as a great relief and after brief negotiations we managed to change $20 at 10,000 *córdobas* to the dollar, not the best black-market rate though still 1,500 higher than the official one.

Next we took a taxi to the central station to get information about buses to Somoto. We were told to come back at nine the following morning to buy tickets for a bus that would leave in the afternoon. At long last, we could see the light at the end of the tunnel and we started to feel that it wouldn't be too much longer before we could leave Nicaragua.

Early the next morning, we purchased bus tickets without any problems and decided to celebrate with a meal at McDonald's – in spite of all the US trade embargoes, they actually had a McDonald's franchise in Nicaragua! The Swedish guys in the adjacent room joined us and we all had an enjoyable time, exchanging travel tales over meals that consisted of Big Macs, French fries and soft drinks in plastic beakers that had to be returned to the counter when we finished dining.

After lunch we returned to Chepito's, packed our things and went to catch the bus. We had a trouble-free trip to Somoto, where we got a room for the night, and then the following morning, on the 365th day of my world trip, we finally crossed the border.

'So, I guess that was a bit of a relief,' said Nick.

'Why? What do you mean?'

'Well, after all this time in hospital, you don't want people to think you've started going crazy and you can't remember who they are.'

'No, Nick, she didn't think I was going crazy. I think she just realized I was genuinely surprised to receive a call from her.'

'Oh, right. And a nice surprise like that makes all the difference when you're stuck in here, doesn't it?'

'Yeah, I suppose that's true,' I agreed. Then as I lay back on my bed, I started to think that maybe the worst was over. My time in hospital was coming to an end. I was on the border of going home.

16 *Beach Bag*

Although my father had started administering his course of physio-therapy four days earlier, I'd now been deemed fit enough to begin my formal hospital rehabilitation. They had removed the stitches the previous day and I was ready to receive a course of treatment from a qualified physiotherapist. My friend Manel had visited me that morning and told me that someone from his department would be coming after lunch with a machine designed to exercise a knee joint. This was very good news and made me feel I was another step closer to going home.

As promised, early that afternoon a lady arrived with a strange-looking contraption, which she placed on the bed alongside my left leg. Then, foregoing the usual pleasantries, she simply announced, 'It's time to begin your rehabilitation.'

I watched in silence while she got herself organized, a task performed with a cold efficiency that gave the impression she would rather have been elsewhere. A few moments later she said there was a problem with the electrical supply of the machine. Her somewhat terse explanation left me a little unsure if she was going to get an extension lead or an adapter, though I understood she would return shortly.

'Well, I think I'll leave you to it,' my father said just after she'd left the room.

'Yeah, sure, there's no point in hanging around. I mean, you've already done *your* bit. You got me this far, didn't you?'

'No, it's not that. It's just that I don't want to get in the way, that's all,' he explained. 'I think I'll go out and join Nick on the balcony for a chat and a smoke.'

'OK, I'll see you a bit later then.'

'Yeah, I'll come back in half an hour or so,' he said, giving my shoulder a gentle squeeze. Then he turned towards the door but just before leaving he added, 'And make sure you let her know when you reach an eight on our scale, won't you?'

'Yeah, don't worry, Pops. I'll let her know exactly how much pain I'm in.'

A couple of minutes later the physiotherapist returned with an adapter in her hand. She plugged the machine in and made a few adjustments, presumably to calibrate it to the length of my leg but it was difficult to tell since she made no attempt to explain anything. Then once everything appeared satisfactory, she lifted my leg, slid the machine into position beneath it and said that we were ready to make a start.

This machine consisted of a footpad at one end that was connected to other end by two horizontal pistons. Underneath my knee there was a small bar between these pistons that would be forced to rise when they contracted, thus causing the knee joint to bend. This mechanism was controlled by a hand-held dial which regulated the contraction of the pistons, therefore allowing you to choose the degree of flexion. The basic principle was the same as the treatment my father had been administering, except he'd used a rolled up hand-towel in place of the small bar, his arms had done the job of the pistons and our scale of one to ten had 'regulated' the degree of flexion.

Before we started I already felt quite uncomfortable, perhaps a three or four on our scale, but I simply assumed this was because my leg was now in a slightly different position. However, the moment she turned the hand-held dial, I wished I had spoken sooner. An intense pain shot through my leg at a level that was way off our scale and all I could do was scream. It was so severe that I couldn't even begin to explain that something had to be wrong. A scream was the only sound that would pass my lips.

'Don't be such a baby,' she said as the machine brought my leg back to horizontal.

'No! No! I can't! I can't!' I sobbed but then, to my horror, she turned the dial again.

This time tears began flooding down my cheeks and it's the only time I remember ever crying as a result of physical pain throughout my entire accident experience.

By then she'd started to realize that maybe I was a bit uncomfortable. With a look of contempt spread across her face, she put the dial down and lifted my leg out of the machine. Then she placed it on the floor under the bed and promptly got up and left without saying another word.

While I lay there, alone and still crying, my whole body began trembling in an uncontrollable spasm as the pain continued to throb through my leg. My vision became hazy, making me think I was about to lose consciousness, and more than anything I wished my father were with me.

'Are you OK?' came a voice from somewhere to my right.

I slowly turned my head and saw an elderly Spanish lady standing in the doorway. She must have been passing my room on her way to visit another patient and had stopped on hearing the sound of sobbing.

'No– I– no,' I stuttered in an effort to reply.

As she moved closer, her expression of concern told me that she understood I was in agony. Unable to talk, I raised my right hand and she immediately responded by taking it in hers and began caressing it gently whilst softly whispering words of comfort. I started to cry even harder, though this was more in response to her warm-hearted kindness than the result of any pain I was feeling. It was as if the touch of her hand on mine somehow drew the discomfort from my body.

I don't know how long I held her hand . . .

. . . but at that moment it was the only thing I could do. I quickly forgot the pain of my recent injuries and simply tried to reassure her as best I could.

'Don't worry, Christie,' I whispered. 'It'll be all right.'

'But I had everything in that bag,' she sobbed.

'Don't worry, please don't worry. Believe me, we'll be able to sort it out.'

However, as we sat there on the moonlit beach in silence, I began to wonder if it really would be that easy to solve the multitude of problems that had suddenly been imposed on us through a brief moment of negligence. I felt it was such a shame to be so unlucky on the penultimate day of a glorious two-week stay here, on Viti Levu, the main island of the South Pacific Republic of Fiji.

It's a beautiful island with a pleasant tropical climate and is populated with an interesting mix of people. About half of the inhabitants are indigenous Fijians whereas the other half are Indians, mostly fourth-generation descendants of the indentured labourers who were imported to Fiji during British colonial days to work on the sugar plantations. But the equal balance between these two remarkably different racial groups was a very recent change in the cultural make-up of the country. For nearly 50 years the indigenous people of Fiji represented an ethnic minority in their own land. Then on May 14th 1987, just over a year before Christie and I arrived, the Indian dominated government had been overthrown in a bloodless military coup.

During the preceding months, many Indian-owned businesses had been petrol-bombed and there had been violent attacks on Indian communities. It was another chapter in Fiji's chequered history, a country where racial segregation continued into the second half of the twentieth century and a law still applied that prevented land ownership by anyone who wasn't native Fijian. Upon the abolition of indentured labour in 1919, this law forced the Indian community to move from agriculture into business holdings, trade and bureaucracy, where their innate business acumen eventually led to a significant strengthening of economic and political power. The indigenous Fijians subsequently began to perceive this as a threat to their landholdings, and resentment coalesced around the *Taukei* movement, leading to the violent attacks and a military coup.

Yet in spite of all the recent civil unrest, Fiji still appeared to be a wondrous tropical haven in the eyes of a visitor on its shores for the first time. I also found it didn't take me long to develop an affection for the very affable, laid-back, native Fijians, whereas the Indians a tourist came into contact with could be rather tiresome due to their almost incessant desire to make money.

We spent our first two days there at a resort just a few miles south of Nadi, the third largest town in Fiji and home to its international

211

airport as well as being the principle tourist centre. It wasn't the most attractive part of the island, set in a barren landscape against a mountainous backdrop on the west coast of Viti Levu, but it was a popular first-stop on the backpacking circuit. Upon arrival, we had taken a courtesy bus to the Seashell Cove resort, where the facilities included a campground, a swimming pool and a bar that boasted the best 'happy hour' on the island.

Once we'd pitched our tent, we prepared an evening meal over a camp-fire and dined under the stars next to a moonlit sea that gently swayed back and forth. Then we decided it was time to sample the infamous 'happy hour' and made our way to the bar, situated among a cluster of South-Pacific-style cabins rented by those tourists travelling on a more mid-range budget.

On entering this appealing little tavern, we found it to be crowded with numerous Aussies, Brits and Americans. They were all engrossed in excited conversations punctuated with bursts of raucous laughter, and virtually everyone had large brown bottles of Fiji Beer in hand. Just before reaching the bar, we suddenly saw the source of all this revelry: frog races! In the centre of a wild group of rollicking merrymakers, there was a long table decked out with a racetrack of about half a dozen lanes, and through this frenzied mob I could just make out one or two of the slimy, green-backed competitors as they hopped their way towards the finish line. This weekly 'sports' event was obviously a big crowd-puller, and judging from those spectators who were screaming the loudest, it also involved betting.

We bought a couple of half-priced drinks and then almost instantly found ourselves 'adopted' by a family of blond-haired, bronzed Californians. It appeared that the parents, clothed in tie-dyed T-shirts and wrap-around sarongs, were still living in the sixties and probably looked much older than they wanted to. In contrast, their teenaged son was sporting the trendy surf labels of his generation and I also concluded that all three of them had begun practising hand-to-mouth skills with the local brew quite some time earlier that day.

'So, you guys just arrived then?' asked the mother, a woman who had the kind of face that said one eye was remembering while the other was looking towards the future.

'Yeah, just flown in from Hawaii,' replied Christie.

'Hawaii! Rode some killer swells there last year, man!' exclaimed the father with an excitement that made his unkempt, greying pony-tail quiver, though I noticed the tresses that were long at the back had virtually disappeared on top. 'So, you guys from Hawaii then?'

'No, I'm from Montana and Steve is from England.'

'Cool! Did you here that?' he said, turning to his son. 'We got a guy here from London!'

They went on to explain that they had come over for a surfing vacation – there were one or two good surf breaks here, although you needed to take a boat to the offshore, fringing reefs in order to ride them – but unfortunately Air New Zealand had lost their surfboards en route, thus leaving them with nothing to do . . . except drink. We only stayed with them for a couple of beers and then retired to our tent for an early night, feeling very tired at the end of a long day's travel.

As I was drifting off to sleep that night, I reflected on the journey I'd just completed. This was the first time since I started travelling that I'd flown somewhere new without feeling nervous. Backpacking is very different to a package holiday; nothing is planned, nothing is confirmed. When you reach your destination, there aren't any holiday reps at the airport waiting to whisk you off to your hotel whilst talking you through a two-week itinerary of activities and excursions. You have to organize everything for yourself, solve each problem as it arises.

But this was the first time I'd taken a flight with somebody else. I'd had travelling companions overland before, but never anyone seated beside me when a plane began its approach to a place I only knew as a name on a map. This time I'd been with Christie, and while enjoying her company immensely I felt I'd missed out on that gut-churning feeling just before arrival that somehow made me feel so alive.

After a second night at the Seashell Cove, we awoke early as a salt mist came up from the ocean giving the air a crisp and healthy smell. We had a quick breakfast and then packed up our things in preparation for a 30-mile bus trip to a town called Sigatoka. On reaching this farming community, we did some shopping at the local produce market and then took a taxi to the southern coast, an enormous expanse of sand dunes.

From the coastal roadway we started a long and demanding hike across this undulating landscape, struggling with heavy backpacks and bags full of shopping while a fierce white glare came off the dunes, forcing us to squint. Following an hour of strenuous physical exertion, we finally stumbled over a sand bluff that dropped off sharply to a virgin beach with sand as white as salt and soft as flour: Kulukulu Beach.

Our plan was to spend a few peaceful days of solitude on this strikingly beautiful beach, yet less than ten minutes after we'd set up camp a little Indian boy appeared. He said his name was Bobby, told us he was the son of the taxi driver who'd brought us here and asked if there was anything we needed. We told him we'd done our shopping before taking the taxi – but thanked him for his concern – and then waited for him to leave. We presumed he had fulfilled his father's request to see if there was any more money to be made from the two tourists, yet much to our surprise and annoyance he simply sat down on the sand and made himself comfortable.

He stayed with us until well after dark and would only leave when we finally managed to persuade him it was time for us to go to bed. Then at daybreak the next morning, I unzipped the tent flap to find him snoozing on the sand, right outside the door! This was more than my patience could withstand, particularly in the light of the intimate act Christie and I had just shared not two feet from his dozing head. I woke him up and with as much self-restraint as I could muster, I politely asked him to leave because we needed to bathe ourselves. He complied without complaint, though returned less than half an hour later and once again remained at our sides until sundown.

We had initially planned to spend four or five days on Kulukulu Beach, but 48 hours with our little Indian 'chaperone' was the limit of our endurance. We recommenced our journey along the south coast and spent the next couple of days at a very comfortable backpackers' hostel that was a little out of the ordinary. It was situated on the waterfront and the accommodation comprised a collection of attractive bungalows that provided guests with the partial privacy of a four-bedded dormitory and their own lounge, kitchen, bathroom and patio.

Our next stop was Suva, the capital of Fiji. It's one of the South Pacific's largest and most sophisticated cities, and during the nineteenth century it was a major centre of trade. As a result, there are many colonial-era buildings that contrast with numerous Hindu temples and Muslim mosques, giving the city a distinctly multicultural ambience. Even so, we only stayed there for two nights because we were still looking for what we had hoped to find on Kulukulu Beach. We wanted to get a bit closer to nature.

Consequently, we decided to visit one of the islands off the east coast of Viti Levu. An island named Ovalau was the most popular amongst backpackers but we thought it might be too developed and instead chose a smaller one further to the north called Naranu-i-Ra. We'd read that this island was very sparsely inhabited and had no shopping facilities of any description, so we first went to a supermarket and bought enough supplies to see us through a few days on a 'desert island'. Then we boarded a bus and began our journey around the east coast.

This bus took us on a five-hour drive through a luxuriant landscape of tropical rain forests, the complete reverse of the scenery at our point of arrival on the other side of the island. It was also quite a demanding ride. Despite the luscious vistas, the bus continually jolted in ruts, potholes and deep stagnant puddles while bouncing us up and down on a hard and unyielding wooden seat. Obviously, the roads on this part of the island had yet to be improved to a standard suitable for vehicles of this size.

After a very late lunch, we changed to a smaller bus and travelled to Voli Voli, the northern-most village on Viti Levu. We arrived just in time to see a beautiful, deep orange sunset, and then boarded a fishing boat for the final leg of our journey to the Kon Tiki resort on Naranu-i-Ra.

As we came ashore, an ageing, grey-haired hippie from New Zealand strolled out of the darkness and introduced himself as George, the proprietor of this low-budget beach resort. He showed us to our accommodation, which consisted of a petite thatched-roof hut, and then gave us a brief tour of his estate. It was an appealing jumble of cabins amidst an undulating grove of coconut palms, hammocks swinging between many of them, and the amenities included a clean shower room and a well-equipped kitchen, all at the very reasonable price of $3 a night.

It had been a long and tough day's travel so we freshened up, had a quick meal and went straight to bed for a well-earned rest. But even though both of us were extremely tired, we'd hardly had a chance to fall asleep before we were roused by a strange noise coming from somewhere in our hut. Struggling to control my feelings of frustration and annoyance, I got up to investigate and discovered that a mouse was nibbling through the contents of our food bag. Fortunately, I managed to evict this uninvited guest without too much trouble and we were finally able to get the sleep we so desperately needed.

We spent four days on this island and in many ways it was the highlight of our stay on Fiji. It couldn't quite offer the solitude we'd hoped to find on Kulukulu Beach, but this resort was far from crowded and had a very homely atmosphere. We also found a beach hidden on the opposite side of the island that the other guests seemed reluctant to frequent. This was quite surprising, since there was a fantastic colourful reef just 40 yards offshore, where we snorkelled every day, but at least this provided us with an element of exclusivity. Our evenings were spent relaxing in a hammock, chatting with other travellers and drinking a sufficient amount of Fiji Beer to guarantee a good night's sleep, with or without uninvited mice. And to add to our contentment, there weren't any annoying little Indian boys shadowing our every move.

Unfortunately, our days in this tropical paradise passed far too quickly. It soon became time to leave, so we reluctantly began the trip back to Nadi, repeating our original route, only this time in reverse.

When we had almost completed this journey we decided to spend our penultimate night on Natandola Beach, in spite of a warning in our guidebook that said it was inadvisable to camp there due to thefts by local villagers. We arrived just after lunch, and once we'd set up camp we spent the afternoon swimming and sunbathing, enjoying our final taste of the tropics before taking a flight to New Zealand.

It was another stunning beach, which didn't seem at all threatening until the late slant of sun turned the palm fronds a green-gold colour and the locals started returning to their village. We attracted quite a lot of attention from them as they wandered along the dusty road that bordered the beach, and one or two even came over to warn us of the dangers of camping there.

Eventually, after sundown, we agreed that it might be safer if we moved to the other end of the beach. That way we would be a lot further from the village and less conspicuous to the locals. We had almost finished packing up and were struggling to get the tent back into its bag when a young lad suddenly emerged from the bushes close by. He immediately grabbed Christie's knapsack, which was sitting on top of her backpack, and then disappeared into the obscurity of the trees.

I frantically set off in hot pursuit but by then it was quite dark and I had great difficulty seeing him. In addition to this, I also had another disadvantage. I was barefoot and unlike the shoeless robber, whose thick-skinned feet were accustomed to such terrain, I soon discovered that running over broken branches, rocks and stones was extremely painful. After a very short time, the soles of my feet became cut and bruised and these injuries quickly brought me to a halt.

Once I had given up my chase, I suddenly realized that I'd left Christie alone on the beach. I had no idea if our thief was a one-man operation or if, at this very moment, a group of his accomplices were helping themselves to the rest of our possessions while she watched in terror, powerless to stop them. Ignoring the discomfort of my lamed feet, I hurried back and to my immense relief I found her sitting on the sand between our two backpacks on a deserted beach.

However, this image stopped me in my tracks for a moment. Although it clearly *was* Christie sat there, she looked so different. She had lost that wild, sensual air that had initially attracted me to her when we'd first met on Hawaii almost five months earlier. I couldn't believe it was the same girl I'd watched boldly fend off the occasional amorous advance from a male patron of the bar where she worked, but always with a lively wit that would avoid offence or humiliation. All that confidence seemed to have disappeared. Now she looked so weak, afraid and insecure . . . almost childlike.

I ran over and knelt down beside her, then took her hand in mine and tried to comfort and reassure her as best I could.

'Don't worry, Christie,' I whispered. 'It'll be all right.'

'But I had everything in that bag,' she sobbed.

'Don't worry, please don't worry. Believe me, we'll be able to sort it out.'

'No, Steve!' she cried. 'I had my passport, my traveller's cheques and my ticket in that knapsack!'

'It's alright, really, just try and calm down. Tickets and traveller's cheques can easily be replaced and we'll go to the American Embassy in Suva and get you a new passport. It'll just delay us a bit, that's all. Please believe me,' I begged but she didn't reply.

As we sat on the moonlit beach in silence, I couldn't help thinking that, in truth, we really did have some major problems. And the most immediate of these was finding a safer place to spend the night. It was a backpacker's nightmare – losing money, traveller's cheques, a plane ticket and more importantly, a passport containing visas – and it had happened without the possibility of even being able to return to the safety of a hostel or a hotel room. My own depression left me unable to find any more words of reassurance and I looked up into the clear night sky feeling completely helpless.

'I love the stars,' I mumbled, giving voice to a private thought. 'There's no right or wrong in them; they're just there.'

'What was that?'

'I said I love–'

'No, I meant that noise,' said Christie in a voice that was quivering with fear.

Suddenly, I heard the rustle of someone in the bushes behind us. Just as I turned round to investigate, an object came flying through the air towards us and landed on the sand no more than a few feet to our right. Then a few seconds later, a boy ran out of a nearby cluster of trees and off towards the village.

We both stared at this object, stunned into silence: it was Christie's bag! For some strange reason, the thief had returned the spoils of his crime and my immediate response was one of gratitude. 'Thanks,' I shouted as he disappeared into the darkness.

Christie briefly sifted through of the contents of her knapsack and found that the only things missing were a camera, a personal stereo and a penknife. We'd been robbed by a thief with a conscience. He had taken the things he could use or sell but had realized that the other documents were important and had returned them rather than dump the bag in a bush somewhere. Being robbed is not something anyone wants to happen, yet that night I couldn't help feeling at least mildly lucky that it had happened to us in the way that it had.

Even though the majority of our problems had vanished just as quickly as they'd appeared, we still needed to find a safer place to spend the night. After Christie had cleaned the cuts and grazes on the soles of my feet and stuck a few plasters over the deepest ones, we finished packing up and began hiking up the beach. It took almost half an hour to reach the other end, where we set up camp again, but we still felt very nervous and we knew it wouldn't be easy to sleep that night.

While we sat there in front of our tent, chatting about trivialities in an effort to ignore our anxiety, we saw four young lads walking past us at the water's edge. Instantly, we became filled with apprehension, believing them to be another band of thieves, and our agitation was heightened when two of them turned back and started heading straight towards us. Yet once they'd reached our tent, they politely asked if they could sit with us and talk.

These two boys were Indian, which was a little reassuring in one sense. The nearby village was native Fijian – segregation laws no longer applied but rural communities were still exclusively one race or the other – and the boy who had robbed us was one of its inhabitants. Following a few minutes of very edgy conversation, we began to relax and told them the story of our recent untimely encounter. On hearing this story they seemed truly shocked and concerned, so much so that one of them offered to let us stay at his house for the night. In fact, it wasn't an offer, he *insisted*. He claimed that this stretch of beach was particularly dangerous and gave several accounts of other travellers' misfortunes in an attempt to convince us it was the right thing to do. He even told us that a few backpackers had stayed at his house after being robbed, and eventually our distrust started to diminish. In the end, we accepted his offer and began packing up again.

As soon as we reached his house, he woke his parents and siblings to announce our arrival. Almost immediately, the whole family got up and started to prepare food and drinks, giving us a warm reception beyond our wildest expectations. They all sat with us well into the early hours, listening with interest to stories of our travels and of life in our homelands, and I felt completely overwhelmed by the sincerity that was evident in their heartfelt concern. Despite all the experiences of our contact with Indians during the brief time we'd spent in Fiji, I felt sure that *they* weren't doing this for any kind of financial gain. They desired nothing more than the peace of mind that comes to those who help someone in distress.

The next morning we were served a cooked breakfast with hot sweet tea and, again, the whole family was present, ready and willing to assist us in any way possible. Before we left I really wanted to offer them some money, at least to pay for the food we had eaten, but unfortunately we only had a small amount of local currency left. We were travelling on a tight budget and the rash decision to ignore the warning in our guidebook and camp on the beach the previous night had been taken due to financial constraints. All we had was enough money for our bus fare back to Nadi and a night in a cheap hotel before leaving Fiji the following day.

However, my inability to provide any kind of gratuity left me feeling a little ashamed. This discomfort was also intensified by my awareness that they were not a wealthy family and I knew I couldn't leave without offering something. Consequently, I gave one of their sons my fishing rod, to another a set of snorkelling gear, and to the eldest son, he who had rescued us the night before, I gave the address of my grandmother in England. I know this may appear to be a trivial offering but he had talked at length about a vast collection of pen-friends he had established all over the world. I thought an elderly English lady would be an interesting addition to his collection, and several months later I learned from my grandmother that they were still corresponding, so my gift wasn't as insignificant as it may have seemed.

When we left at just after eight that morning, it was quite an emotional farewell. I can still picture the whole family, grouped in front of their tin-roofed, breeze-block abode, all waving until we hiked out of sight.

'They were really genuine people, weren't they?' I said to Christie as we approached the junction of the main road to Nadi.

'Yeah, they sure were,' she agreed. 'And we couldn't a met 'em at a better time, could we?'

'No, you're right. When you're on your last legs, there's nothing better than being helped by a complete stranger.'

Eventually, my body stopped trembling, the pain in my leg subsided and the tears dried up. Nevertheless, she continued to caress my hand for quite some time, and I felt so much calmer, safer and reassured through simply holding the hand of a complete stranger.

17 *Exit Visa*

I didn't know what time it was. I'd lost my watch in the accident and since then I had been in hospital, a place where time wasn't important. However, it felt like dawn was about to break and I could hear one or two noises in the corridor outside as the hospital slowly began to wake up.

I'd woken up quite some time ago. At some point during the early hours of the morning I'd been roused by the recurrent nightmare of a lonely midnight walk through a chilling darkness and had been unable to get back to sleep. But this wasn't due to any kind of distress. Many days earlier this dream had ceased to be a source of anguish and that night it had taken on a more symbolic meaning. I'd woken up just as my father had taken my hand in his and promised to bring me home. Subsequently, sleep had become impossible because this was true: my father *would* be taking me home very soon. My physiotherapy had progressed without further complications and I could now walk short distances on crutches and bend my left leg sufficiently to sit comfortably. The previous morning Doctor Ruiz had told me that he would sign my discharge forms the following day, so that night had been my last in this hospital. Finally, I could start thinking about rebuilding my life, about actually *having* a life again.

As I lay there filling the time with happy thoughts of going home, I realized that another chapter in my life was coming to an end. I had lived a somewhat unconventional life full of numerous adventures in foreign places, where I'd met many different people and gone through a multitude of varied experiences. Yet in some respects my time here in hospital had been another of those adventures. I had met many people, made some new friends and undergone countless experiences, most of them unpleasant but also one or two that were rather more agreeable.

And there was one agreeable experience that stood out above all others: hospitalization had given me the chance to spend a long time in the company of my father. We had always been very close, though somehow through my accident we'd become even closer, and while I knew this part of my life would always be overshadowed by negativity, I saw that as something very positive.

In one way, I almost felt lucky to have had the opportunity to spend so much time with him at this later stage in my life, a life throughout which I'd always been so independent and quite often so far away. As I thought about it more, something came to mind that now made much more sense. It was a Latin American saying I had first heard in a salsa song several years earlier: '*No hay mal que por bien no venga*' – There's nothing bad that doesn't happen for a good reason.

Eventually, the door opened and the cleaner arrived so I guessed it was approaching six o'clock. She greeted me with a quick nod of the head, looking a little surprised to see me wide awake at such an early hour, and then set about her duties. She started in the bathroom, where she emptied the rubbish bin, cleaned the fixtures and fittings, and swept and mopped the floor. Then she came back into the main room and first collected up any rubbish before starting to sweep the floor.

Through lack of any other entertainment at such an early hour, I was watching her quite closely as she went through her practised routine. I became fascinated by her professional approach to such a mundane task, intently watching the broom as it firmly swept back and forth in an aggressive rhythm, and then . . .

. . . the camera panned up the broom handle to a face that looked familiar.

'He looks a bit like someone I know,' I mumbled, though I was thinking aloud and didn't expect a response from those who were watching the programme with me. But when the camera cut to another performer coming onto the stage from the opposite side, I immediately jumped up and screamed, 'That's Luke! I know him! I used to be in this group!'

Catalina and her parents all turned and looked at me, noticeably surprised at my sudden outburst of excitement.

'I know him,' I repeated, exercising considerable self-restraint as I sheepishly lowered myself back onto the sofa. 'It's a group called Stomp and Luke is the leader. I just can't believe they're at the Oscars!'

It was spring 1996 and I was watching the Oscars with my girl-friend and her parents at their home in Medellín, Colombia. The three of them still looked very confused at my unexpected display of enthusiasm, so I turned to Catalina and quickly explained in English how, for a short time, I had become a member of the group that was currently performing on television.

'Why you no tell me this before?' she asked.

'Well, I guess it never came up in conversation. This was about three years ago, when I was still living in Brighton, and a lot has happened since then.'

'But is a beautiful story, I like very much. I not know that my boyfriend is a famous man!' she said with a broad, sensuous, dimple-cheeked smile that never failed to melt my heart.

'I'm not famous, Catalina. I only did a couple of shows with them during the Brighton Festival along with a dozen or so others who'd been recruited for the occasion. It wasn't a big deal.'

'No, Steve, this is a very important group and for this reason they make a show now, on television, in the ceremony of the Oscars. You wait, I explain my parents that you were in this group and they, too, are very happy.'

Catalina began translating the story to her parents, Julián and Fanny, while I sat and listened. I always loved watching her when she became so animated, talking excitedly with both hands, and it was a mannerism she shared with her little sister that was such a contrast to the regal serenity of their mother. I also enjoyed listening to her voice, the lyrical tones of a *paisa* Spanish accent distinctive of all residents of the province of Antioquia, the cultural heartland of Colombia.

Once she had finished, presumably after adding one or two 'Latin American' embellishments, it appeared to have aroused her parents' interest and they started watching the group's performance a lot more closely. I continued to watch with them, still extremely excited that some people I knew were performing at such a prestigious ceremony. It gave me a fantastic feeling of justice to finally see them receiving the recognition they truly deserved. During the month I had worked with them I'd been very impressed by their ability and professionalism, and above all by Luke's creativity.

As a percussionist, it was easy for me to become inspired by a show based on rhythm, yet I could also see that it had a much broader appeal. Using dustbins, brooms, tea chests, buckets, oil-drums, drain-pipes, pots, pans and even the proverbial kitchen sink, this group took everyday noises and turned them into a throbbing, energetic, musical extravaganza. It was a show that included an imaginative mix of theatrical rhythmic pieces, often with an element of humour, so you didn't need to be a percussionist to enjoy it. Now it appeared they had really made a name for themselves and I was overjoyed to see them reach a level of success that was in accord with their expertise.

When the performance was over, Catalina's parents asked me all about my experiences with the group, and then we still continued to chat a little longer in preference to returning to the TV programme.

'So, have you got everything ready for tomorrow?' asked Julián. He was a short, cuddly man with a middle-aged paunch and a calm, controlled temperament (the antithesis of a stereotypical Latino) who had continually displayed a responsible concern for my well-being since the day of my arrival the previous year.

'Yes, everything is prepared and packed,' I replied.

'And you've got all your documents in order?'

'Yeah, of course. I've had long enough to do that, haven't I?'

'Yes, you certainly have,' he agreed. 'So, what time does your flight leave?'

'At half past two.'

'And will Catalina be able to take you to the airport?' asked Fanny.

'Yes, we've organized everything,' I confirmed.

'What about your friend? When does he arrive?'

'He lands in Bogotá on Sunday morning and we should be able to get a flight back here the same day without any problems. Besides, I have to be at work on Monday morning anyway.'

'Well, we hope everything goes OK. These official people can be a bit difficult at times.'

'Yeah, tell me about it.'

The next morning, I was due to fly to the Colombian capital to try and rectify my visa problem. It had taken a lot of time and patience to get this far and I hoped everything would go smoothly in my final battle with the bureaucrats. I was very happy with the life I was building for myself in a South American country that is so misperceived by the rest of the world.

When people think of Brazil, it conjures up the image of a densely forested, lowland basin bordered with coconut-strewn beaches full of tall, tan, bikini-clad beauties. Argentina is seen as an enormous flat plain of agriculture and livestock production, while Bolivia is believed to be a land of gaunt mountains populated with pan-pipe players. All of these perceptions are very close to the truth, and Colombia, too, has many of these features. But none of them is the first thing that comes to mind when most people contemplate this country.

Colombia is the northern-most country of South America. It's sandwiched between Venezuela and Brazil to the east, Ecuador and Peru to the south, and has both Atlantic and Pacific coastlines leading up to its northern neighbour Panama. The eastern half of the country is an almost uninhabited expanse of lowland jungle and swamp. Four ranges of the Andes run through the western half, forming deep longitudinal valleys inhabited by the majority of the country's population, and the north is an area of broad lowlands along the Caribbean Coast.

Its diverse economy is based on a mix of agriculture, mining and manufacturing. Traditional crops include flowers, sugar cane, bananas and rice, and Colombia is only second to Brazil in world coffee production. Manufacturing industries are made up of agriculture-related activities, such as food processing, and the clothing industry is also very important – even Levis jeans are assembled in Medellín after the material has been cut and sent from the USA. Colombia is the largest Latin American producer of gold and platinum, and petroleum also represents a dynamic sector of the economy, yet before I'd come here the mere mention of the country's name had always produced the same response: cocaine.

However, my ill-informed English friends couldn't have been more wrong. I'd seen more of this drug during my student days in Brighton than over the past six months in the world's 'Capital of Cocaine'. Certainly, the drug was produced here, but these people had to live with the problems this industry created and I'd never encountered a more contra-drug culture. None of my friends here had ever seen any cocaine, let alone actually tried it.

I had come to Colombia following my girlfriend's return to her homeland. We'd been together for almost a year in England but she'd had to go back home to continue with her university degree. I hadn't been prepared to let this bring our relationship to an end, so a couple of weeks later I had flown out and joined her.

In many ways, of the four backpacking trips I made, this one had been the easiest. All I'd had to do was buy a ticket and get on a plane. Upon arrival I was collected at the airport, accommodation had been arranged at Catalina's family home, and I already had a large group of friends who were all ex-students of the English school where I'd been working in Bournemouth. In addition to this, I'd managed to find a job with absolutely no difficulty at all and had started teaching English to executives at a paint company in the city.

Just over a year earlier, I had spent some time in the neighbouring country of Venezuela, so before coming here I thought I knew more or less what Colombia would be like. In contrast, I was surprised to find a country that was much cleaner, more organized and populated with harder working people than my previous South American experience had led me to expect. As a consequence, I found it very easy to feel at home in a country where the people worked hard, played hard and tried their hardest to make me feel at home.

I was also particularly happy to be able to continue my relationship with Catalina, a sweet-natured girl who'd captured my heart the very first day we met. I'd been introduced to her in a pub in Bournemouth by a Japanese student I had gone there to meet. On hearing that she was Colombian, I'd told her of my passion for Latin American music and also of my recent trip to Venezuela. At that time, she had only been in England for a couple of weeks and was consequently very pleased to have met someone who had such an affinity for her part of the world.

Now, for the second time in my life, I was once again in that part of the world. But this time I was in a very different situation; this time I was living with a South American family. It didn't take me long to establish a close rapport with her parents – Julián in particular, with whom I shared one or two personality traits and also a penchant for fishing – and I soon developed a brotherly affection for her siblings Ricardo and Clarita. After a very short time, I began to feel like one of the family and we often spent the weekends away together at their villa in the countryside. This was very much the custom in Colombia, a country where the family unit was so much closer than I had experienced in Europe, or in many other parts of the world for that matter. You never felt alone in Colombia.

Unfortunately, a problem had arisen concerning my visa. Although I was working here, I didn't have the necessary papers for employment; I only had a three-month tourist visa. When my permission to stay in the country was on the point of expiring, I'd tried to apply for a further three-month extension at the DAS office – the Department for the Administration of Security. Catalina had assisted me with this daunting task (DAS agents were more like 'secret police' than immigration officers) and we'd driven from one side of the city to the other in order to reach this office. Medellín is situated in a long valley of the Central Cordillera, facing forbidding mountain barriers on nearly all sides. Catalina's family home was in El Poblado, a clean, modern, middle-class neighbourhood on the eastern slopes of the valley, while the DAS office was located in a more run-down, intimidating area to the western extremes of the city.

Once we'd found this office, we went straight to the reception desk and Catalina explained my situation. We were given the necessary application forms, which she helped me to complete, and then I was told to wait for an interview with a DAS agent, fortunately giving me time to prepare for any questions I might be asked.

During the ensuing interview, the agent enquired about my reason for staying longer. It was a question I had anticipated and I told him it was because I wanted to continue with a Spanish course I was taking at the university where my girlfriend was studying. Despite feeling sure that Colombia didn't have a problem with black labour flooding over from the UK, I'd been in a similar situation on a few occasions in the past and felt obliged to dispel any suspicions he might be entertaining about my activities in the country.

'But you have a tourist visa, not a student visa,' growled the DAS agent, a menacing man with a hatchet face and a lantern jaw.

'No, you don't understand. It's just an informal course to help foreigners learn basic Spanish,' I explained.

'A tourist is a tourist, a student is a student. You cannot study on a tourist visa.'

'But it's not a university degree or anything like that. I only want to try and improve my Spanish a bit, that's all.'

'This is not possible. You must stop immediately,' he commanded. 'You cannot continue until you have the necessary visa.'

'So how do I apply for it? What do I need to do to get a student visa?'

'I can give you a list of the documentation we require and the procedures you have to follow,' he answered with an air of detachment. Then he reached over to a filing cabinet, pulled out a faded, photocopied, information sheet and passed it over to me.

'But my tourist visa expires *next week*,' I sighed in frustration. 'Will I be allowed to stay here while I make my application or do I have to leave before the date stamped in my passport?'

'This is not a problem,' he replied with a not-quite-kind smile. 'Can I see your passport, please?'

'Yes, of course,' I said, handing him my identity document.

He briefly flicked through it, then picked up a rubber stamp from the clutter on his desk, printed something on the next clean page and handed it back to me.

'I have given you a three-month extension,' he announced. 'That should be sufficient time to apply for a student visa.'

'Er, OK, thanks,' I mumbled and made a hasty exit.

I was confused. I had gone to this office to ask for a three-month extension to my tourist visa and that was exactly what I'd received, *without* going through the customary process of application forms and payment. The forms I'd completed in the reception were still with me; the DAS agent had lost interest in them the moment he discovered I was studying Spanish. But what concerned me most was that he had considered three months as 'sufficient time' to follow the procedures necessary to procure a student visa.

Nevertheless, as Catalina began translating the information sheet he'd given me, I started to understand why. I needed a bank statement showing proof of sufficient funds, though this wasn't too difficult to obtain. I had to get a medical certificate from an approved doctor, which was a little costly but, again, not a problem. However, I also required an enrolment certificate for my Spanish course and documentation to prove that the university was paying taxes. This was rather more difficult and a lot more disconcerting.

Unbeknown to me, my visit to the DAS office had resulted in the university being raided by government agents from that department. During this foray, every foreigner in the building had been ordered to produce their documentation for inspection, which had led to the expulsion of four students and one teacher, and the university had been fined due to their failure to meet legal requirements. I felt terrible when the secretary of the language department told me this, but luckily they didn't hold me personally responsible and supplied the documents I had requested.

Despite suffering extreme embarrassment at the university through the indirect consequences of my predicament, there was still one more document I needed. And this one was considerably more difficult to acquire. The Department for the Administration of Security required a letter from the British police showing a clean criminal record. This letter had to be translated into Spanish, and both the original and translation had to be notarised by the Colombian Consul in London.

This was a very time-consuming process, hence the three-month extension to my tourist visa, and also not an easy task to orchestrate from Medellín. In the end, my parents managed to obtain a suitable document from the British police, which they sent to one of my Colombian friends in London, who translated it, took care of the necessary officialdom at the Consulate and forwarded everything on to me.

Now, at long last, after waiting nearly two months, I had all the requisite documentation and was ready to make a trip to Bogotá, where I could submit an application for a student visa.

Purely by chance, my moment of readiness coincided with the arrival of a friend from England. Sean and I had first met during our late teens when we both had part-time jobs at a Tesco's supermarket. Like me, he was quite a seasoned traveller and had visited me while I was living in Key West as well as making a grand tour of Canada.

But we also had a Colombian connection. Before I left England we had been sharing his flat in Bournemouth together with Catalina and Luisa, another Colombian girl who was studying there. He'd become romantically involved with Luisa and had consequently decided to come out and visit all three of us.

My plan was to fly to Bogotá the following afternoon, a Thursday, where I had arranged to stay at the home of another ex-student from Bournemouth. I'd have a full day to resolve my visa problem before spending the weekend with Patricia and her family. Then I would meet Sean at the airport on Sunday morning and bring him back to Medellín with me.

The next day, Catalina drove me up through steep, thickly forested mountains to the airport and I got a flight to Bogotá. Patricia met me in the arrivals lounge and took me to her family home, where I was introduced to her parents and subjected to an evening of the warm, Colombian hospitality to which I had now become very accustomed. She also told me she'd already investigated where we needed to go the following day and had made the appropriate plans, so the first stage of my visa visit went without any complications.

The next morning, I was woken at dawn with a hot cup of coffee and on climbing out of bed I received my first surprise of the day. The climate of Medellín is like that of an eternal English summer but the Colombian capital is situated some 3,000 feet higher. As a result, early morning temperatures can be somewhat wintry, yet none of the houses are equipped with central heating. Eventually, I managed to drum up the courage to strip off and take a shower. Then I got dressed, had some breakfast and was ready to face the bureaucrats of Bogotá.

On arriving at the Ministry of Exterior Relations, I was first informed that exterior relations with British ministers were good, therefore British citizens didn't require a letter from the police. I had waited nearly two months for a document that wasn't even necessary! Then, at the apparent whim of the Ministry's expertly trained and helpful staff, I spent the next six hours getting my documents photocopied and notarised, completing application forms, getting photographs, getting the application forms and photographs photo-copied and notarised, giving fingerprints which had to be photocopied and notarised, until I was ultimately informed that it would take about three weeks to deal with my application because the whole process proceeded at the speed of Dutch elm disease while officials worked out what to do with all the photocopies.

By then my head was spinning, so that evening Patricia and one of her cousins took me to Galería Café Libro, Bogotá's most popular salsa venue, in the hope of relaxing me with an evening of Latin music and Cuba Libre. The following day we left a city paralysed by traffic and laden with fumes, and retreated to the majestic tranquillity of her family's country villa in the mountains. Then on Sunday morning I met Sean at the airport and we took a flight back to Medellín.

A few weeks later my passport was hand delivered to me by another of Patricia's cousins, who had come to Medellín on business. As soon as he gave it to me, I thumbed through the pages and found that the Ministry of Exterior Relations had issued me with the student visa I so desperately needed, dated May 2nd 1996 and valid for one year. My visa problem had been resolved.

That evening I returned to the university with my passport in hand, very relieved that I could finally re-enrol for a Spanish course. The moment I entered the office of the language department, the secretary recognised me and began explaining something that simply staggered my imagination. Apparently, due to the problems I had unintentionally created for the university, their lawyer had done some research and discovered that a new law had been introduced in December 1995 permitting foreigners to study Spanish on a tourist visa. I didn't need the student visa! It had all been for nothing. It was just a pity that the government had overlooked notifying DAS officials of the change in the law. Bureaucracy at its best.

So my life in Colombia slipped back into a routine of hard work and serious studies from Monday to Friday, followed by fun-filled weekends with family and friends in a country that was incredibly rich and diverse in landscape, culture and customs. I truly believed I had found a place where I could settle down.

But Colombia wasn't a country without problems. The repercussions of something that had happened earlier that year had started to affect everyone, including me. Back in March, the US Congress had voted against renewing Colombia's export certificate. This was an agreement that permitted Colombian industries to export products to the USA without paying taxes, and in return Colombia had to do everything in its power to combat the narcotics industry. Unfortunately, it had recently been revealed that the Colombian president Ernesto Samper paid for his election campaign with drug money. The United States had demanded his resignation, though of course he'd refused, and this certificate had been suspended, despite the recent arrest of the most powerful drug baron in the country. This had had a devastating effect on the country's economy, since the USA accounted for three-quarters of their overseas markets, and Colombia's exports fell by 40% in less than four weeks. Now the whole country was beginning to feel the effects of America's decision.

Initially, I was torn between two countries. Everywhere I went I heard people berating the United States, and possibly even voicing their anger a little more loudly whenever I was present, as virtually every westerner in Latin America is automatically perceived as a North American. Yet it was something I'd seen in every third-world and developing country I had ever visited. These downtrodden nations all share one thing in common. Outside their American Embassies you invariably find two groups of people: an enraged riotous mob protesting American intervention and a patient line of men and women waiting for American visas, and it seems they all swap places alternate days.

The whole world loves to hate America. Everyone criticizes their far-reaching political power and cultural dominance while simultaneously buying Nike trainers, Adidas sweatshirts and the latest Hip Hop releases so they have something good to wear and listen to on their next holiday in Disney World. And in respect to the poorer countries of the world, I once read or heard their relationship with America being described in the following way. It's like that infatuation many of us developed at some stage during our teens for another student who was a few years ahead of us. There was nothing we could do to impress them or win their affections, so we chose the opposite tack and did everything in our power to annoy and frustrate them, just to get their attention.

I'm neither pro- nor anti-America. It's a country I lived in for about a year and a half, a period of my life that I enjoyed immensely, and I've returned a few times since then on holiday. I accept that they are the most powerful nation on this planet – the world's policeman – and will admit that I sleep a little more soundly each night through the peace of mind this security provides.

But I also understand that they're not perfect. It's not the *best* country in the world, and at times it's easy to become angered and frustrated by their brash, loud, heavy-handed disposition. Yet if *your* country is unjustly invaded by a maniacal tyrant, who are you going to call? Canada? Britain? France? No. In our heart of hearts, we all know the answer to that question.

Nevertheless, back in 1996 I felt they'd made a mistake when they closed the door on Colombia. One of the unfortunate effects of this poverty enforced by American foreign policy was that the number of kidnaps had begun to increase. (This country only holds second place in coffee production but it's the world leader in kidnappings.) I was a foreigner who was working for a very big Colombian company and was automatically a prime target, even though I was nothing more than an English teacher. Consequently, Julián repeatedly warned me to be very careful every time I left the house, implored me to make sure I wasn't being followed and advised that I travelled to work by a different route each day.

Having grown up in the stability of Europe, I found 'paranoia' a difficult tendency to assume. No matter how hard I tried, I simply couldn't get into the habit of continually looking over my shoulder. I went through two or three months of tormented indecision, constantly surrounded by numerous reminders of my own vulnerability. Everyone here seemed to know someone who'd been kidnapped – a friend, a colleague or even a family member – and I could still remember an evening with Catalina, about six months into our relationship, when she recounted the horrific story of her own kidnap.

She was about fourteen at the time, and had gone to a commercial centre with a friend on a Saturday morning shopping jaunt. Just as they were coming out of this centre, she was grabbed by a couple of professional body snatchers and whisked away to their secret hideout. Her friend instantly phoned Julián, who contacted a special branch of the police force that had been formed for the sole purpose of dealing with abductions. Luckily, this group of specialists managed to find her after no more than a few hours, although the two kidnappers, a man and a woman, were subsequently executed right before her innocent, adolescent eyes.

Despite the emotional scars of this terrible ordeal, Catalina had been quite fortunate as not every kidnap victim in this city walks away in one piece. I'd recently seen a Colombian film set in Medellín called *La Virgen de los Sicarios* – The Assassin's Saint. It tells a fictional story but was filmed in the style of a documentary and there's one particular image that I've never been able to forget. Through the centre of Medellín runs a river, and in one scene of the film there's a lingering shot of a sign on its banks that reads, '*Por favor, no arroje cadáveres aquí*' – Please don't dump dead bodies here.

One afternoon my own nervousness was significantly intensified by an incident that happened as I was returning home for lunch. I was walking from the Metro station towards Catalina's house along a wide, tranquil avenue split by a small stream that flowed down its centre in the shade of large flamboyan trees. I'd almost arrived when I noticed a car about 30 yards up the road that appeared to have broken down. I was just on the point of going over to offer some assistance but a strange sensation stopped me in my tracks. Something didn't feel right. I quickly realized that the neighbourhood security guard, a rotund friendly man who was always seated on a garden wall with a shotgun in his lap, was nowhere to be seen. Then, as I peered at the car ahead of me, suddenly my heart missed a beat. Immediately, I understood why it was stationary.

On the far side, standing with his left foot resting on the front bumper, was a man pointing a pistol through the windscreen at the driver. Then another man came into view, as he walked round to the driver's side, where he opened the door, pulled out the terrified female occupant, aggressively pushed her towards the back of the car and forced her to open the boot. He reached inside, retrieved a medium-sized holdall, roughly jostled her back to the driver's side, shoved her inside and then gently closed the car door with the same delicacy I've seen displayed by all Colombians whenever they enter or exit an automobile. Finally, these two bandits mounted a small motorbike and made their escape, their faces adorned with malicious smiles.

All of this had happened in broad daylight in a respectable neighbourhood not 20 yards from the house where I was living. It forced me to accept the truth. If something like this was possible, how could I ever feel safe here?

A few days later I made the most difficult decision of my life: I decided I had to leave the girl and a country I adored. I knew Catalina would never forsake her homeland. It was something we'd discussed a few times in the past and she had always remained adamant that her future lay in Medellín. She was studying international business for the sole purpose of eventually entering the family business, so I knew I could never persuade her to come with me or even join me elsewhere when she'd finished her studies. That was quite simply not an option.

I tried to persuade myself I could put it down to experience – that thing you get when you don't get what you want – but where Colombia is concerned, I've never been able to do this. It's a country that, even today, remains in a special place in my heart. Something in me is still there. I've never forgotten Colombia, not for a moment.

Once the decision had been made, I then had the painful task of telling those who were close to me. In one respect, this was made a little easier because nobody tried to convince me it was the wrong thing to do; there was no counter argument to put forward. Then two weeks later, a small convoy of cars drove up through the mountain range to the east of Medellín as a group of Colombians accompanied their English friend, El Gringo Latino, to the airport.

I felt very touched to receive so much loyal support from the people with whom I'd shared the most precious year of my life, yet it made my departure that much more distressing. I don't think I'll ever forget that day, as I waited in the departure lounge surrounded by so many people who'd had such a profound effect on my life. I was overcome by a debilitating sense of grief and when my flight was finally called I honestly felt like a man being called to the executioner – a dead man walking. I've never felt so sad.

'I've never felt so happy,' I said to my father with tears in my eyes. 'Finally, I'm getting out!'

'That's right, son. It's time to go home.'

'Time to go home,' I sighed. 'So, do we have wait for an ambulance?'

'No, I've talked to the doctor and he said we can take a taxi, but hang on a minute. Where's the *main man*? Where's Nick? I thought he'd be here to see us off.'

'No, they've taken him somewhere to do a special scan; there was some kind of complication. Anyway, I'm sure we'll see him again. But listen, Dad, there's . . . er . . . there's something I wanted to say.'

'What's up? Is everything OK?'

'Yeah, fine, it's just that . . . well . . . I wanted to say thank you. Thanks for being there.'

'Come on, Stevie,' he said with awkward embarrassment. 'I'd have thought we were beyond that stage by now.'

'No, Dad. We'll never be beyond that stage.' Although the words 'thank you' did little to express what I really wanted to say, I knew that a man of his generation might feel more comfortable if I left my deeper thoughts unvoiced.

A few moments later a nurse arrived with my discharge forms, a prescription for painkillers and a note with the date of my next session in rehabilitation. Then my father picked up my bag, put out a hand to steady me as I stood up, and we walked out of that room for the last time . . . together.

As we slowly made our way along the corridor towards the lift, many of the nurses bid us a fond farewell and in some ways his face was probably more familiar to them than mine. I'd spent the past two months in a hospital bed, whereas *he* had spent that time constantly coming and going, finding a nurse whenever a problem arose or a doctor when it was something more serious. Consequently, he knew everyone there even better than I did.

I realized he must have been filled with the same happy relief that I was feeling. He was getting out as well. I felt so proud to have a father who would do anything for me. Even though my childhood had been littered with family problems, splits and divorce, he had always been there to offer support. And now, due to the actions of an irresponsible Canarian lad, he'd instantly dropped everything, jumped on a plane and endured two very long, lonely and painful months watching his son pull back from death's door. He'd spent two months away from his wife and his normal life, in a country where he didn't even speak the language. And he'd done all of this without complaint; he'd done all of this for me.

I'm sure most people put their family ahead of anyone or anything else in their lives. It's human nature. It's the way we're made. Yet I had spent the majority of my adult life away from my family. I'd been travelling all over the globe, visiting places my father had only seen through the postcards I'd sent him or photos I had taken, meeting people he only knew of through the stories I'd told him of my life on the road. But during these past two months I'd learned one important thing that I was sure he had never imagined. Despite my world of experience, *he* was my north, my south, my east and west, the sun of my skies . . . he was the best.

18 *Leaving Lanzarote*

I felt quite impressed, as I sat in the departure hall of Lanzarote's new airport. It had opened just a few weeks earlier so I'd never seen it before, and this vast edifice filled with the smell of fresh paint was a dramatic contrast to dwarfed, redundant building next door. Not only was it much larger but the contemporary design exaggerated this spacious ambience due to the high ceilings and an abundance of light that flooded through the wall of windows behind me. The overall effect was to fill the passenger with a wonderful sense of relaxation, which I imagine came as a welcome relief to those who were nervous of flying.

I was waiting for my father. He'd gone in search of the desk where the travel agent had told us we would be able to collect the wheelchair he had reserved for me. Twelve days had passed since I'd been discharged from hospital and we had spent that time preparing for the journey we were about to commence. Apart from booking tickets for our flight to London, I'd had to get permission to leave the island from my general practitioner as well as the doctor at the social security office in order to receive sickness benefits while I was away. I'd also met with the lawyer my father had engaged and given a statement in the presence of the court doctor to fulfil all the legal requirements of my case for compensation.

In addition to these bureaucratic duties, I'd been continuing with a course of physiotherapy, though not at the hospital under the super-vision of a trained professional. My rehabilitation had been conducted at home by my own personal physiotherapist. This had come about as a result of an unusual Spanish health care regulation: social security covers all medical treatment except for injuries sustained at work or in car accidents. Consequently, the insurance company of the guy who'd crashed into me was responsible for my medical expenses, and we had taken a document to their local office to authorize ambulance transportation to and from hospital for my rehabilitation sessions there. Unfortunately, they had chosen not to sign this document and my father had therefore decided to continue with his own course of physiotherapy at my flat.

In many ways, the past two weeks had been a very pleasant experience. I'd enjoyed being with my father 24 hours a day, just the two of us living together away from the rules and regulations of an institutionalized hospital. It was also reminiscent of that time during in my late teens when my mother had taken up a nursing position in Bermuda. Except this time there was one big difference. Unlike the routine of shared responsibilities we established during our cohabitation some 15 years earlier, this time we couldn't split the day-to-day chores of shopping, cooking and cleaning because I was completely dependent on him for everything. All manner of everyday tasks such as going to the toilet, having a shower or getting dressed required his assistance, and I couldn't even put on my underpants or socks without his help because I still couldn't bend my left leg far enough to do it alone.

Evenings had been spent at the flat, chatting or watching videos over dinner – my father also has an aversion to fish, so I never had to complain about the menu – and we'd occasionally met friends for a drink, but only soft drinks for me as I hadn't yet regained my taste for Cuba Libre. Then, once we'd completed all the medical, legal and bureaucratic requirements to enable me to leave the island, we were ready to make the journey home. The travel agent had booked a wheelchair for our use here, and my mother had made similar arrangements for our arrival at Gatwick Airport, where she would be waiting to take us back to Bournemouth. Finally, we were leaving Lanzarote.

'I've got a bit of bad news,' my father said as he approached pushing a wheelchair.

'What do you mean? The flight hasn't been cancelled, has it?'

'No, it's not that. The lady at the desk told me you might not be allowed to take the flight because you haven't got a fit-to-fly stamp on your medical form.'

'What? That's crazy! Both my own GP and the social security doctor have given me permission to leave the island. They wouldn't have done that if I wasn't fit enough to get on a plane.'

'Yes, I know, but she said that you need a stamp on the form, in English, stating that your medical condition is stable enough for you to take a flight.'

'Even Doctor Ruiz said I could fly, and he was the man who operated on me!' I shouted in frustration. 'What the hell is this woman talking about?'

'I don't know, but just try and calm down, OK. She said we've got to go and wait by her desk, so follow me, it's over there.'

As he pushed our luggage trolley, I struggled to get to grips with the alien task of wheeling myself at his side, and when we reached the desk I asked him to see if he could find out exactly what the problem was.

It transpired that airline regulations required all passengers taking a flight after hospitalization to have a stamp on their discharge form stating that the patient was fit to fly. This stamp was issued by all doctors in private practice on the island and airlines deemed it necessary for insurance reasons. Our predicament stemmed from the fact that a passenger in my situation was an almost unique occurrence. Any tourist who had an accident on holiday would probably be treated at a private hospital where doctors provided patients with a fit-to-fly certificate before they returned home. My situation was different. I was an island resident who'd been involved in a near-fatal car crash and had been treated by Spanish doctors in a state hospital where such certificates were unheard of.

Now all we could do was wait. My father had been told that the only option open to me was to seek permission to board from the crew of the plane. If permission weren't granted, we would have to try and get the necessary document from a British doctor and fly another day. The crew of our flight hadn't arrived yet and we could do nothing until they appeared. Then the lady at the desk would be able to explain the problem to them and await their decision.

So we waited, and waited, and waited. From my wheelchair I could see the queue of people checking in for our flight, and as I watched that queue get smaller and smaller I became more and more worried and frustrated. More than anything, all I wanted was to return home and be amongst family and friends.

I really wanted to see all my friends again. They'd already received news of my accident and many had sent cards and gifts, so my home-coming promised to be a party I would never forget. But there was nothing I could do except wait . . .

              . . . at the roadside in the stifling heat of a tropical afternoon, and stick my thumb out each time a car passed. It had taken me nearly two days to get this far and I still had a long way to go, but I simply *had* to be in Sydney for New Year's Eve. So many of my friends from Brisbane would be there that my arrival promised to be a party I would never forget.

I was in northern Queensland on the east coast of this vast island continent. In two days I'd only managed to hitch a couple of hundred miles and I still had a further 1,300 left to cover before reaching my destination. As I sat there with a T-shirt stuck damply to my back, feeling tired and frustrated, I started to wonder if maybe this time I had planned a journey that was a little too ambitious. This wasn't just another 'day-trip down the Florida Keys'. This time I'd given myself five days to hitchhike 1,500 miles, and on paper it had appeared quite possible. But now I was way behind schedule and a New Year's Eve in Sydney was beginning to look unlikely.

I had arrived in Australia a few months earlier, in mid-September, having flown to Sydney from New Zealand. After a winter in a ski resort, my longest exposure to cold climes in almost two years of travels, I was desperate to once again feel the warmth of the sun on my skin. However, when I arrived in Sydney, springtime temperatures were still quite mild so I had taken an overnight bus to Brisbane, the capital of the 'Sunshine State', Queensland.

I slept through most of this journey and I didn't wake up until dawn was breaking. As I opened my eyes and my dreams faded away, I became very confused by the image on view in the eerie, faint light of sunrise. Despite being in a country famous for its endemic fauna such as the iconic kangaroo, koalas and emus, galloping alongside the bus was a large herd of camels! Apparently, due to its favourable climate and terrain, Australia is the world's largest camel breeder and the only place on Earth where wild camels can be found.

My decision to travel to Brisbane hadn't been solely the result of climatic considerations. My financial situation had also had significant bearing on my choice of destination. New Zealand had been a lot more costly than I'd anticipated and now I was on the other side of the world with no ticket home and just a couple of hundred dollars left in my money-belt. Consequently, employment was my primary concern and Brisbane, a city that until recently had been little more than an overgrown country town, had now become one of Australia's most progressive centres and was currently hosting the world's leisure fair Expo '88. The enormous workforce required for such an undertaking had led to a dramatic increase in employment opportunities and within a matter of days I'd taken up two full-time positions.

It was a challenging timetable that left me with little time (or energy) for anything else, outside the pursuit of making money. Every weekday morning I awoke at a quarter to six and travelled to a northern suburb, where I worked in construction as a painter. I usually finished at around 4pm and would return to the hostel for a bite to eat and a short *siesta* before starting my evening job.

This particular nocturnal livelihood was a new experience for me that had come about purely by chance. As is so often the case, someone had wandered into the backpackers' hostel looking for a prospective new employee. This was on my second day there, so I'd instantly offered my services before even hearing what the job entailed, though I soon learned that this young entrepreneur had started a business interest linked to the exposition being staged in the city. He needed someone to man one of his hotdog stalls outside the main gates of Expo. From that day onwards, I spent every night of the week selling bun-wrapped frankfurters from eight to midnight on weekdays and until three in the morning at weekends; a job that made me so much money that I began to feel like a car mechanic who'd just discovered the insurance company.

Five weeks later, this short period of intensive employment left me with over $3,000 in my recently opened bank account. My preoccupation with finances had temporarily been abated and I could enjoy a wild, end-of-Expo party at the hostel with a worry-free mind. It was a fancy dress *fiesta* I'll never forget and the costume I wore was a combination of my exaggerated English humour mixed with an Americanism: I went as a 'rubber man', dressed in a dustbin liner adorned with dozens of inflated condoms. It didn't quite achieve the impact of my penis at The Hat Party, but only one other person was aware of this. Sharon, one of my flatmates in Queenstown, was also staying at this hostel.

The following day marked the start of a massive backpackers' exodus from Brisbane, the vast majority heading north. I, too, began a month-long journey up the coast, now in the pursuit of pleasure. It was a gratifying trip and a much-needed holiday after the long hours of hard graft during the preceding weeks.

My first stop was Stradbroke Island, just off the coast of Brisbane. From there I travelled north to a town called Mackay and stayed at the Ko Huna Resort, a luxury Polynesian-style beach resort with a backpackers' bunk-house at only $10 a night. After a weekend there, I continued up the coast to Airley Beach and happened to run into Sandy and Claire, two English girls I knew from the Brisbane hostel. Sandy decided to join me on a trip to Hook Island, an uninhabited island on the Great Barrier Reef, where we spent five sun-filled days on the beach, a period of carefree camping that once again rekindled my memories of *Lord of the Flies*.

On returning to Airley Beach, we met up with two more familiar faces from Brisbane: an electrician from London named Glenn and a fair-skinned 'sweaty sock' called Stewart. Glenn's profession matched his personality perfectly – he really was a *live wire* – and his appearance, mannerisms and playful disposition constantly reminded me of the comic actor Norman Wisdom.

Together, the five of us travelled up the coast to Tulley, a small town that had been crowned the 'Banana Capital of Australia'. Due to the abundant availability of casual work, it was a popular stopover on the backpacking route north, and I chose to relax while the others went banana picking in the surrounding plantations. Although not the type of person to shy away from hard work, I'd been suffering from lower back pains, a sporadic affliction that started in my teens, and had decided it would be unwise to take up this very physically demanding form of employment.

A few days later we made the final leg of our journey to Cairns, the backpacker Mecca of the Far North. This town had once been a sleepy tropical backwater but was now amidst a period of rapid development. I had heard about the current growth in the tourist infrastructure and had intended to find work there in construction. Unfortunately, it was brimful of backpackers seeking employment, making it very difficult to secure a position without the necessary papers, so I travelled a couple of hours further north to the lesser-known tourist town of Port Douglas, situated on the edge of a spectacular rainforest. Luckily, I managed to get a job there as a painter and was subsequently joined by Glenn and Stewart, who had found work as groundsmen at one of the hotels. Then the three of us remained in Port Douglas until the Christmas holidays.

For the festive season we travelled back to Cairns and spent a truly memorable Christmas Day on Green Island, another island on the Great Barrier Reef. In a country where the seasons are reversed, many Australians I'd met had talked about spending Christmas on the beach, but *we* really took this to the extreme.

I remember sitting on the warm, soft sand in the shade of coconut palms – a turkey sandwich in one hand and an ice-cold beer in the other – and thinking about my family back in England. I could clearly picture them sitting around the dining-room table, pulling Christmas crackers and wearing silly paper hats. Then as they were getting ready for the Queen's speech, I was swimming in a crystal-clear ocean and feeding Christmas cake to the colourful tropical fish that surrounded my submerged body. I even went snorkelling amongst a shoal of a dozen sharks, having first been assured that they were vegetarians. It was my kind of a Christmas.

After a rather boozy Boxing Day in Cairns, I said goodbye to my two pommy mates and set off with the plan of following the same route back down the coast, this time using a thumb instead of a bus ticket. Yet now, less than two days into this journey, I couldn't help thinking that maybe the bus ticket might have been a better option.

As I sat at the roadside, trying to calculate whether the reunion in Sydney would still be possible if I spent the night at a backpackers' hostel nearby, a rental car pulled over a little way down the road. I got up and wandered towards it, unsure if they'd stopped to offer a ride or for some other reason. When I reached the car I saw that the driver and passenger were two guys over from Papua New Guinea – PNGs as the Aussies call them. The passenger wound down the window, asked me where I was going and then told me to jump in. My luck had changed. I had got another ride.

Through my experiences of hitchhiking I've met many interesting people, since the type of person who's usually prepared to pick up a hitchhiker isn't someone you would describe as dull or conservative. Nevertheless, my trip with the PNGs certainly stands out as unique.

Jeff, the passenger, was a short, skinny, balding man with a comic-strip face and a little-boy smile. He spoke English quite competently but was unable to drive, whereas his heavy-set, wild-eyed companion Ronnie had a driving-licence but he didn't understand English. This meant that Jeff had to translate every single road sign along the way, and on many occasions this resulted in us coming to a virtual standstill while he translated 'vital' information such as the location of a Pizza Hut restaurant in the next town a few miles down the highway.

Following a couple of hours of this unnerving stop-start routine, we pulled into a self-service petrol station. Ronnie drew up alongside a petrol pump, turned the engine off and then waited. The three of us sat there for what seemed like an eternity until I asked Jeff the reason for this delay, and his reply came as quite a surprise: Ronnie was waiting for someone to come and put the petrol in! Presumably they didn't have self-service petrol stations in Papua New Guinea, and despite my detailed explanation of the set-up, it was obvious neither of them felt confident enough to actually pump the petrol for themselves so I got out and did it.

As we drove into the night, at one point we came to a complete stop. Then Ronnie opened his door, jumped out of the car and started doing press-ups in the middle of the road.

'What's he doing?' I asked Jeff, once again feeling very confused.

'He is feeling sleep and now he tries to wake up,' he explained.

'What?' I exclaimed. 'Look, tell him I've got a driving-licence and I can drive for a while if he wants to have a rest.'

'No, is not possible. Now is the first time he drives a new car and he wants to do all the driving for him.'

'OK, but just let him know the offer is there. And do you think you could tell him to get out of the middle of the road?'

'Why? Do there is more cars that drive so late in the night?' he asked with surprise.

'Well, er, it's possible,' I replied, knowing full well that one of the enormous Australian 'road trains' could come hurtling round the bend at any moment.

Eventually, just after midnight, Ronnie submitted to the need for sleep and we stopped in a small town called Rockhampton. I quickly realized that the alien task of organizing accommodation would be way beyond the limit of their experience, so I started thumbing through my *Lonely Planet* guidebook. In the end, we managed to find a van park recommended for backpackers, and rented a caravan for the night at a price of $8 a head. However, even though they appeared to be very naive, I was still a bit worried that I might wake up the following morning to find that Jeff and Ronnie had absconded with my backpack.

I couldn't have been more wrong.

The next morning I was woken up at half past five by two confused PNGs asking me where they could wash themselves and what we were going to do about getting some breakfast. After I'd arranged our basic necessities, we made a very early start on the final leg of the journey to Brisbane, their ultimate destination.

Once we were out of town, having negotiated a complicated and confusing grid of junctions and road signs, I decided to get some more sleep. A few hours later I was woken by a very excited Jeff, who announced that we'd reached 'Brisbane City'. The moment I glanced through the window, I recognized the neighbourhood because it was where I'd been working as a painter just a few months earlier. It was a quiet residential area to the extreme north of the city and we still had quite some distance to go before we would reach 'Brisbane City'.

As we gradually got closer to the centre, Jeff's translations became more and more animated with the increasing number of road signs and junctions. Then, finally, we reached the brow of a hill and they got their first glimpse of the city centre – a mass of shimmering high-rise apartment and office blocks – and even today I can still picture their faces filled with wide-eyed amazement. They had the same expression that I imagined filled *my* face on that bus ride to the south coast of England when I returned home from Thailand. It was the first time they'd ever seen a real-life modern city.

At this point the process of translation became more complicated. I first had to give directions to Jeff, which he then translated to Ronnie, and by the time we had reached the central bus station all three of us were sweating profusely. Fortunately, we made it there without any mishaps, and after helping them get in touch with some friends who lived locally I was ready to leave them to fend for themselves. Even so, as I shouldered my backpack and said farewell, I couldn't help feeling like a father leaving his kids at the gates on their first day of school. Both of them looked so nervous and vulnerable that I found myself wondering how they would have ever made it this far if they hadn't picked me up the previous day.

Despite the desire to stay with them until their friends arrived, I had a pressing engagement in two days time with another 600 miles left to travel. I took a city bus south to Surfer's Paradise, spent the night there and then continued down the coast the following morning. It took me several rides to reach a town called Port Marquarie, and the final one was from three young guys who had also commenced their day's travel in Surfer's Paradise.

We reached town at around dusk and all decided to camp out on the beach. Early the next morning, woken by a crisp chill I hadn't felt in more than three months, I asked one of the lads to drive me back to the main highway so I could carry on with my trip. It was the morning of December 31st and I only had another 250 miles to go. At long last it looked like I might actually make it. Sydney was within my sights.

I waited for about half an hour, feeling very cold and hungry, then much to my relief a car stopped just a little way ahead of me. I immediately ran forward, desperately hoping they would be able to take me at least as far as Newcastle, the next main town on my route south. The last thing I needed at the start of that day was a disappointing ride just a few miles down the road.

When I reached the car, they had already wound the window down and I could see there was a young couple inside whom I subsequently learned were from Colombia.

'Hi, where are you going?' asked the driver.

'I'm trying to get to Sydney by tonight,' I replied. 'I've got a big party to go to there.'

'Sydney? Yeah, we're going to Sydney. We can take you there.'

'You can take me to Sydney?' I exclaimed in disbelief.

'Yeah, sure, jump in. We can take you.'

'They can take you,' said the lady at the desk.

'They can take me?' I exclaimed in disbelief.

Yeah, sure, they said it wasn't a problem so you'd better go and check in right away.'

'Oh, that's fantastic,' I sighed, 'and thanks ever so much for all your help.' Then I turned to my father and joyfully announced, 'She says we can go!'

'Yes, Steve, I heard her,' he replied, and I could see in his face that he was just as relieved as I was. Although, in our own way, each of us loved this island, we were both very happy to be going home . . . to be leaving Lanzarote.

19 *First Day*

Today is January 15th 2000: my anniversary. The accident happened a year ago today. I'm back in Lanzarote now. I returned in September last year. I spent six months in England; six months of hospitals, doctors, physiotherapists, eye specialists and facial surgeons, but my physical recovery has finally come to an end. I've still got a long way to go, though. I've only won the first battle on the long road back to a normal life and it's a war that will continue for many years to come.

I underwent plastic surgery in England. It wasn't something I'd requested, or even considered. This was partly because the question of cosmetic surgery had never been raised while I was in Lanzarote, and I imagine the insurance company footing the bill for my hospitalization there would never have agreed to such a costly procedure. But in addition to this, throughout that entire period my left leg had always been my singular concern. Any other injuries had been considered as secondary. My sole preoccupation had been to walk again (and also to dance) so once I'd had the operation on my leg and returned to the UK, those worries diminished quite rapidly.

Nevertheless, another medical complication soon took their place: I still had severe double vision in my left visual field. As a British citizen, the cost of health care wasn't an issue while I was in England because I was covered under the National Health. Consequently, my doctor arranged for a consultation with a facial surgeon at the hospital, seeing as this problem was a result of the fractures I'd sustained to my face which had altered the position of my left eye. During the course of this consultation, the surgeon asked me a very simple question.

'Why do you want to have an operation on your face?'

'Well, I can't see properly and I was told that this is the only way to cure my double vision.'

'Yes, that's true,' he replied, 'but is it the *only* reason why you want to have facial surgery?'

He had asked me a question that, until that moment, I had never actually asked myself, and this made me pause before answering. The reflection I saw when I brushed my teeth each morning wasn't quite the same as the one I had used to see before my accident. And even though I wasn't grossly deformed, I'd begun to notice that one or two heads would occasionally turn as I passed people in the street.

'Well, I suppose I wouldn't mind having a face that looked, you know, a bit more like it used to,' I replied.

'That was the answer I needed to hear,' he said with a smile that expressed relief.

Subsequently, I underwent two operations. The first was a five-hour marathon of surgery to reconstruct the left side of my face and reposition my eye, and the second was a shorter, aesthetic operation to implant a bone transplant into my left cheek. A team of very gifted facial surgeons performed both operations and the results were more than satisfactory.

So, I've got the face of the man who used to be me; it's just that the person behind it is not the same as before. My double vision has been cured, I can walk quite normally, even dance a little too, and you can only see my scars when I'm at the beach. Yet there are other scars that no one can see, and I don't know how long it will take for those to heal. Maybe some never will.

But . . . I'm still here.

However, whenever I'm alone the same questions always return. Why did it happen to me? Why was I chosen to be on that stretch of road at that particular time on that unlucky night? And why didn't I die? It scares me not to know my place in this world, to not know why I'm here. All in all I've had a very full life; it's just that it doesn't mean anything. I haven't really done anything all that notable with the short time I've spent on this planet, so why am I still here? Why did I survive that car crash?

In that car crash, during those few, brief seconds preceding the moment of impact, I didn't see my whole life flash before me. It was more like it kind of crept up on me as I began to emerge from post-traumatic delirium. It was during my time in hospital that I relived so many of the experiences that had made my life what it was; that had made *me* what I was. It was an intense period of reflection that showed me all I'd learned through my travels, while also opening my eyes to one or two other things hidden deep within my subconscious, so deep that only the trauma of a near-death encounter could bring them to the surface. It was a thought-provoking journey along a winding road of discovery, although it didn't reach its conclusion once I'd recuperated in the UK. It wasn't until I returned to Lanzarote that I started to see the true value of the trip I had made.

During my first month back on the island I spent many hours each evening rereading my travel diaries and reviewing the pages of the scrapbooks I had compiled. I took myself once more on a journey through my past, through all those years I had spent travelling and learning about the world. I'd always known that these experiences had taught me a great deal, and I could see it was an education I had put to use almost every day ever since.

In my professional life, I knew that whenever I walked into a classroom filled with students from the four corners of the earth, I could very quickly put all of them at ease. I'd travelled through and lived in so many parts of the world that I could instinctively respond to their cultural differences in addition to anticipating what problems someone from their part of the world might encounter whilst living and studying in my homeland. Certainly, there are many other English teachers who've done the job long enough to acquire a sophisticated understanding of the needs and preferences of students of different nationalities. It's a distinction of a good teacher. But on the other hand, it isn't quite the same as experiencing those cultures firsthand. There's only so much you can learn about a different way of life through working with people who live theirs that way.

My private life had also been influenced quite considerably by travel. The music I listened to, the books I read, the clothes I wore, even the food I cooked were all a reflection of things experienced on the road. On reaching adulthood, many people draw up the map and then, for the rest of their lives, they leave the boundaries exactly as they are. But I hadn't been prepared to do this, to remain the same until my dying day. Instead, I had chosen to join the first generation of backpackers, and it's a decision I have never regretted.

Even so, the 'journey' I made in hospital through the first half of my life didn't only remind me of all I had learned and experienced in the outside world. It showed me one or two truths that were a lot closer to home, things about my own family.

It gave me the chance to see my father in a completely new light. Of course I'd always loved him dearly and thought of him not just as a dad but also as my best friend. Yet I'd never realized he had such depths of caring, concern and understanding. The idea of deep conversations about one's hopes, fears, dreams and aspirations was a thing that had been born long after he'd reached adulthood, so it was a side of himself he had never shown before. In fact, during that time we shared in hospital, I only saw an oblique version of it and I doubt this will ever happen again. But at least it did happen . . . once.

Then there was my sister Nikki. There was so much about our relationship as adults that I'd never understood until now. Indeed, I'd never seen the connection between this relationship and my decision to expel our biological mother from my affections. But now, as I reflected on the past six months I had spent in England, I finally began to understand the consequences of our shared history.

On two occasions during my convalescence at our family home I'd become incensed by flippant comments she had made, and on each occasion it was very obvious she was extremely surprised by my choleric response. But she wasn't to blame. She had only been treating me in the way that she'd become accustomed to a long time ago. How could she be aware of the changes that had taken place within me? How could I expect her to understand that the trauma of my accident had ripped away the thick skin I'd been forced to grow during my adolescence at the hands of our biological mother?

But this presented me with a new problem. In the past I'd made a little deal with myself about Nikki. I had decided that I would always accept her as she was and our relationship as it stood. Unfortunately, due to my accident, this little deal would now be considerably harder to keep. It had become another of the scars I would have live with.

Despite all this enlightenment, though, one thing still remained the same as it had always been. Even though a near-death experience can often lead to a reconciliation, a healing of past wounds, as far as my biological mother was concerned I was absolutely certain this would never happen.

Whenever I thought of her – a very infrequent occurrence – one memory inevitably came to mind. It was a story her second husband (another ex-husband) had once told me of a visit the two of them had made to my grandparents' house. While he was in the kitchen chatting with his mother-in-law and she was in the living room with my grandad, he suddenly heard screams coming from the lounge and immediately went to investigate. As he opened the living-room door, he was shocked to find his wife beating her own father over the head with one of her stiletto-heeled shoes, blood pouring down the face of this poor, defenceless, aged man. Even though the reason for this horrific outburst of violent anger remained a mystery, I was certain that I never again wanted to get close to a woman who was capable of attacking a frail man in his mid-seventies with the ferocity she'd displayed that day.

So, the aftermath of my accident had given me a lot of answers. Admittedly, I'd already had knowledge of some of them, though there were one or two others that, well, I hadn't even been aware of the questions. Nevertheless, deep in my gut there was still one nagging question that had yet to be answered. Why was I still here? I'd gone through an intense period of enlightenment but what should I do now?

I knew exactly what I should do today: I went to see Nick. He's back in hospital again, so I decided to pay him a visit. I thought the hospital was the best place for me to be on a day like today; the place where, one year ago, it had all ended . . . and started once again.

Nick's still fighting the first battle on his road back to a normal life. He's been very unlucky, there were a lot of complications, and in the end Doctor Ruiz had to make what must have been an immensely difficult decision for a doctor with such a deep-felt desire to help his patients to the best of his abilities. Next week he's going to amputate Nick's left leg.

But I feel that Nick is the type of man who will be able to survive this trauma. There's a spirit inside him that not many of us possess. Somehow I'm sure he'll leave this hospital with his cheeky grin still intact. And no doubt those he leaves behind will also find themselves smiling whenever they think of him, just as I do as I write this very sentence.

When I arrived at his room, he didn't give me the welcome of a bitter man full of regret. He greeted me as . . . as only Nick can.

'Hey! Steve! How's it going?' he exclaimed, the moment I walked through the door. 'I hear the locals have started locking up their daughters again, now that you're back on the streets.'

'Hi, Nick. It's good to see that you haven't changed.'

'Nope. They can cut off whatever they like and I'll still be the same,' he declared. 'Well, almost anything, anyway. So, what brings you here then?'

'You know, just thought I'd come and visit my old room-mate. And it's my anniversary, the fifteenth of January, so I thought *here* was a good place to be.'

'Of course! Happy birthday, mate. Happy second birthday!'

He was right. I understood exactly what he meant. A year ago today I'd come very close to death, so close that all the doctors had thought I really would die. But I didn't. I had cheated my extinction and been reborn. Today *was* my birthday.

However, as I sit here in my flat and I think about it more, I see things in a slightly different way. For me, 'half-time' is over. I've had time to recuperate from the first half and reflect on the game so far. Now it's time to get back out on the pitch and start playing again. It's time to start the second half. It's the first day of the rest of my life.

But as I trot through the dark tunnel towards the brightly-lit pitch ahead of me, I don't feel the urge to recommence the game yet. Maybe the best part of my life is over and I don't want to get up and start the bad part. Or maybe I still haven't recovered from all the injuries I sustained in the first half. I'm carrying too much inside of me that still needs to be resolved, and while I'm a beach boy at heart, no man is an island, so maybe I should share all I've learned with those who are close to me.

Perhaps I also need to extinguish the anger that still festers deep within me. I have to put right a miscarriage of justice by revealing the true circumstances surrounding that ill-fated night, one year ago. Before I can start playing again, I need to be at peace with everything that happened in the first half. Maybe I should write it all down. Maybe *that's* why I'm still here:

I went to a football match once . . .